# Looking Backward

# Looking Backward

A CRITICAL APPRAISAL OF
COMMUNITARIAN THOUGHT

*Derek L. Phillips*

PRINCETON UNIVERSITY PRESS

PRINCETON, NEW JERSEY

*Library of Congress Cataloging-in-Publication Data*
Phillips, Derek L.
Looking backward: a critical appraisal of communitarian thought /
Derek L. Phillips.
p.   cm.
Includes bibliographical references and index.
ISBN 0-691-07425-9
1. Community—History. 2. Liberalism—History.
I. Title.
HM131.P438   1993
302—dc20       92-36381

*For Eliot Freidson,*
*a good friend*

———————————

# CONTENTS

# ACKNOWLEDGMENTS

IN WRITING this book I have received help from many people. Some are friends. I would like to thank Eliot Freidson, Joel Nelson, Gil Loescher, and Robert Louden for reading portions of the manuscript and giving me useful criticisms and suggestions. Others are (or were) strangers. They are scholars to whom I wrote explaining my project and asking if they would be willing to read draft chapters. Although they knew neither me nor my work, they generously agreed to make their expertise available to someone outside their own disciplines.

The political scientists Richard Matthews and John Wallach read several chapters and gave me the benefit of their special knowledge. I am grateful to both. The historians Susan Reynolds, Paul Finkelman, and J. R. Pole saved me from numerous errors in my attempt to examine communitarian thought from a historical as well as a philosophical perspective.

Susan Reynolds, a specialist on the Middle Ages, provided several pages of detailed and incisive criticism, as well as some excellent suggestions for improving the chapters. It was clear from the very first sentence of her comments that improvement was certainly necessary: "I have read your draft chapters with great interest. I think what you are doing is immensely interesting and useful. But—here it comes—although I find great merit in your attempt to grapple with the middle ages I think that as it stands it does not quite work." If it works better now, and I think it does, it is due largely to the wonderfully helpful comments of Susan Reynolds.

Paul Finkelman and J. R. Pole provided similarly pointed criticism of my chapters concerning seventeenth- and eighteenth-century America. Finkelman wrote that "overall, I like what you are doing, although I think the arguments can be sharpened." Indeed they could, as he went on to show. He listed several instances where my use or interpretation of the historical evidence was open to challenge, noted some lack of clarity about time and chronology, and alerted me to mistakes about certain factual matters. J. R. Pole was equally forthright in his critical comments on factual and theoretical matters, and in warning me not to fall into anachronism when arguing from history. I learned an enormous amount from these two scholars.

I also profited from the comments of Craig Calhoun, Donald R. Kelley, Lawrence C. Becker, and Will Kymlicka, each of whom read the manuscript in its entirety for Princeton University Press. Calhoun, a sociologist, made me realize that this book will be of more interest to political theorists and philosophers than to sociologists. I have revised it with that in mind. His comments were also useful in helping me specify and distinguish my main arguments. Donald Kelley provided thoughtful criticism and suggestions from a historian's perspective, and Lawrence Becker offered sound advice about tone and balance. Will Kymlicka read the manuscript twice and made a variety of useful suggestions. Among other things, he provided some good ideas concerning organization and made me see the need to better integrate the historical and political critiques of communitarian thought.

These various readers are not responsible, of course, for the ways that I have acted on their criticisms and suggestions. But the manuscript has certainly been improved by their comments. It is a pleasure to thank them all for their time, insight, and encouragement. Together, they have given me a deep sense that the community of scholars is real and good-spirited.

Ann Wald, the philosophy and political theory editor at Princeton University Press, worked closely with me and patiently saw me through the various stages of the evaluation process. I am highly appreciative of her advice and support, as well as her suggestions for improving the manuscript. My thanks to Bill Hively for his help in preparing the final version of the manuscript for publication. I also wish to thank the Rockefeller Foundation for the opportunity to work on this book in the peace and comfort of its Villa Serbelloni at Bellagio.

My greatest debt is to my wife, Klaske Muizelaar, whose intellectual and spiritual companionship has given me so much. Her patience, encouragement, and understanding have sustained me through the years that I wrestled with the completion of this book. Beyond gratitude, she has my love.

# Looking Backward

———————————

# INTRODUCTION

WE ARE always dreaming, it seems, of community. For almost everyone, the word *community* has a very positive connotation indeed. It evokes images of personal relationships characterized by warmth, care, and understanding; of shared values and moral commitments; of social cohesion and solidarity; of continuity in time and place. But community is no more. Sociologists and other academic experts have written volumes about the disappearance, decline, erosion, and eclipse of community. Its loss is widely mourned.

The longing for community is today widespread, and a return to community is often seen as a solution for the ills of modern society: relationships that are transitory, impersonal, and segmented; the loss of feelings of attachment and belonging; the absence of meaning and unity in our lives; the sharp dichotomy between public and private life; the isolation and alienation of the individual.

Whatever the exact terminology used, individualism is viewed by many critics as a disease of the modern world, and liberalism as the political philosophy in which it manifests itself. The atomizing tendencies of individualism and liberalism, it is often claimed, stand opposed to ideas of common interests, the public good, collective attachments, group loyalty, respect for tradition, patriotism, and similar attributes. In short, the evils of individualism and liberalism are contrasted with the virtues of community and communitarianism.

But a concern with the disappearance of community is not really new. It has been a persistent theme in political and social thought throughout much of the nineteenth and twentieth centuries.

It was expressed by Tönnies as a shift from gemeinschaft to gesellschaft, by Durkheim as a shift from mechanical to organic solidarity, and by Weber as a move from traditional-sacred to rational-secular social orders.[1] Each of these theorists believed that the social ties which previously held people intact had disintegrated, thus leaving the individual exposed, unprotected, and unregulated. The absence of community continues to receive attention from sociologists.

The loss of community is today a favored topic of discussion for many others besides sociologists. It has been the focus of voluminous commentary by philosophers, political scientists, legal scholars, historians, and psychologists in recent years. In one way or another, all emphasize the

3

special importance of communitarian values. Although most of them focus on American society, the search for new forms of community affects all Western societies today.

However, not all writers who place an emphasis on community should be counted as communitarians.[2] And while there is no set of necessary and sufficient conditions that distinguish full-fledged communitarian theorists from others who advocate community, there is considerable agreement about which of our contemporaries *are* in fact the major communitarian thinkers.

Two names are always included in discussions of communitarian thinking today: Alasdair MacIntyre and Michael Sandel.[3] A third name that is usually included is that of Charles Taylor.[4] Along with these three theorists, my focus here will be on *Habits of the Heart*.[5] This book, written by four sociologists and a philosopher, has received considerable attention since its publication in 1985.[6] In fact, as Christopher Lasch points out, "No other book has done so much to bring the communitarian critique of liberalism to general attention."[7]

There are differences among the positions taken by MacIntyre, Sandel, Taylor, and Robert Bellah and his collaborators, some of which will be noted as I go along. But these theorists are all highly critical of political individualism and liberalism, and emphasize very similar features in characterizing social groups as communities.[8] They are all also social reformers who intend their work to produce changes in our ways of thinking, and—more importantly—in our conduct and social arrangements.

Although I give most attention to the above theorists, my inquiry has implications for all those writers who posit the existence of widespread community in the past, ascribe a massive change to a disintegrated present, and emphasize the moral urgency of realizing community in contemporary society.[9] Let me now turn to what MacIntyre, Sandel, Taylor, and Bellah et al. actually say about these matters.

In his broad attack on liberal politics and liberal society, MacIntyre writes that modern man "is a citizen of nowhere, an internal exile where he lives."[10] More and more, "modern liberal political society can appear only as a collection of citizens of nowhere who have banded together for their common protection."[11] The individualistic self, observe Bellah et al., has become increasingly detached from its social and cultural contexts.[12] Taylor speaks of "loss of meaning, fragmentation, the loss of substance in our human environment and our affiliations."[13] Sandel offers similar observations about modern society being characterized by radically isolated individuals, who are absolutely free, unencumbered, and on their own.[14] To reverse these trends, they all agree, requires the renewal of community.

4

These scholars argue that there were times when community was prominent. They advance the historical thesis that there have been periods in which community reigned and things were in good order. Like others who have written about community in the past, they view three specific historical periods as exemplars of community: classical Athens, the Middle Ages, and the founding period of America.[15]

The Athenian polis was a point of reference for many of the major nineteenth-century social theorists. They saw it as a community in which the citizen interacted with others in pursuit of the human good and political development. But it was medieval society that served as a more influential model for Comte, Weber, Simmel, Durkheim, and Tönnies. They all saw the Middle Ages as made up of a network of communities in which people lived together in peace and harmony.

MacIntyre, too, refers to the existence of community in early Athens and in medieval Europe. In those earlier periods, he says, shared traditions and practices assured a common morality as guidance for people's behavior. Individuals lived in particular communities with their own specific institutionalized forms, and everyone contributed to the realization of the community's shared goals and projects.[16] MacIntyre laments the loss of the classical tradition best captured by Aristotle's definition of the polis, where citizens were bound by ties of affection made possible by "a wide range of agreement . . . on goods and virtues."[17]

In both classical Greece and the Middle Ages, says MacIntyre, shared standards and values provided a sense of meaning and a degree of stability that are absent in contemporary life. These earlier societies were unified by a shared understanding of the common good, and were peopled by virtuous individuals who were willing to renounce their own partial claims in the interest of the whole community. In short, there was widespread agreement in the past on "man-as-he-could-be-if-he-realized-his-*telos*."[18]

Like MacIntyre, Sandel says that morality and social organization have to be based on people's shared understandings. In championing community and civic republicanism, he emphasizes the crucial significance of those allegiances arising for individuals "as members of this family or community or nation or people, as bearers of this history, as sons and daughters of that revolution, as citizens of this republic."[19] In early America, according to Sandel, community was widespread. As America grew, however, the form of community had to change.

Speaking about the need for a strong sense of national community as the United States developed from its founding into a modern industrial society, he writes:

If a virtuous republic of small-scale, democratic communities was no longer a possibility, a national republic seemed democracy's next best hope. This was still, in principle at least, a politics of the common good. It looked to the nation, not as a neutral framework for the play of competing interests, but rather as a formative community, concerned to shape a common life suited to the scale of modern social and economic forms.[20]

But, says Sandel, this project has failed. By the mid-twentieth century, the shared self-understandings and common purposes necessary for community had largely disappeared. Nevertheless, because of these ideological origins in America's past, Sandel believes it possible to revitalize public life and restore a sense of community.

In *Habits of the Heart*, Bellah and his associates refer to early America as a community in which people participated widely in a common life. Through active involvement in common concerns, the individual was enabled to overcome any sense of isolation and the general tendency to pursue his or her private interests. In agrarian America, they say, the basic unit of association was the local community.

The founders of the Republic pressed for widespread democratic participation and emphasized that a republic needed a government "that was more than an arena within which interests could compete, protected by a set of procedural rules."[21] A republican government could survive and flourish only if animated by the spirit of virtue and concern for the public good.[22] In the words of the authors of *Habits of the Heart*: "The premise of the system was that the virtue of the people would lead them to choose for their officials and representatives men who would be great-spirited enough to place the public good above their own, or their local region's, special advantage."[23] Individual dignity, political participation, and American citizenship were all anchored in the ethos and institutions of the community.

We are surely all familiar with the thesis that community was once widespread. But familiarity is not necessarily truth. Was community indeed dominant in the three periods so often chosen as points of comparison: classical Athens, medieval Europe, and early America? One of the recurrent phrases in the communitarian standpoint is "Once there was . . . ," followed by an assertion about various aspects of life in the past. They argue, then, that community once reigned supreme and things were in generally good order in earlier times—at least better than they are today in the United States and other modern societies. My concern is with the validity of this thesis.

6

But it is difficult to determine the prevalence of community in the past without knowing what community *is*. Despite the attention given to the crucial importance of community, one is struck by the overly abstract and strongly ideological flavor of much communitarian writing. It lacks an explicit theory of community, and seldom specifies what is meant by community. The term is variously used to refer to a large number of interconnected elements, both structural and normative.

Given its many associations, the term *community* is somewhat vague and imprecise.[24] This makes it difficult to know what is purportedly missing in our urbanized and industrialized societies today. Still, it is possible to catch the drift of the communitarians' criticisms if we keep in mind that they are reactive. And part of what they are reacting to is the fragmentation and alienation perceived as the prevailing condition of contemporary society.[25] Liberal society is fragmentation in practice, while community is the opposite. Yet these scholars seldom specify the meaning of community.

A pair of questions need to be raised, then, about current discussions of community. First, we have the *definitional* question: What is meant by community? What are its common attributes or characteristics? Community is obviously an enormously "open-textured" concept that needs to be clearly defined. As Raymond Plant notes, "Of all the concepts in terms of which we characterize, organize, and constitute our social and political experience, the concept of community seems to be the one most neglected by social and political philosophers."[26]

Second, we have the *historical* question: Was community indeed prominent in classical Greece, medieval Europe, and early America? In asking this question, I am concerned first with the claims of contemporary writers and then, in later chapters, with the descriptions of Tönnies, Durkheim, and other nineteenth-century social theorists. How accurate are the accounts of community presented by communitarian writers today and by scholars of the previous century? Were those communities, for example, so all-inclusive and continuously harmonious as is often suggested?

I take the title of this book, of course, from Edward Bellamy's famous utopian novel of 1888: *Looking Backward*.[27] This futuristic novel concerns a young man who awakens from a trance-induced sleep of more than a century to find that the misery of American life as he knew it has been transformed into a society of harmony, stability, abundance, and fellow feeling.

Bellamy's *Looking Backward* was a bitter denunciation of the social, economic, and political conditions of his time. In that regard, he had much in common with the concerns of contemporary communitarians. But Bellamy's book actually looked *forward* to a communitarian "golden age" in the year 2000, while communitarian writers today look *backward* to various golden ages of the past in their search for the ideal society.

In the following chapters, I draw on a great deal of recent historical scholarship in order to estimate the extent of community in the past. My aim is to draw a sociological portrait of life in those three periods so often mentioned by communitarian scholars. Only by detailing the deeper structures of social life and the dominant patterns of culture in these earlier periods can we learn what is different now from what has gone on before, and what is the same. To understand how things have changed, we require historical perspective. The bulk of this book, then, represents a sort of sociology of the past.

This is not, however, my only concern. Communitarian writers appeal to the historical existence of community to support their arguments concerning the "renewal" of community. They want to show that such an ideal is possible by establishing that it was once widely realized. In other words, contemporary communitarians look to the past for reassurance and guidance about the present world.[28]

But even if community was once widespread, that does not mean that it is a viable option today. Thus, a third question needs to be asked, this one a more purely *sociological* one: What are the conditions necessary for the realization of community and the mechanisms needed to maintain it? Questions about homogeneity, differentiation, and social control, for instance, are obviously of direct relevance to the existence of community. None of the scholars being considered here gives any systematic attention to the matter of the conditions for community.

Although I devote much attention to the historical question about the actual prevalence of community in earlier periods and to the sociological question about the conditions for community, my ultimate and deepest concern is with a fourth question: the relevance of community and communitarian thinking for our *moral* and *political* life. Is community an attractive possibility for us today? As noted, communitarian writers criticize the widespread individualism so dominant in the modern world and emphasize the need for community in its place. They also invoke a communitarian approach as an alternative to the extreme individualism and abstract formalism that they perceive as the prevailing theoretical position in political and moral philosophy today.[29]

Like Durkheim and several other nineteenth-century social theorists, communitarian thinkers today are interested in regenerating public life, in reanimating concern for one's fellows, in assuring harmony in contemporary life. Liberal society, they insist, is morally impoverished. Community is the necessary solution. They agree with Durkheim that "to experience the pleasure of saying 'we,' it is important not to enjoy saying 'I' too much."[30]

Much communitarian writing today is designed as a postmortem on the doctrine of liberalism. With its recurrent emphasis on the supreme value of communal affiliation, communitarian thinking is highly critical of the liberal commitment to individual rights. Sandel is quite forthright in arguing that we must give up the "politics of rights" for a "politics of the common good."[31] Other communitarians share his view.

In examining the politics of the common good later on in this book, I will consider communitarian thinking as an alternative to the liberal perspective in political and moral theory. What would be the consequences of bringing community into being? What would be the contours of that common moral life that communitarians advocate? What would be the practical implications for social arrangements in contemporary society? How would this help ameliorate injustice and alleviate human suffering?

Only after we have specified the characteristics of community, examined the historical record as to its prominence and the accuracy of the accounts presented by the scholars being considered, and investigated the conditions necessary for creating and maintaining community will we be able to offer an informed judgment about the crucial question concerning the viability of community in contemporary society.

In my view, the adequacy of the sorts of theories set forth by MacIntyre, Sandel, Taylor, the authors of *Habits of the Heart*, and other communitarian writers, the concrete possibility of realizing the ideal of community apparently held by so many people today, and the very desirability of such realization require answers to the questions raised above. This book aims to provide these answers.

# UNCOVERING THE
# COMMUNITARIAN IDEAL

MacIntyre, Sandel, Taylor, Bellah and his collaborators, and many other writers advocate community as a normative ideal. Yet, only the last-named specify what they intend by the term. It is important, then, to examine carefully what these different communitarians have to say about the attributes of community. For there seem to be some features that are basic in the conceptions set forth by the various communitarian writers. My interest is to distill a definition of community from the specific characteristics that communitarian scholars—either implicitly or explicitly—include as central to the notion of community. Thus, I will examine their writings in order to learn what *they* mean by community.

## I

Alasdair MacIntyre speaks of a community having the "realisation of the human good" as its shared aim,[1] of a community as envisaging its life as directed toward a "shared good" which provides it with its common tasks,[2] of communities in which people together pursue a "common good."[3] What is clearly crucial for MacIntyre is that there be "a community whose primary bond is a shared understanding both of the good for man and of the good of that community and where individuals identify their primary interests with reference to those goods."[4] Throughout *After Virtue*, one finds frequent reference to various elements that suggest the content of MacIntyre's community ideal. Among those attributes of community most often mentioned are a shared history, shared practices, shared meanings, a common tradition, and common ideals about a life together. In his more recent book—*Whose Justice? Which Rationality?*—he speaks of community as being "held together by sympathetic feeling and by coincidence of interest."[5]

Michael Sandel echoes much of what is said by MacIntyre. Community, he says, is marked by "a common vocabulary of discourse and a background of implicit practices and understandings."[6] He, too, characterizes community partly in terms of what is good for individuals and for the community itself. Sandel contrasts what he terms the "constitutive conception" of community with those conceptions of community where individuals cooperate either simply for the sake of achieving their private ends or in order to attain certain shared final ends.[7]

With regard to his own conception of community, Sandel writes: "to say that the members of a society are bound by a sense of community is not simply to say that a great many of them profess communitarian sentiments and pursue communitarian aims, but rather that they conceive their identity—the subject and not just the object of their feelings and aspirations—as defined to some extent by the community of which they are a part."[8] For the members of a genuine community, he adds, "community describes not just what they *have* as fellow citizens but also what they *are*, not a relationship they choose (as in a voluntary association) but an attachment they discover, not merely an attribute but a constituent of their identity."[9] Although he goes further than MacIntyre in specifying his conception of community, Sandel does not provide an actual definition of community.

Charles Taylor also refers frequently to community in his work, without specifying what he sees as its contours. In *Hegel*, he emphasizes "the moral obligations that I have to an ongoing community of which I am a part," and says that it is in virtue of the community's "being an ongoing affair that I have these obligations; and my fulfilment of these obligations is what sustains it."[10] It is essential, says Taylor, that man achieve his true identity in the public life of a community. In fact, "our highest and most complete moral existence is one we can only attain to as members of a community."[11] One of the great needs of the modern age, he says, is the achievement of communities that "can become again important centers of concern and activity for their members in a way which connects them to the whole."[12] In *Sources of the Self*, as well, Taylor refers to the crucial importance of a defining community.[13] But he does not say what it is.

Robert Bellah and his colleagues in *Habits of the Heart* differ from other communitarians in that they do offer a concrete definition of community in their glossary of key terms, although they unfortunately provide no extended discussion of it. They state:

> *Community* is a term used very loosely by Americans today. We use it in a strong sense: a *community* is a group of people who are socially interdependent, who participate together in discussion and decision making, and who share certain *practices* . . . that both define the community and are nurtured by it. Such a community is not quickly formed. It almost always has a history and so is also a *community of memory*, defined in part by its past and its memory of its past.[14]

It is no coincidence that the ingredients in this definition have much in common with the views of MacIntyre, Sandel, and Taylor, since Bellah et al. draw explicitly on the writings of these three scholars. Given the many similarities in the conceptions of community held by these different writers, it is appropriate to consider carefully the various elements contained in the definition above.

As they make clear in their book, Bellah and his collaborators conceive of a community as a group of people whose relationships are tied to a common territory. Like other communitarian writers, they see shared locality or place as having a unique community-engendering power. In a genuine community, they emphasize, people's affiliations are not the sort that are formed entirely voluntarily or broken at will. A common locale helps assure that people's ties to other community members are to some extent unwilled and nonvoluntary. Bellah et al. hold that groups based on freely chosen associations cannot replace "natural" inherited groups in maintaining the "moral order."[15]

From the perspective of communitarian theorists, only those forms of association that are based in part on locale are communities in the full-blooded sense. Thus, they would not consider the Arab community, the international community of scholars, or all those people who have a common interest in stamp collecting to be communities. Such persons do not share a common locale. Furthermore, they relate to one another solely on the basis of the interests that they have in common and not as members of a group with a rich texture of interconnections.

Bellah and his associates sometimes speak of a community as being national in scope but generally use the term in reference to more limited collectivities. Similarly, MacIntyre variously speaks of the community in terms of the city-state and local territory as well as in terms of kinship and religious groups.[16] Sandel also gives special emphasis to the importance of inherited membership for genuine community.[17] Taylor does the same. These scholars generally acknowledge that the modern state is too complex and heterogeneous to constitute a viable site for the re-creation of community. Instead, they place their hope in smaller, local collectivities.

Bellah and his colleagues' definition of community in terms of its being a group, then, refers partly to the territorial dimension of people's relationships. Here they combine aspects of the two major usages of "community" in the sociological literature. One, the territorial, conceives of community in terms of locale, physical territory, geographical continuity, and the like. The other, the relational, conceives of community in terms of the quality of human relationships and associations.

Like other communitarians who call for the return of community, Bellah and his associates place special emphasis on its relational aspects. At the same time, however, they also refer to it as a geographical entity. This is consistent with ordinary speech, where the term community usually refers to the people with whom we identify in a locale. Obviously, however, locality is not sufficient to turn a population into a community.

To continue with the definition set forth by the authors of *Habits of the Heart*, they say that a community is a group of people who are *socially interdependent*. This implies that in their involvements with one another people have some of their important needs and interests met by other group members, and that their actions have direct consequences for those with whom they regularly interact.

Certain shared behavior patterns are an ingredient of community. Thus, for a group of people to constitute a community, say Bellah and his associates, they must *participate* "together in discussions and decision making." This emphasis on mutual involvement and participation is a common theme to all writers on community. Sandel argues that we are all defined by our political associations, and MacIntyre emphasizes that traditions and practices can be maintained and understood only if all members of the community are regarded as competent participants in the ongoing process of shaping them. These writers follow Aristotle in viewing man as an active political agent whose humanity is realized through such activity.[18]

Bellah and his associates specify that community involves people sharing certain *practices*. Elsewhere in their book, they define practices as "shared activities that are not undertaken as means to an end but are ethically good in themselves."[19] Among other things, these practices define the patterns of loyalty and obligation that keep the community alive.[20] These practices help establish a web of interconnection by creating trust, joining people together, and making each individual aware of his or her reliance on the community.[21] Sandel and MacIntyre also give special attention to shared practices as central elements of community.[22]

Noting that a real community is not quickly formed, Bellah and his associates say that it almost always has a history and so is also a *community of memory*. A "community of memory" does not forget its past. "In order not to forget that past," we are told, "a community is involved in retelling its story, its constitutive narrative, and in so doing, it offers examples of the men and women who have embodied and exemplified the meaning of the community."[23] As they observe, MacIntyre speaks of the same thing in stressing the importance of the past, shared history, and common traditions. Sandel, too, emphasizes a shared history and common memories.

For these communitarian scholars, then, the shared collective values are uncovered from the traditions and practices of the group. These common values are deeply rooted in the history and ongoing activities of the community. People are members of a community and share its traditions and practices *before* they are able to explicitly recognize and reflect on what they have in common.

MacIntyre, Sandel, Taylor, and various other writers suggest that a true community requires that the bonds between the members rest on their mutual recognition or "we sense" of belonging together. This psychological dimension is absent, however, from the definition of community set forth by Bellah et al. in *Habits of the Heart.* Yet it is clear that they, like other scholars advocating community, place a high value on a shared emotional connection as an element of community. This shared sense of community—of how we see ourselves, of who and what we are— is, then, an additional characteristic in the conception of community espoused by various communitarian thinkers today.

## II

The definition offered by Bellah et al. as well as the writings of MacIntyre, Sandel, and Taylor all include four particular characteristics as central to community: a common geographical territory or locale, a common history and shared values, widespread political participation, and a high degree of moral solidarity. These four elements together make up the normative ideal of community common to communitarian thought. For these writers:

> A *community* is a group of people who live in a common territory, have a common history and shared values, participate together in various activities, and have a high degree of solidarity.

Let me now consider each of these four elements at greater length.

The *first* ingredient of community is a common territory. Although some social scientists today argue for the irrelevance of locality, communitarian writers conceive of community as being tied to place. They see a common territory as having unique community-engendering power. A common locale, in their view, helps assure that the various shared aspects of community arise from that form of life in which, as Sandel puts it, "the members find themselves situated 'to begin with.' "[24] Communitarian writers argue that inherited membership in a group creates a far stronger and more meaningful sense of attachment than does the sort of membership based on voluntary choice. People are seen as naturally and unselfconsciously identifying themselves with those with whom they share a territory, and as unquestioningly accepting the demands of the particular form of life into which they are born. As will be seen later, nineteenth-century social theorists also emphasized the importance of location.

14

The *second* characteristic of community is that the individuals who compose a community have a common history and shared values. Included are various attributes mentioned by communitarian scholars: traditions, practices, common understandings, and conceptions of the common good. A common history—with a specific background of events, activities, victories and defeats, successes and failures—helps assure consensus about where people come from and who they are. Common origins and common experiences are seen as providing the basic framework for individuals to understand and relate to one another. According to contemporary communitarian writers, as well as classical sociologists like Tönnies and Durkheim, the members accept and internalize the community's shared values and standards. Thus people in a genuine community comply with the norms, and external sanctions are generally unnecessary.

The *third* characteristic of community is that members participate widely in common activities. Advocates of community stress the importance of community members being involved in discussions and decisions about the most desirable form of collective life for themselves. Like Aristotle, they hold that only the public sphere admits of general deliberation about how people are to "be" together.

Community, from this perspective, involves the idea of collective, participatory engagement of people in the determination of the affairs that directly concern them. Benjamin Barber, whose work contains communitarian elements, points to a dialectic relationship between the nourishing of community and participatory civic activity: "Community grows out of participation and at the same time makes participation possible; civic activity educates individuals how to think publicly as citizens even as citizenship informs civic activity with the required sense of publicness and justice."[25] Community requires, then, that people be actively involved in common talk, common decision making, and common action.

Some writers on community emphasize the necessity of direct, intimate, face-to-face relations as a defining characteristic of community. But the communitarians being considered here do not include regular face-to-face relations as an element in their conception of community. They are agreed that in a modern state, and even in smaller localities, it is unrealistic to expect all members to have face-to-face contact with one another, and equally unrealistic to expect the sort of intimacy that is associated with people's relations with loved ones and close friends.

They share Aristotle's view that there are degrees of intimacy among members of the community who do not all know one another equally well—or even know one another at all. As I will make clear in a later chapter, the population of Athens in the fifth and fourth centuries B.C.

ran into the tens of thousands. Although Aristotle does say that those sharing membership in the *polis* are friends of a sort, they are not bound together by feelings of warmth and personal intimacy. He makes it clear that it is "impossible to be an intimate friend of many."[26] "For that reason," he continues, "it is also impossible to be in love with many people: being in love means to have something like an excess of friendship, and that is only possible toward one person. Accordingly, intimate friendship is only possible with a few people."[27]

But an inferior type of friendship, based on the sharing of interests, can exist among fellow citizens. What Aristotle calls "political" friendship is a species of friendship based on utility or shared interests among fellow citizens who are neither close friends nor relations.[28]

The communitarian thinkers being considered here do not, then, see a genuine community as requiring direct, face-to-face relations among people who care deeply about one another. Instead, they emphasize the importance of there being widespread opportunities for everyone to participate in the important affairs of the community, in collective decision making, and in the exercise of power.

The *fourth* and final characteristic of community is that it has a high degree of solidarity. The dimension of solidarity represents a combination of two elements found in the normative conceptions of community advanced by various communitarian writers: social interdependence and the "we sense" of belonging together. Bellah et al., for example, define community partly in terms of it being "a group of people who are socially interdependent."[29] But social interdependence, by itself, is not really a distinguishing characteristic of community. After all, each and every one of us is socially interdependent, whether it be in the family, the neighborhood, the workplace, or elsewhere. We all depend on others; others depend on us. It is a sociological truism that we cannot even conceive of a person separate and absolutely alone in the world, independent of other people. For human beings are not and never were, of course, atomic, separated, completely self-sufficient creatures.

Nor are they (or we) creatures for whom all other persons have the *same* significance. Thus, it is not enough to emphasize—as do Bellah and his associates in their formal definition of community—the importance of social interdependence for community. The sense of personal attachment or emotional involvement that Bellah and others speak of as an aspect of close personal interdependence must also be included.

Sandel emphasizes that community involves "fraternal sentiments and fellow feeling."[30] The element of solidarity in the above definition of community concerns, then, the extent and direction of people's fellow feeling and mutual concern for other persons. People who share membership in, say, a village or a town can be expected to think and speak of "our" village or "our" town. It will be an object of common identification for them.

Beyond this, communitarians argue, being a member of a community involves interdependencies that impose nonvoluntary moral obligations and create relationships of reciprocity. Community members ought to share a general and diffuse sense of solidarity with everyone else in the community: from those with whom they are most intimate to those in circles most removed from them personally. As members of the community, their responsibilities should run both to all other individual members and to the community as a whole.

Solidarity involves special concerns and moral obligations that are absent in people's relationships with individuals from outside the community. Bellah et al. mention those practices of commitment that "define the patterns of loyalty and obligation that keep the community alive,"[31] and MacIntyre and Sandel emphasize the special moral bonds between people who share membership in a community. These special ties were also seen as important by social theorists a century ago.

Solidarity is obviously limited and delimited by relation. Sandel makes this clear when he argues that those special loyalties, allegiances, and concerns one has as a member of a community go beyond the obligations one voluntarily incurs and the "natural duties" one owes to human beings more generally.[32] People owe more to some than to others simply because of the attachments and commitments constituting shared membership in a community.

The different communitarian writers all emphasize the *special* quality of people's obligations or duties toward others in the community. And, one way or another, they distinguish them from those sorts of obligations that individuals voluntarily incur through promising, consent, or voluntarily joining a group, as well as from those natural obligations that individuals may have to all other human beings.

Communal solidarity involves certain attitudes held in common by all members of the community. As noted, communitarian thinkers regard the group's obligations as *special*. They are seen as holding only within the community and as different from those obligations arising from voluntary commitments or owed equally to people outside the community. People's obligations and responsibilities toward the community are also viewed by communitarian thinkers as *personal*: they run not just to the community in a collective sense but also from each member to each other member. Members are expected to act in certain ways toward one another, to respond to each other in particular ways, and to value each and every person as a member of the group.

It is this normative ideal of community, then, that I will use in examining the historical question about the extent of community in classical

Greece, medieval Europe, and early America. This means *concretely* that I will be reviewing evidence relevant to the four elements contained in the normative conception advanced by communitarians: a common territory, shared values, collective participation, and social solidarity. Without these characteristics, they believe, a collective of persons does not constitute a genuine community.

## III

In referring to the prevalence of community in the past, sociologists, political theorists, philosophers, and others share certain assumptions about the four elements of community. They seem to assume, for example, that people in the periods being considered here inhabited a comparatively immobile world. Whereas people today change residences with great frequency, people in earlier periods are viewed as having been permanently settled in one place. Thus, it is argued, men and women in the past were much less dissociated and separated from one another than is the case today. But were people then really so permanently located and settled?

It is also assumed that in the periods being considered there was far greater consensus about values than exists in modern society. Communitarians believe that, partly because of the absence of geographical mobility, individuals shared the same traditions, practices, and conceptions of the common good. Marriages were stable, and children easily acquired the dominant values and customs from their parents.

Political participation, communitarians assume, was much more extensive in earlier periods. There was considerably more opportunity for individuals to be actively involved in various decisions that concerned their lives and well-being. In contrast to the apathy that we witness today, it is argued, people took their responsibilities as citizens very seriously. Are these assumptions correct?

While modern society is dominated by extreme individualism and self-centeredness, communitarians believe that earlier periods were characterized by fellow feeling and mutual concern. People were concerned with the good of the community and its individual members, and relationships of loyalty and obligation were dominant. Communal solidarity, it is assumed, helped preclude disagreement and conflict. Consensus about the good life, and thus about how people ought to live, assured that men and women inhabited a single moral culture. How accurate are these assumptions?

In my exploration of community in the past, I presume that certain *human needs* are experienced by people everywhere.[33] The needs for food and water, for periodic rest or sleep, for shelter in the sense of protection against the climate, for movement and exercise, to excrete, and to maintain one's body are common to all human beings. We can generate a list of such basic physical needs simply by considering what "human beings" must have if they are to continue to live and function. Failure to meet these physical needs will cause suffering for any human being.

Every society has the problem of meeting these basic needs. The survival and well-being of people also depends on their being able to meet certain *social* needs and to solve common problems of life. These problems arise because we are human beings and because the world is as it is. They are common in all times and places. As Stephen Toulmin points out, "the possibility of understanding the actions, customs, and beliefs of men in other milieus rests on our sharing not common 'sensations' or mental 'images,' but rather human *needs and problems*."[34]

These needs and problems arise whenever and however a number of human beings attempt to live together and reproduce their kind. We can think here of problems of family maintenance, the socialization of the young, the regulation of sex, control of violence and other forms of social deviance, authority relations, the allocation of work and labor, the distribution of status and other rewards, the provision of goods and services, and the care of the sick and needy. These social needs exist as much for a Stone Age society as for a modern industrial one.

In examining the three periods of concern to me, therefore, I will consider the different dimensions of community in terms of these sorts of universal problems. Organizing my exploration of community on this basis allows me to compare and contrast, at least roughly, across time and space.

Moreover, it provides an opportunity to make an initial judgment about the significance of a *politics of the common good*. As I noted in the Introduction, Sandel and other communitarians argue for the superiority of a politics of the common good over a politics of rights. Although both of these theoretical perspectives are concerned with the political realm, they also usually provide a justification for the sorts of legal, economic, and social arrangements that their advocates see as politically and morally preferable in regulating society.

Sandel points out that in some instances the two theories may lead to different arrangements or policies. In others, the two may give competing arguments in support of similar arrangements or policies.[35] But liberals usually defend their preferences by appealing to rights as protections for the needs and interests of individuals, while communitarians appeal to the common good.

In addition, communitarian thinkers say that societies not only should be, but often *have been*, organized and regulated by a politics of the common good. As I noted earlier, part of their argument for this perspective is that its superiority has been demonstrated in the past. Consequently, I will be concerned to see if there were justifications or legitimations for something akin to a politics of the common good in early America, medieval Europe, and ancient Greece.

Although I will not provide a detailed discussion of the implications of my historical analyses for the attractiveness and viability of a politics of the common good until chapter 8, a concern with this perspective informs my use of the materials in the chapters dealing with community in the past. Not only am I interested in whether or not there was something along the lines of a politics of the common good in each of the three periods, but I am also concerned with how the historical evidence about community relates to this.

Communitarian writers emphasize the importance of a common good based on shared purposes and standards that are fundamental to a people's way of life. Both individual conduct and a society's institutional arrangements, they argue, ought to be in accordance with a shared conception of the common good. They say that certain communal practices and ends can be accepted by everyone as the basis for a politics of the common good. The preferences and actions of individual men and women are to be evaluated in accordance with their contributions to that common good.[36] And the same holds true with regard to a society's institutional arrangements.

From the perspective of communitarians, the four central features of community enable and sustain a politics of the common good. At the same time, they hold, a politics of the common good helps assure the features of community. They argue that a *common territory*, the first of these features, is crucial in defining people's individual and collective identity. People who share the same locale, communitarians believe, unquestioningly accept the way of life into which they are born. They argue that a way of life that is found, rather than chosen, is defined by a shared conception of the common good. Communitarians claim that people in earlier periods did, in fact, usually remain in the particular place where they grew up.

But even if the historical evidence should show that there was little or no geographical mobility in the earlier periods, this is not sufficient to support communitarian assertions about people being embedded in and strongly attached to the way of life in which they found themselves "to begin with."

It could have been the case, for example, that different towns and villages had strict rules forbidding people from leaving and outsiders from moving in. Had this been true, the *absence* of movement would not accurately reflect people's attachment to the local way of life. What we have to know is whether people could have moved elsewhere had they wanted to.

Conversely, of course, historical evidence indicating the *presence* of considerable mobility does not establish that communitarians are mistaken about people's attachments. After all, individuals may have preferred to stay in their original locale but had to leave purely because of economic necessity. Only evidence showing that people chose to move because of dissatisfaction with the way of life where they lived counts against communitarian claims about people's attachments to their town or village.

What is at issue here is both the extent of social mobility and its relationship to a politics of the common good. This relationship goes in two directions. On the one hand, people being tied to the place or territory where they originally found themselves may or may not have enabled the achievement of a genuine politics of the common good. On the other hand, the presence of such a politics of the common good may or may not have assured that people would remain where they were.

Exactly the same line of reasoning holds for the other three main features of community. We need to know the extent to which people in the three time periods had a common history and shared the same values, participated in the important affairs of their town or village, and showed a high degree of social solidarity. And, further, we need to consider evidence pertaining to why people did or did not conduct themselves as communitarians say they did. Otherwise, it will not be possible to determine whether or not the four central features of community and a politics of the common good enabled and sustained one another.

What this means, then, is that my historical examination utilizes evidence concerning both *what* actually happened in early America, medieval Europe, and ancient Greece, and *why* things occurred as they did. Although I may sometimes err in the direction of giving more historical detail than is absolutely necessary, I attempt to provide enough to place community and a politics of the common good in the perspective of the time.

## IV

I make no pretense of having mastered the mass of historical literature relevant to the periods that concern me. But I have become familiar with many of the classic and standard works, as well as with many recent books and articles relevant to the problems at hand. My use of these materials reflects what Peter Novick terms an "elite bias," in that I give most attention to historical work that has received widespread recognition among historians.[37]

This does not mean that there is anything like complete consensus within the historical profession about the correctness of their findings and conclusions. Reading widely on the history of early America, the Middle Ages, and classical Greece, as well as on issues of methodology and epistemology as discussed by historians, has taught me that there is probably as little consensus among historians as among sociologists, philosophers, and political theorists today. But even in the absence of consensus, some stories about the past seem to stand up much more successfully to careful scrutiny than others.

As Michael Kammen shows in some detail, the contours of recent historical thought and scholarship are strongly different from those of past decades. Although he speaks specifically about significant work in American history, it appears to me that the same general pattern of change has occurred in other areas of historical scholarship as well. Kammen notes a "declining concern with traditional political history—the narratives of public institutions, officials, and their competition for power," on the one hand, and "a notable awakening of interest in social history," on the other.[38] "In contemporary historiography," writes Kammen, "social history has come to focus on the examination of changes in social structure, mobility, bonds of community, social order and dis-order, intergenerational relationships, the history of the family and childhood."[39]

Along with an increase in studies of one or another subdivision of social history—often the oppressed and the historically inarticulate—there has been a remarkable growth in the writing of local history, in-depth investigations of a locality. These studies have been important in challenging the conventional wisdom about various periods and subjects of concern to professional historians. American history, especially, has witnessed an increase of local studies where we hear the voices of women, the poor, and people of color. Many of these recent investigations have been strongly influenced by Marc Bloch, Georges Duby, Emmanuel LeRoy Ladurie, and other European scholars whose studies have come to be regarded as major classics in reconstructing the past.[40]

There is, as Kammen points out, no consensus among historians about the most appropriate way of doing any kind of history.[41] As will be seen, I draw on a wide variety of sources in attempting to ascertain the prominence of community in different times and places. Some of these are earlier works that appear not to have been successfully challenged by new evidence. But many of them are important, original, and often methodologically innovative works that have appeared in the past two decades or so. They utilize such sources as tax assessments, wills, deeds, estate inventories, lawsuit testimony, voting records, notaries' registers, and other documentary evidence, as well as maps and aerial photographs, the analysis of themes found in paintings, and the examination of archaeological objects.

My examination of the historical evidence about community sets the stage, so to speak, for later consideration of the preconditions for community, the consequences of community, and the possibility of restoring community in the modern world. It is to the historical evidence that I first turn in the next several chapters. I begin with America and look backward.

# ONCE UPON A TIME IN AMERICA

ACCORDING TO many communitarian thinkers, community was prominent in the critical period of America's founding. At the local level, there were close personal ties among people, a general concern for one's neighbors, and a sense of responsibility for their welfare. At the national level, there was a strong sense of shared purpose that helped to shape a common life. The founding fathers, we are told, were part of a republican tradition that had its earliest roots in Aristotle's *Politics*.

These communitarians draw on the work of several prominent historians who posit the omnipresence of classical republicanism or civic humanism in the critical period of America's founding. Those advocating this "republican synthesis" argue that the moral foundation of the American republic can be found in that tradition of political philosophy which draws on the writings of antiquity, on Machiavelli, and on eighteenth-century "Country party" thinkers in England.[1]

Central to this tradition was the belief that ultimate authority is rooted in the community at large. Much emphasis was placed on "virtue" as an ideal stressing preference for the public good over personal advantage, love of country, and a readiness to serve. Also central was the belief that man is by nature a being who achieves moral fulfillment by participating in a self-governing republic.

This republican system of ideas stressed further the omnipresent danger to society and the polity from corruption by luxury and power, respectively. A concern with the public good, with the development of virtuous citizens through their participation in civil life, and with the health of the wider community were important aspects of this republican tradition.[2]

But even if it is true that the founding fathers were themselves guided by republican values, this says nothing about the attitudes and behavior of most Americans at the time. Contemporary communitarian thinkers give considerable weight to that historiography of the founding period which has focused on the language employed in essays, letters, speeches, and other forms of discourse in late eighteenth-century America. They pay far less attention to the question of whether republican discourse is an accurate representation of the social and political reality of that period.

MacIntyre says that republicanism represented an attempt at a partial restoration of the classical tradition. Central to republicanism in eighteenth-century America was "the notion of a public good which is prior to and characterisable independently of the summing of individual desires and interests." For the individual, writes MacIntyre, virtue "is nothing more or less than allowing the public good to provide the standard of individual behaviour." In addition to allegiance to the public good, he says, republicanism was guided by a "passion for equality."[3] Members of the community were assumed to possess equal rights and privileges, and to bear equal obligations to one another. MacIntyre claims, then, that Americans in the founding period were guided by a concern for the public good and the welfare of their fellows.

Like MacIntyre, Bellah et al. associate republicanism with equality and allegiance to the public good. "Classical republican theory from Aristotle to the American founders," they assert, "rested on the assumption that free institutions could survive in a society only if there were a rough equality of condition, that extremes of wealth and poverty are incompatible with a republic."[4] The republican ideal, say the authors of *Habits of the Heart*, was a self-governing society of relative equals in which all participated.[5] It is because of the sense of public solidarity in the founding period, they argue, that recovery of the insights of the republican tradition is so crucial today.[6]

William Sullivan, one of Bellah's associates in the above book, gives detailed attention to republicanism and its importance in his own book: *Reconstructing Public Philosophy*.[7] He says that an emphasis on individual dignity, mutual respect, universal participation, and mutual responsibility were common elements in the republican tradition in America.[8] The republican founders "sought to promote civic virtue through an active public life built up through an egalitarian spirit of self-restraint and mutual aid."[9] The "rediscovery" that America's founding was strongly shaped by the republican tradition "makes possible new conceptual analyzes as an aspect of the historical interpretation."[10] Further, argues Sullivan, republicanism must be the essential core for an effective public philosophy and a viable community in America today.[11]

Michael Sandel also champions republicanism, virtue, and community. And he, too, draws on those historians who have seen republicanism in America's founding. "If the 'republican school' is right about our ideological origins," he states, "then perhaps there is hope for revitalizing our public life and restoring a sense of community."[12]

But is the republican school right? And are the new communitarians right about America's origins? In trying to answer these questions, I will be concerned with the sociopolitical reality and not with the language of late eighteenth-century American politics. My focus will be on the general membership of society rather than on the founding fathers. What, I am asking, was life like for most people at the time?

Did people have a sense of common purpose and allegiance to the larger community? Were their actions guided by a shared commitment to the public good? Did they value the general welfare over their own personal advantage? Was there a rough equality of conditions at the time? Were people concerned with avoiding the temptations of power and luxury? Was there collective, participatory involvement of people in those decisions that directly concerned them? Was there, that is, access to a political arena in which people could participate and fulfill themselves as citizens and human beings? Did their behavior reveal a sense of concern for their fellows? What, I want to know, was the extent of communal solidarity at the time?

How true, in short, are the assertions of communitarian writers about the historical reality of late eighteenth-century America? In attempting to answer this question, in particular as it pertains to the revolutionary and constitutional periods of America's history, I have spread my net much wider and drawn on a far larger number of historical investigations than have the new communitarians.[13]

The authors of *Habits of the Heart* draw very heavily on Tocqueville for their portrait of early America, although they do make some reference to more recent historical studies. But neither they nor other communitarian writers mention those in-depth case studies in which professional historians have tested the conventional wisdom about America's past. Nor do they mention at all recent research by economic historians and historical demographers.

Several books in social history have focused on the social structure, patterns of authority, and social relationships in particular villages, towns, and regions in seventeenth- and eighteenth-century America. As Kammen points out, "American historians are examining smaller units of society in greater detail than ever before."[14] In addition, other historians are producing much more detailed knowledge about population patterns and the geography of early America.

In the rest of this chapter, I draw on studies by social historians of specific villages, towns, and regions as well as on a considerable amount of historical evidence concerning family composition, social stratification, political participation, and other aspects of social and cultural life in America's colonial years as well as in the founding period. Then, in the following chapter, I turn to a consideration of the claims of contemporary communitarian thinkers in the light of what historians today have concluded about the reality of life in eighteenth-century America. By going into some detail about these matters, my intention is both to be able to estimate the extent of community at the time and to provide an accurate picture of American society more generally.

I

At the end of the colonial period around 1775, the total population of the thirteen colonies was roughly 2,350,000. Excluding Indians, about 53 percent of the colonies' inhabitants in 1775 lived in the North and the rest in the South.[15]

Of the total population, about 20 percent were black slaves and 1 percent were free blacks.[16] While blacks made up less than 3 percent of the population in the northern colonies, they constituted more than 40 percent of the South's population. About 56 percent of America's inhabitants were children and people younger than twenty-one, with the rest of the population being split evenly between adult men and women. In general, the population was very young; only some 5 percent were forty-five or older.[17] This differed somewhat among the various colonies.

Most American families made their living in agriculture, with the agricultural sector engaging 80–90 percent of the work force at the time of independence.[18] The size of farms and the value of land varied greatly between regions. The small subsistence farmer, doing all his own work and owning no slaves, was especially prevalent in the northern colonies. Large farmers were more often found in the South, where the soil was richer and where they utilized slave labor. It was there that one found the largest landowners (planters) and most of the slave population.

Next to farmers, artisans were the second most prevalent occupational group in the colonies.[19] A wide variety practiced their crafts in every farming village of the North and on most southern plantations. In large cities, there were literally dozens of different crafts. Carpenters, weavers, coopers, masons, blacksmiths, tailors, shoemakers, and the like varied enormously in their earnings. Obviously, those who hired themselves out did less well than those who had their own business. As a category, however, artisans were not very well-off. Shopkeepers earned more than most farmers and most artisans. Together with the local innkeeper, they were frequently men of some importance in many towns.

In 1775 only a tiny professional class existed in colonial America, consisting of clergymen, doctors, lawyers, and teachers. The lawyers in particular were often men of considerable wealth. Some of these professionals, as well as some rich merchants, and many extremely rich planters in the South, were often accorded nonmilitary titles such as "gentleman" or "esquire." Such titles were accorded only to men of property.[20] It was this small group that made up the wealthy elite in the late colonial era. This was especially so in the southern colonies. As Morgan emphasizes, Americans in the eighteenth century always distinguished the "better sort" from the "middling sort" and from the "poorest sort."[21]

Not surprisingly, colonies of different size, geographic location, conditions of settlement, historical experience, forms of government, population composition, and wealth were quite dissimilar. The thirteen colonies were distinct entities, separated from one another by inadequate systems of intercolonial transportation and communication, divided by suspicion and regional jealousies.[22]

Since it would be extremely difficult to consider each of the different colonies at length, I am going to provide a detailed description of Massachusetts and Virginia. My main concern, of course, is with the period around the time of the Revolution. But to understand life for people at that time, it is necessary to consider the colonists in Massachusetts and Virginia from the earliest years.[23] Furthermore, there are some scholars who see Puritan Massachusetts as the major source of community in America.[24] I select these two colonies because they have been more thoroughly studied than any other colonies, because the established leaders of Massachusetts and Virginia charted the course of the Revolution, and because the two states would fight out their differences into the Civil War.[25] Thus, the Massachusetts and Virginia colonies demand close examination.

## II

Thomas Bender points out in his *Community and Social Change in America* that much American historiography has been shaped by a picture of community breakdown.[26] According to this model, early New England was composed of a series of locality-based, small, closed, self-contained, tightly knit, Puritan commonwealths, characterized by shared values, political consensus, bonds of sentiment and mutuality, a managed economy, and a general lack of differentiation. This has long been a persistent stereotype of seventeenth- and eighteenth-century New England. References to early New England call up visions of small villages of wooden frame or Georgian brick houses, located around the town common or green, where God-fearing, freedom-loving, and idealistic Puritans or Yankees participated as equals in town-meeting democracy.

As Bender notes, book-length studies by a dozen or so American historians are in agreement that there was indeed community in early New England. But they disagree as to when it broke down. The earliest collapse, observes Bender, is said to have occurred in the 1650s, while other historians locate the breakdown in the 1690s, 1740s, 1780s, 1820s, 1850s, and even in the 1920s. Bender himself argues that it was not until 1870 that a locality-based pattern of community was destroyed in American society.[27]

The historians whom Bender discusses have an essentially sociological conception of community. Very much like Durkheim and Weber, they give primary emphasis to the crucial importance of what is shared or held in common by a people: locale, history, values, beliefs, attitudes, commitments, modes of thinking, understandings, and the like, which assure consensus, cohesion, mutuality, and a concern for the common good. In one way or another, they all emphasize the loss of community. But I begin with a prior question, concerning the extent to which community actually existed in early America.[28]

### Massachusetts: The Early Years

All too often, little detailed information is provided about the backgrounds of the early settlers in America. In fact, it is only since 1965 that historical demographers in the United States and England have begun to produce work concerning the population history of early America.[29] This is important in understanding what happened thereafter.

Although there were a few Spaniards in Florida, a small number of Dutch in the New York area, and a few hundred settlers in Plymouth, emigration on a large scale began with the so-called Great Migration from England in the 1630s. Based mainly on the studies of early parish registers in England and census counts in America for the British government between 1623 and 1775, there is now much more detailed knowledge about the early settlers than was available twenty-five years ago.

Approximately 155,000 people left England for the mainland American colonies in the period between 1630 and 1700. About 116,000 emigrated to the South and 39,000 to the North in the period.[30] They included a small but unknown proportion from Wales, Scotland, and Ireland. The peak level of emigration to the colonies was in the 1640s and 1650s, and it then continued at a substantial but declining level in the following decades. As Wrigley and Schofield make clear, people left England for a variety of motives. Many left in search of greater freedom to worship as they wished, but poverty and a hope for greater economic opportunities were probably the most important motives.[31]

Around one thousand English immigrants arrived in Massachusetts in the year 1630. On the basis of reports from English explorers in the early years of the seventeenth century, the English had developed an image of

New England as a rich and abundant land, with an ocean teeming with fish, excellent harbors, large expanses of fertile lands, thick forests, and docile and cooperative natives.[32] On the eve of permanent settlement in New England, some of those leaving England focused on nationalist expansion; others on adventure, speculation, and economic gain; and still others on religious freedom.

Those English men, women, and children arriving on the shores of Massachusetts in 1630 were a composite of English society at the time, including nobility, representatives of the urban middle class and mercantile interests in London, men from the law and the ministry, many yeomen, artisans, and laborers, and a large number of indentured servants.[33] It appears that around 10–15 percent of the passengers bound for Massachusetts during the great Puritan migration of the 1630s were servants, and they constituted about a third of the initial work force.[34]

By the end of 1630, the Puritan colonists were dispersed among seven settlements: Salem in the north, Dorchester in the south, and between them Boston, Medford, Charlestown, Watertown, and Roxbury.[35] Plymouth, settled earlier by the Pilgrims, by that time had about five hundred persons. Between 1630 and 1640, there was considerable dispersal from the Puritan-dominated settlements around Massachusetts Bay throughout southern New England. Religious disputes and jealousies among the Puritan leaders, political rivalries, dissatisfaction with the amount of available land, and commercial ambitions were among the motives giving rise to emigration to areas outside the jurisdiction of the Bay Colony.

During the second decade, the desire for cheaper land and other economic interests brought people to move from both Massachusetts Bay and Plymouth to sites westward and northward, as numerous new towns were created throughout the colony. By 1660, a population of more than twenty thousand was spread over nearly fifty different towns.[36]

Groups of settlers from various English regions differed in both their social backgrounds and experiences and their motivations for emigrating to America. These differences were often reflected in the kinds of agriculture that they practiced and the strength of their religious concerns.[37] But they all came with a shared culture to some extent and, especially, a shared language. They brought with them the values and experiences of Englishmen of their time.

However strong their religious impulses, an emphasis on control of their own individual destinies was common to most of them. Alan Macfarlane, who has traced family and landholding patterns back to the thirteenth century, argues that ordinary people in England have always been "rampant individualists, highly mobile both geographically and socially, economically 'rational,' market-oriented and acquisitive, ego-centred in kinship and social life."[38] Other contemporary historians agree that many of the leading Puritans were "adventurers who shared the accumulative acquisitive instinct abroad in England at the time."[39]

The first settlers brought with them, then, both religious and social values. As Puritans, they were committed to living a personal life subject to the divine commandments and God's will. Each individual was expected to prepare him- or herself for an active, disciplined, and responsible life in society. The tension between the sins of self-interest and the demands of Christian morality was recognized, and every individual was responsible for his own conduct. Every person had the obligation to assure God's will through the operation of his or her conscience.

For the Puritans, America was the best refuge for God's people; it was to be the "new Israel." They emphasized love, peace, and cooperation among those who shared their religious beliefs. In the early period of settlement, however, the right to share in the government was restricted to those "visible saints" who were the proven elect. Only those who could establish before the church elders their sainthood and ability to lead the kind of life enjoined by the strict precepts of the Puritan ethic were admitted to the Congregation.[40] But even among those devout Puritans who could qualify for church membership and enjoy the franchise, the proportion of those who had any voice in the colonial government was very small. George Haskins estimates that around 1640 it could not have been more than 7 or 8 percent.[41]

Although their religious values emphasized mutuality, these Puritans also emphasized a hierarchy of relationships among their members. They came from a society that was highly stratified and characterized by a clearly differentiated status hierarchy. At the top of English society was the monarchy, followed by the nobility. Then came those gentlemen who constituted the gentry. The primary characteristic of a gentleman was that he need not work with his hands but could employ others to do the necessary labor for him. Not more than 4 or 5 percent of the population belonged to the gentry and to those above them in the social hierarchy. As Peter Laslett points out, this "tiny minority owned most of the wealth, wielded the power and made all the decisions, political, economic and social for the national whole."[42] Below them were the merchants, followed by the yeoman class, husbandmen, artisans, laborers, and servants, with paupers being at the bottom.[43]

This ancient order of English society was seen as eternal and unchangeable, reflecting the natural hierarchy of social distinctions. Society was viewed as a living organism in which each of its component parts performed the functions necessary for the welfare of the whole. The king was the "head" or the "father" of his subjects, ruling paternally over his children. And the nobility and the wealthy gentry, as well, were seen as making important contributions to the health and survival of all. Those below them in this natural hierarchy performed much more modest—though socially necessary—functions.

It seems clear that this doctrine was very much akin to the "politics of the common good" that I mentioned in the previous chapter. Each member of English society was expected to fulfill the function that he or she was allotted, because each functioned for the sake of the greater whole and not for his or her own sake. Social arrangements were justified, then, on the basis of the capacity of different groups and individuals to contribute to the common good of the society. Such a justification or rationale is always required, since there may be some who will question the rightness of higher rewards for the privileged and submission and obedience for others.

In general, kings, rulers, statesmen, and the wealthy and privileged in all societies justify the dominant social arrangements by emphasizing their special contribution to the functioning, health, or harmony of the social whole. But as Durkheim has emphasized, this in itself is not enough. He points out that "what is needed if social order is to reign is that the mass of men be content with their lot. But what is needed for them to be content, is not that they have more or less but that they be convinced that they have no right to more. And for this it is absolutely essential that there be an authority whose superiority they acknowledge and which tells them what is right."[44]

In England during the early seventeenth century, there was an authority whose superiority was acknowledged and which told people what was right: the Church of England. The people of England were literal Christian believers, all the time. Ordinary people and the privileged alike, notes Laslett, "looked on the Christian religion as the explanation of life, and on religious service as its proper end."[45] It was the church that authorized and justified the unquestioning subordination which characterized the patriarchal arrangements so dominant in England at the time. Such arrangements were, in fact, required by the content of Christianity itself.

Attendance at service and communion was compulsory for everyone. Children were required to take communion before the age of twelve (later fourteen), and were required to know the articles of faith, the Lord's Prayer, and the Ten Commandments by that time on pain of excommunication.[46] Obviously, then, religion was central to everyone's life from an early age.

Every parish priest had the stated duty to teach the children in his flock the catechism. In every one of the ten thousand parishes in England, writes Laslett, there gathered "the group of adolescents from the houses of the gentry and the yeomen, the husbandmen, the tradesmen, the labourers and even the paupers to learn what it meant to be a Christian." And every single one of them had to learn by heart the following words from the catechism of the Church of England: "My duty towards my neighbour is to love him as myself, and to do to all men as I would they should do unto me: to love, honour and succour my father and mother: to submit myself to all my governors, teachers, spiritual pastors and masters; to order myself lowly and reverently to all my betters."[47] These words, learned by all Englishmen three centuries ago, helped assure that the habit of obedience to the head of the authoritarian family was extended to the heads of the social and political order.[48]

Thus, those men and women arriving in early Massachusetts brought with them this same habit of obedience. Supported by the faithful devotion of all those settlers who lived by their own labor, the natural-born leaders of these Puritan settlers constituted the ruling minority. The hierarchy of wealth and status among them was as inevitable, they believed, as it was desirable. In fact, land was initially distributed on the basis of men's status back in England. Granting more land to the rich than the poor rested on consensus as to who were the most deserving.

David Allen's very detailed examination of the settlers of five Massachusetts towns from different English regions reveals considerable economic stratification in each of them. And differences in wealth were accompanied by differences in the amount of land that men had. The wealthiest 10 percent of the original settlers controlled anywhere from 31 percent to 56 percent of the allotted land in these Massachusetts towns, while the bottom 50 percent held only 8–14 percent.[49] Some men arriving in Massachusetts had no land at all.

By granting more land to the rich than to the poor, each town's settlers set the framework both for the status structure and for economic developments in the colony. As James Lemon observes, "the middling and lesser sorts accepted the differences as part of the customary social design."[50] This, as we shall see, had a very significant impact on what occurred thereafter.

Thus men who had been wealthy or prominent in the localities from which they came continued to be so in Massachusetts. As long as the gap between high and low was not too extreme, hierarchy was not viewed as a threat to peace and harmony. Compared with the vast distances in the English social hierarchy, the distribution of wealth and status in these villages represented experiments in controlled similarity.[51]

As already noted, the first influx of Puritans resulted in the creation of half a dozen small towns in the immediate vicinity of Boston. Later settlers lived in other villages scattered throughout the colony. These villages were characterized by a striving for uniformity and the avoidance of conflict. Each had its own formal bylaws, serving to protect the common interests and prevent disorder. Peace, unity, and stability were the ideal to which they aspired. Although there was consensus that economic betterment would remain differential, it was assumed that everyone could improve his economic position.

The same men were likely to be leaders in the village, the church, and the colony, and the three forms of power reinforced one another. Deference from ordinary folk to those of high rank was expected. Most people accepted the special capacity of elite members to speak with authority on important public issues and fill the highest positions on the basis of their wealth, status, and personal prestige. A hierarchical social model was dominant, and with it a set of assumptions that stressed deference to social superiors. "The government of Massachusetts," Haskins writes, was "a dictatorship of a small minority who were unhesitatingly prepared to coerce the unwilling to serve the purposes of society as they saw it."[52]

The same model dominated the marital relationship. Just as in seventeenth-century English families, the husband wielded absolute authority. The wife owed him obedience in secular and religious matters alike.[53] In fact, the law restricted the rights of women to act independently of their husbands. A woman could not enter into a contract or write a will without her husband's consent.[54] If she earned money outside the home (as did some women in Boston, for instance), the husband had the right to all such earnings. Massachusetts lawmakers opposed separate property rights for women during marriage.[55]

As today, the nuclear family was the standard household unit. One married couple and their own children always formed the core of the family, and usually comprised its full extent. Only rarely was the home shared with someone from an older generation or single siblings. The average age of marriage was twenty-one or twenty-two for women and twenty-five or twenty-six for men in Massachusetts.[56] The average couple produced a total of eight children, of whom at least three-quarters survived to adulthood.[57]

The rural farmstead, occupied by a single household, was the standard unit of settlement for most persons in the seventeenth and eighteenth centuries. Farmsteads were sometimes clustered next to one another in a village but were more often separated by contiguous fields. Initially dispersed, these individual farmsteads eventually coalesced into loose rural neighborhoods or settlements. There seem to have been several reasons for such dispersion. Most important, argues Lemon, was the desire of many early settlers to exercise control over their own land and over their own production.[58]

Although it has often been assumed that "open-country" landscapes were seldom found in seventeenth-century Massachusetts, it now appears that this pattern of settlement was present from the earliest times. Lemon cites recent research showing that most initial settlements were dispersed and that there were only about twenty-eight agricultural villages (where homesteads were clustered on small home lots, surrounded by open fields and common meadows and pastures, and where church buildings, taverns, and stores were also clustered) formed in the early decades of New England.[59] Even most of the village houses were stretched out along a broad street, rather than being closely gathered around a meetinghouse.

Whether or not a town began as a dispersed settlement, dispersion was soon widespread. In contrast to our idea of a town today as being a small city or small urban center, a "town" in New England was essentially a large tract of land with a defined legal status, privileges, and responsibilities.[60] Initially a town was assigned to a group of settlers, frequently coming from the same region of England. After the initial settlement of a few towns in the 1630s and 1640s, most towns were created by a group of men petitioning the ruling colonial body to establish a new settlement.

If permission was given, a tract for the new settlement was delimited, and a committee of proprietors allotted land in accordance with men's wealth and status, and also decided how the fields were to be utilized. Some of these towns received very large original tracts. Dedham, one of the largest, had an original tract of almost two hundred square miles.[61] Andover had about sixty square miles, and many of the other towns were large and spread out. In most towns, the house lots assigned to each family for house, garden, and storage buildings comprised the initial town center or village.[62]

Usually not long after settlement, the unallotted land outside the village center passed into private ownership through a series of divisions. The wealthier settlers were in a position to acquire an increasingly disproportionate amount of the available land. In most villages, the initial differences in material condition were soon magnified by the richer settlers' rapid accumulation of available land. This had an important impact on subsequent relations among the early New Englanders.

Chunks of land appropriated by companies, proprietors, and speculators were organized into "fee-simple" lots of varying size for sale. Lemon notes that fee-simple ownership had been developed prior to 1600 in

England and "denoted the nearly absolute right of the owner to, and the exclusion of all others from, the use of that piece of property, as defined by deed."[63] Such private land was rapidly enclosed and marked by fences, walls, and blazes.

A settler's total acreage was very often spread in several parcels around the original village plot, and such dispersal meant that much time was spent traveling from field to field. This very quickly spurred farmers to move from the village plot to locations closer to their fields, and sons often chose to move to land farther away in order to establish households independent of their parents.

Even laws requiring everyone to live within a certain distance of the town meetinghouse had little effect on stopping men from moving away from the center, as the laws were ignored and ultimately unenforceable. The breakdown of the original town-congregation method of settlement had already begun, as farmers moved from the village to their increasingly outlying farmlands.

Farming was not the only activity that drew people away from the town center. For example, gristmills and sawmills had to be erected at sites where waterpower was available, and trading posts had to be established at locations between towns, thus drawing people around them.

Such population dispersal not only challenged the primacy of the original center but also gave rise to conflicts. Those people living in the outer community came to resent having to travel to the town center to attend church and school, and thus demanded such facilities for themselves. Where the outlying population grew large enough, its inhabitants were often granted permission from the parent village to become a precinct of the original town and eventually to become an independent town.

One way of dealing with the conflict arising from so many people dispersing to new areas outside the original town center, then, was to create new towns. "This process of town subdivisions operated well enough for several decades," writes Douglas McManis, "but by the end of the seventeenth century, the original towns began to oppose bitterly further reduction of population, territory, and revenues."[64]

But however a town was created, there was everywhere an ideal of active participation by all eligible adult males in the town meeting that governed each village. Attendance at town meetings was generally compulsory, but not all men were allowed to vote. At the outset, only freemen had a vote. After 1647, however, nonfreemen who were over twenty-four and who had taken the resident's oath of fidelity to the colony might vote on certain issues in town meetings.[65] Women were excluded altogether from such meetings. Most towns elected a group of "select men" to manage their affairs in the periods between meetings. The selectmen enjoyed almost complete control over all aspects of local administration.

The earliest meetings appear to have been concerned mainly with the admission of new settlers and the allotment of land. Later, talk at the town meetings was of road repair, field surveys, schoolmasters' salaries, and the like. There was also a concern with how to deal with those who threatened the harmony of the town or village. For instance, fines were instituted against anyone borrowing another's possessions without permission or cutting down trees on the common land. These town meetings were dominated by the gentry and wealthier merchants, especially in the backcountry towns. Most of the men attending were essentially passive and usually left most decisions to the selectmen.

People had to apply for admission to the town or village in which they wished to live, and those who were disapproved had to move elsewhere. Settled villages often told strangers to move on, and moved them on if they did not go voluntarily. The law was used to keep vagrants and unsupported people out of the town or village limits. "Poor persons were aided if they were members of a townsman's family," writes Kenneth Lockridge, "otherwise sent packing no matter how hungry they might be; the town would take care of its own but would not risk expense or scandal by entertaining impoverished outsiders."[66]

From the first decade, the ideal of the close harmonious community, founded on mutual consent, was threatened by people leaving to seek their future elsewhere. Shortly after their founding, many towns saw a considerable amount of out-migration. Some of this occurred because of dispersal to outlying areas, some because of the pursuit of growing economic opportunities elsewhere by wealthy townsmen, some because of the lack of any opportunities for the town's poor residents, and some because of disagreements or conflicts.

In the five Massachusetts town studied by Allen, he found that all experienced out-migration in the early years. Even in Rowley, which had the lowest level of emigration, one-quarter of the original landholders moved elsewhere within the first decade or so. At least some of them, says Allen, went "to start or join newer communities further inland that may have offered greater opportunities for economic advancement."[67] Newbury had an even higher level of outmigration, with 36 percent of the original landholders leaving. Along with limited economic opportunities, Allen mentions other forces working against stable communities: the social fragmentation created by dispersal to outlying areas to find land, conflicts over the lessening amount of available land, and religious controversies between conservatives and evangelicals.[68]

Internal conflicts, the rapid turnover of land, and the stimulation of distant economic opportunities had even more profound effects in the two largest seventeenth-century towns than elsewhere in Massachusetts. If it was difficult to realize the Puritan social vision in the agricultural villages with their seasonable rhythms and settled routines, it was even more difficult in the port towns of Boston and Salem.

### Boston and Salem

Midway across the Atlantic, John Winthrop—the first governor of colonial Massachusetts—addressed his friends aboard the *Arbella*, the flagship of the 1630 migration: "We are a company professing ourselves fellow members of Christ and we ought to count ourselves knit together by this bond of love, and live in the exercise of it."[69] These colonists intended to create an ideal community, what Winthrop called "A model of Christian Charity," a new Jerusalem, a city upon a hill.

Winthrop envisioned a model society in which men and women would subordinate themselves to the public good. There was to be one church where everyone attended and listened to the word of God. The church was to serve as a unifying social and political organization as well as a haven for the settlers' souls. Everyone in the community would work together, pray together, and see to one another's spiritual and physical welfare. Such was the blueprint of how Winthrop and the other leaders wanted their ideal community to develop.

But soon after landing in Massachusetts, the settlers were forced to disperse around the Bay. Eventually Winthrop and about 175 men, women, and children settled on a hilly peninsula that the Indians called Shawmut. Because the name Boston had been selected earlier for the central community, this name was given to the city upon a hill. From the beginning, the town grew steadily: to around 200 by 1631, approximately 300 by the end of 1632, 400 by the end of 1633, and to more than 600 by the end of 1635. It then doubled in size between 1635 and 1638, and had a population exceeding 2,000 by the end of the decade.[70]

Town and government were originally synonymous. Except for servants, all adult males participated in governing the community when called upon. All shared in the distribution of land and grazed their cattle on those lands held in common by the town. The protection of the community extended over all men, women, and children, in sickness or want. Initially, then, Boston did seem to resemble the fundamental unity that Winthrop had envisioned: a community to which all belonged "as members of the same body."

This apparent unity, however, was short-lived. Winthrop's ideal of a cohesive community was soon to be disrupted. One of the disrupting factors was the division of land. The original idea was that the first set-tlers would receive land proportionate to their investment in the Massa-chusetts Bay Company, with the paying of passage being accounted an investment.[71] But this policy was never effected in an orderly manner.

By the end of the first decade, Boston's gentry—some thirty families—had received almost one-half of the acreage granted by the town.[72] These rich men engrossed lands of several hundred acres, often taking up resi-dence on the land and directing the activities of their many servants. The holdings of the vast majority of settlers, by comparison, were often very small, and many men commuted to their "places for husbandry" from their homes on the peninsula. Whereas Winthrop's city upon a hill was predicated on the willingness of everyone to put the good of the commu-nity above his own private interests, quarrels about the allotment of land were a source of division from the onset.

In the 1640s as in the 1630s, the Boston gentry dominated the town economically, politically, and socially. But whereas the leaders of the first decade were men with wealth in land, many of the men in the second decade owed their wealth to commerce.[73] In both periods, however, the interests of the gentry were often at odds with those of the generality. And within both groups, there was a jarring of interests. The idea of a single community was gone, divided by "acquisitive men seeking to slake their ambition in the fertile soil and commerce of the New World."[74]

The community sought by Winthrop and the early settlers in 1630 was not to be. "If the crumbling of the Winthropian ideal is to be seen in roughly the first decade of settlement," writes Darrett Rutman, "it is even more clearly discernible in the second."[75] Population dispersal and quar-rels about land increased in the second decade, while church member-ship declined. With a proliferating materialism and individualism, with divergent interests within and between the gentry and the generality, with a division between town and church, and even within the church itself, fragmentation and dispute had become widespread. In Boston, concludes Rutman, Winthrop's ideal of community "was transformed into the reality of modern society."[76]

Like Boston, Salem was to become an important port town in Massa-chusetts. Here, too, an excellent study by historians reveals the extent to which it deviated from the Puritan ideal of community.[77] Founded in 1626, the town of Salem was selected as an attractive site because of its deep harbor and excellent network of waterways. With the flood of Puri-tan immigrants to Massachusetts after 1640, it soon outgrew the narrow neck of land that was its original site. As the population increased, the town selectmen started to make grants of land several miles in the interior. The original grantees of these agricultural regions began to break away to become independent towns in their own right over the following decades. One of these new settlements was known colloquially as "Salem Farms" and its inhabitants as "the Farmers."[78]

Some of these farmers soon chafed beneath the power that Salem Town held over them and demanded a greater degree of autonomy. Salem Town had its own interests, however, and they differed sharply from those of the farmers. The town was crowded into a few square miles of coastal land, and by the 1640s had become a thriving port and commercial center. "But while it was becoming steadily more mercantile," note Paul Boyer and Stephen Nissenbaum, "Salem had no wish to lose control of the rural hinterland which not only increased her tax revenues but provided the food which the Town proper could not supply." When the farmers of Salem Farms showed signs in the 1660s of becoming an independent town, Salem Town took a strong stand against them. Beginning with this fundamental divergence of interest, Boyer and Nissenbaum show, there followed more than a century of conflict between the townsmen and the farmers of Salem Village, as it came to be called.

The tensions arising from the unwillingness of Salem Town to grant autonomy to Salem Village in either legal or ecclesiastical matters acted as a serious disruptive force within Salem Village itself. Some residents identified themselves primarily with Salem Town, while others saw themselves as belonging to an essentially agricultural village. The result was a high level of disarray and internal bickering in Salem Village that continued for several decades. A single group of men had come to dominate the political and economic affairs of Salem: the merchants. "In Salem, no less than Boston," write Boyer and Nissenbaum, "the rise of an internationally oriented merchant class, connected by ties of marriage and mutual interest, spawned a style of life and a sensibility decidedly alien to the precapitalist patterns of village existence."[79]

### Revolutionary Massachusetts

By the end of the seventeenth century, the population of Massachusetts had increased to fifty-six thousand.[80] Since immigration from Europe had ceased to be an important factor after the middle of the century, its growth from a few thousand settlers in the 1630s was primarily the result of natural increase. Accompanying the growth of population was an increasing scarcity of land, and the continued breaking away of outlying areas from the parent towns. These patterns continued into the eighteenth century, along with the development of more and more non-agricultural pursuits, conflicts between agricultural and commercial interests, changes in the locus of authority and responsibility, a more rigid stratification of society, and the emergence of a permanent class of transient poor people.

Just as in the seventeenth century, the family continued to be the dominant colonial institution.[81] The family household was still the main unit of production, with most men still being involved in agriculture. Women began to marry at a slightly older age, and their average number of children declined slowly to five or six.[82] Distinctions between men and women continued to be made in law, in church affairs, and in political and property rights. Hierarchy was still generally taken for granted, and social arrangements took the same pattern as in the seventeenth century. Thus, there were numerous resemblances between the situation in the middle and late seventeenth century and a century later.

At the same time, some obvious changes were beginning to occur. For one thing, villages were becoming larger, and there were many more of them. Yet the majority of towns and villages in the late colonial period still had fewer than 1,000 inhabitants. As late as 1790, there were only twenty-four towns in the United States with a population above 2,500.[83] Even Boston had fewer than 20,000 people. Salem, the most populous Massachusetts town aside from Boston, still had fewer than 5,000 inhabitants. By 1775, Massachusetts had more than three hundred towns.[84] The average town's population at the time was less than 1,500. By our standards today, none of these places was very large. But the changes had considerable impact on the Massachusetts residents of the eighteenth century.

With most people in colonial Massachusetts depending on agriculture for their livelihood, too many people on too little productive land created problems. Since the most desirable types of land were those parceled out initially to the wealthiest settlers or acquired by rich men in the following decades, later divisions and acquisitions involved less desirable land. This land was often marginal for cultivation because of the thin, rocky soils characteristic of much of Massachusetts.

High fertility and low mortality led to an insufficiency of land, with the consequence that an increasing number of farmers' sons had to leave the villages where they had grown up.[85] In Andover, for example, the practice of the first generation had been to bequeath its property to all male heirs, with perhaps a double share to the oldest son. But with a limited amount of desirable land and the inability of most farmers to compete against rich men for that land which was available, the size of farms declined as family holdings were subdivided in the passage from one generation to the next.

Thus while property was passed on to the male heirs in almost every instance in the first generation, it was so for only about 75 percent from the second to the third generation, and 58 percent from the third to the fourth. Consequently, almost half of the male members of the fourth generation—coming to maturity in the middle of the eighteenth century—moved to other towns. They moved because their parents' farms offered them little or no future. To be young in mid-eighteenth-century Massachusetts was often either to be landless or to have insufficient land to support a family.

In the hope of escaping poverty, some men moved elsewhere in the colony. But, of course, other towns had similar problems and did not welcome outsiders. Migrants were discouraged from settling where they didn't belong, and the number of "warnings out" increased greatly during the course of the eighteenth century.[86]

As I noted earlier, there was already a considerable amount of geographic mobility in the seventeenth century. This increased with the passage of time, being much more intense in the eighteenth century. Just as in the previous century, religious and political disputes, personal conflicts, and the lack of opportunities provided reasons for people to move elsewhere. Increasingly, the most common type of movement came to be of family groups. And increasingly also, the movements became longer distance.[87] Between 1760 and 1776, notes Ray Billington, seventy-four new towns were settled in Vermont, one hundred in New Hampshire, and ninety-four in Maine. A very large number of these towns were peopled by migrants from Massachusetts.[88] Although not quantifiable in aggregate terms, says Jim Potter, this mobility "seems to have been at a level that can only be described as rapid and high."[89]

Most people did not, of course, emigrate. But within Massachusetts towns, the locus of authority changed. The town meeting emerged as the actual source of local authority, taking from the selectmen the power which had always been theirs to claim.[90] It became the dominant decision-making body in a town. Men began to assemble for such meetings with greater frequency, and the list of problems treated at each meeting grew longer and longer. Open disagreement became much more common, and the meetings often became acrimonious.

The rules of substantive law were more and more utilized to help sustain peace and order. We have already seen the influence of the law on women and their position of enforced dependence on their husbands. More generally, the legal system supported the idea that a religious establishment should declare and promulgate moral standards for the people, as well as the idea that the courts of law were appropriate instruments for punishing those who violated these standards.

William Nelson shows that about 13 percent of all prosecutions were for such offenses as missing church, traveling or working on Sunday, blasphemy, and profanity. Another 38 percent were for sexual violations: adultery, cohabitation, indecent exposure, lewdness, prostitution, and—most of all—fornication. Crimes of violence accounted for another 15 percent of all prosecutions, and robbery, burglary, and other offenses against property for an additional 13 percent.[91] A considerable quantity of actions were between neighbors. Chronic hostility and personal antagonisms among neighbors was quite common at the time.[92] Yet, as Allen points out, the predominant trend in litigation during the eighteenth century was toward suits involving parties from different towns.[93]

Although most people in eighteenth-century Massachusetts spent their lives within nuclear families on dispersed farms in small towns and villages, there were considerable differences in the sorts of local structures in which people found themselves at that time. Towns and villages differed in size, population density, degree of development, concentration of wealth, distribution of power, pattern of leadership, and in various other ways.

Self-contained villages were less common around 1775 than they had been a century earlier. Those villages that remained small were generally poor settlements, often located in regions with limited natural resources and very little commerce. As the eighteenth century progressed, more and more people came to live in towns rather than villages. What Edward Cook terms "secondary towns" served as centers in the rural counties. These towns had some commerce, being local marketing and service centers for the region. Another type of town was also a local social and economic center, and frequently a county seat as well. Cook terms these "major" county towns.[94]

Along with the three hundred or so Massachusetts villages and towns around 1775, there were also the two urban areas discussed earlier: Salem and Boston. They were far and away the most commercialized centers in the colony. Although they had much in common, Salem and Boston different greatly. Of most importance was the considerable difference in size; Salem had a population of 5,337 in 1775 as compared with Boston's 16,000.[95]

This meant that Boston had a much larger, more mixed, and fluid population than Salem or anyplace else in Massachusetts. There one found a variety of artisans, shopkeepers, professionals, and a large group of successful merchants. As the principal port of the New England coast, Boston was a seafaring, shipbuilding town. Although there was very little manufacturing, much merchandise passed through. It was, thus, very much a merchants' town. Especially in the late colonial period, Boston provided increased opportunities for some persons to better their situation and to increase their wealth and property through competition and/or speculation.[96]

By the time of the American Revolution, the Massachusetts Bay Colony was witnessing a struggle between two different value orientations.[97] At one extreme were those men whose outlook was essentially "local." These were the people living in small, quiet, culturally stable villages and towns in the rural areas of the colony. Being mostly ordinary farmers with little free time and no surplus wealth, they were likely to emphasize what was traditional and Puritan. They were very often suspicious of higher (and not simply English) authority, and struggled against the emerging hierarchies of authority in the name of religious piety, simplicity, and local authority.[98] These farmers resented the shift of more and more revenue and authority to the colonial government in Boston, and felt they were being exploited by the merchants and bankers in Boston, with their close ties to the Bank of England. These intensely local traditionalists attacked the British connection and, in fact, everything that was foreign and "modern."

The "cosmopolitans" represented the other extreme. These men were more likely to live in Boston or Salem, along the coastline, or along the major rivers. They had fine houses, expensively furnished, and often lived in a magnificence that equaled—if it did not surpass—their counterparts in London or Bristol.[99] These men were urbane, well educated, leisured, and well traveled, and their orientation was not so much to their local town or village as to what they saw as an Anglo-American civilization. They were attracted by what was transatlantic, Anglicizing, and by what provided a wider, less constraining perspective, and of course by greater opportunities for the acquisition of wealth and power. Such men believed that the economic health of the province depended on a close alliance between business and government.

Thus, there existed a definite split between two cultural coalitions in late colonial Massachusetts: "one cosmopolitan and reconciled to the future, the other local and forever unreconciled."[100] Of course, not all cosmopolitans lived in cities or expensive areas, and not all locals lived in the country. The important point is that there existed two divergent worldviews in the Massachusetts population.

Having now considered Massachusetts, I turn to the colony that was almost its polar opposite: Virginia. Although less is known about Virginia than about Massachusetts, there is by now sufficient knowledge to make it useful to contrast these two very dissimilar colonies.

## III

### *Virginia: The Early Years*

Settled by entrepreneurs and adventurers rather than social reformers, Virginia became America's first permanent English colony in 1607. The initial party of Englishmen dropped anchor several miles up the James River at a site they named Jamestown. Financed by the Virginia Company in London, the men from the first three ships constructed a fort, laid out their settlement, and began their search for riches. There were no women among them, as the whole venture was a speculative undertaking. Women and children did not begin to arrive until 1609.

The early decades were marked by disease and famine. During its seventeen years in America, the Virginia Company sent over about six thousand persons. Yet, by 1624, there were only twelve hundred English people in Virginia.[101] Although many had given up and returned home, the great majority met an early death in the hostile environment. Things continued to go poorly until tobacco was discovered as a source of tremendous profit. The weed became extremely popular in Europe, and Virginia was soon exporting thousands of hogsheads of tobacco a year.

The cultivation of tobacco required an adequate labor force. To solve the persistent labor problem, the Virginia Company began to import "indentured servants." It devised the headright system to encourage private investors to ship their own servants to America. A "headright" was an offering of fifty acres to investors who would pay the transportation of workers to the colony. The indentured servants agreed to work on company lands for a specific time (usually seven years) in exchange for passage to America and the promise of land.[102]

The category of indentured servant included regular servants, vagrants, convicts, prisoners of war, the poor, men in apprenticeship, and freemen who bound themselves as a means of having their passage paid. Among them were skilled and unskilled workers, young and old, male and female. In the early years, however, the vast majority were young men. Even by 1700 there was still a sexual imbalance of three to two.[103] When a census was taken in 1625, over 40 percent of the Virginia colonists were listed as servants.[104]

The major benefactors of the indentured servant policy were wealthy gentlemen who were in a position to underwrite the cost of passage for several servants. Through the headright system, they acquired vast landholdings. Their wealth also helped them to obtain control over the food and other supplies required by these workers. This allowed these wealthy men to increase their wealth still further. "The successful planters of the first generation," writes D. W. Meinig, "were mostly tough, energetic, rather crudely ambitious entrepreneurs."[105]

Diseases associated with Virginia's subtropical climate took a high toll in the seventeenth century, and life expectancy was much lower than in New England. Because of this, population growth was highly dependent on a constant replenishment from the outside. The sexual imbalance also had consequences for population growth. In some places, the male preponderance was as high as three to one.[106]

And although there were many young women who were between eighteen and twenty-five when they arrived, they had to wait until the end of their servitude (anywhere from four to seven years later) before marrying. This had the consequence that the average age of marriage was at least three or four years higher than in Massachusetts. Resultant family size was also reduced by a higher infant mortality and by earlier parental death. The wife outlived the husband more often than the other way around, and many women were left as the heads of families.[107] Certainly in the early years, marriage was very often a privilege of the socially elite and economically successful.

During the 1680s and 1690s, black slaves from West Africa began to replace English indentured servants as the mainstay of the labor force. By the 1670s, there was considerable labor tension in Virginia between the few rich masters and those many servants and ex-servants who felt cheated, impoverished, and trapped in their legal servitude.[108] It was this, argues Edmund Morgan, that gave rise to slavery. Other scholars argue that Virginia planters shifted to slave labor when the supply of indentured servants was inadequate to meet their needs.[109] In any case, the gradual replacement of white servants by black slaves served—as Morgan also observes—to create a sense of solidarity among all white Virginians. Whatever their economic situation, all white men in Virginia had one thing in common: they were not black.

Contrary to what is sometimes claimed, the African slaves did not share a common background and culture. To the contrary, say Sidney Mintz and Richard Price, "Enslaved Africans . . . were drawn from different parts of the African continent, from numerous tribal and linguistic groups, and from different societies in any region."[110] European traders drew their human cargoes from different areas: Senegambia, Sierra Leone, the Windward and Gold coasts, the Bight of Biafra, the Congo basin, and elsewhere.[111]

These early slaves were transported to America as members of specific cultural groups—Ibos, Falanis, Yorubas, Ashantis, and others—and not simply as Africans. They were, thus, a culturally heterogeneous people from many different tribes and regions. "What the slaves undeniably shared at the outset," write Mintz and Price, "was their enslavement; all—or nearly all—else had to be created by them."[112] In 1700 one-quarter of the Virginia population was black, and this rose to over 40 percent after 1750.[113]

### Revolutionary Virginia

By the middle of the eighteenth century, the Virginia tobacco planters had created a social and economic hierarchy with slave laborers at the bottom, convicts and indentured servants above them, tenant farmers ranked next, above them small landholders and middling planters, and a few large planters in each county at the very top. The slaves, of course, formed the great bulk of the labor force, while the sizable white tenant class was growing, the middle class was comparatively shriveled, and the extremely wealthy planters were small in number during the eighteenth century.[114] Virginia's rapidly expanding staple economy produced a much more stratified social system than was found in Massachusetts at the time.

The huge increase in the number of African slaves in the eighteenth century helped lead to a less transitory white population with a more balanced (though still unequal) sex ratio, and thus more opportunities for marriage and family formation. Mortality rates continued to be high, however, and few couples reached old age together. The death of one spouse often occurred within the early years of the marriage, and remarriage was the norm for survivors. This was especially the case for women.

Virginia remained a peculiarly rural colony throughout the eighteenth century. There was no city and no substantial set of market towns. Compared with Massachusetts, it was less diversified, its wealth more concentrated, and its population more dispersed. While most people in Massachusetts lived in small towns or villages and some in cities, this was not at all the case in Virginia.[115] Even at the end of the eighteenth century, villages and towns contained only a tiny percentage of the total population.[116] Instead, the main points of human concentration in Virginia were isolated habitations diffused throughout the colony. The town meeting, so common in Massachusetts, was unknown in Virginia.

Even more than in Massachusetts, men and women existed in different spheres. While women shared some aspects of the farming activities in rural Massachusetts, this seldom occurred in tobacco colony Virginia. Wives in households too poor to afford bound labor might tend tobacco plants, but slaves performed the bulk of the labor, including household chores. The wives of most farmers had slaves and indentured servants to supervise, and plantation mistresses had responsibility for supervising the largest households in North America. They had to oversee large numbers of household workers in such tasks as preparing food, making clothing, procuring supplies, and caring for the children.[117] But without cities, there was virtually no paid employment for women, as was the case in Massachusetts. Women in Virginia were not expected to enter the labor market.[118]

The rich public life of prerevolutionary Virginia was almost exclusively a male world, with a woman's role being restricted to home and family. Perhaps because women were more scarce than in Massachusetts, they were especially revered in Virginia and were often viewed as an asylum from the world. Men wanted women who were sweet, cheerful, and good-natured. Thus, the private sphere was glorified in a way that it was not in late colonial Massachusetts.[119]

Virginians approved sexual freedom for white men, and wives were expected to ignore their husbands' illicit behavior. Young white men frequently gained their sexual experience through intercourse with black women. And so long as married white men remained discreet, sexual liaisons with slave women met no criticism.[120]

For the vast majority of whites, the usual home site was a field cleared from the woods. Alone in their field and wooded settings, Anglo-Virginia houses typically provided a home for a married pair with their children. Most of these houses tended to be removed from the great waterways and to be located along the lower creeks. "Great men," that is, large plantation owners, on the other hand, took up the best land along the riverfronts, where they built their houses near the most strategic landing places. Many of these plantations, or "great houses," were made up of a large main building and a profusion of separate structures.[121] There was, then, in Virginia a dispersal of the bonds of attachment over wide distances.

These widely separated, one-family dwelling units were one distinctive kind of housing. But there was another type, typical for the slaves who made up some 40 percent of the population.[122] The slave settlements, "huts" and "cabins," sometimes housed a married pair of slaves and their offspring. Toward the end of the eighteenth century, perhaps one-half of slave children grew up in the presence of both parents.[123] But the more general pattern was for these structures to house unmarried persons or a single parent and children. About 40 percent of the slaves lived in a "quarter" with more than twenty other persons, encompassing a plurality of married pairs, parent-child combinations, and unmarried slaves.[124] The slave quarters were often physically close to, but apart from, the houses of the masters. The ownership of large numbers of slaves supplied a secure foundation for the wealth and status of the Virginia elite.

The density of Virginia's population was roughly eight per square mile, in comparison with about thirty per square mile in Massachusetts (excluding Boston).[125] Because Virginia's population was widely dispersed, it in no way resembled the Massachusetts of many towns and villages, where most people had frequent contact with one another. To the contrary, day-to-day contact with people other than immediate family members and slaves was rare for most persons in Virginia.

Compared with the situation in Massachusetts at the time, there was little concern in Virginia with enforcing a moral code. As Jan Lewis writes: "Virginians saw neither duty nor pleasure in regulating the morality of their neighbors. They only hoped to keep disruption of the peace at a minimum. Virginia's peaceable scheme was essentially a private one. Peace would be maintained on the plantation; crime, vice, and immorality were disturbing only when they could not be kept at bay."[126]

Social contacts with others were distinctly intermittent. Nevertheless, there were some contacts. Churches were the most important centers of communal assembly. Such churches were dispersed at frequent intervals in the countryside. They were often located in a cleared area near some crossroads, and in any case had to be accessible by road. The church brought people together not only for worship but also for conducting business activities, consulting about the price of tobacco, discussing the qualities of favorite horses, and enjoying social displays and exchanges.[127]

In addition to the churches, "court day" was another form of communal assembly. Counties were the principal local political entities in Virginia. Since most of these counties were without towns, the courthouse commonly stood at a crossroads. Wherever it was located, it was almost always accompanied by other sorts of buildings: always a lockup, usually a tavern, and sometimes a store.[128] At the monthly court days, the male part of Virginia county society came together for the sum and substance of government at the time—recording transactions, adjudicating disputes about boundaries and entitlement, and otherwise administering "justice."

The county courts translated wrongdoings into indictments for such offenses as bearing a bastard child, for uttering profanities, and for being absent overlong from a parish church. Much of the monthly work of the court was highly routine: most cases involved recovery of debt. The disposition of small-debt cases was determined by juries impaneled by the sheriff from among the freeholders present in the courthouse or outside in the yard. Thus, the local inhabitants—or at least the gentlemen among them—participated to a large extent in the settling of local disputes.

Only slaves were tried in county courts for capital offenses; free persons and indentured servants indicted for a felony were tried in the General Court at Williamsburg. A slave who was tried would be tried for his life (without a jury) by the court. A slave might have been accused of breaking into a storehouse to steal bolts of cloth or some hams or other commodities. If he were found guilty by the judges and they set the value of the stolen goods higher than five shillings, he would be sentenced to hang near the courthouse. But if found guilty with the value of the theft set at less than five shillings, the slave was eligible for "benefit of clergy." This meant that he would be burned on the hand in open court, lashed, and released.[129]

Punishments such as whipping and cropping of ears were reserved for slaves, vagrants, impoverished whites, and women without protectors. Although anyone could be executed, the rich usually escaped such punishment, since they could afford better lawyers. Moreover, those lawbreakers "who commanded money or property or the patronage of someone with those resources were treated with comparative leniency."[130] They could pay fines or post bonds, and were simply admonished to mend their behavior.[131]

The Virginia gentry aspired to a life of complete freedom—from material want, from manual labor, from dependency on others.[132] Property provided the necessary personal independence for such a life. This freedom or independence was viewed as a necessary condition for responsible citizenship and for eventual governmental position.

The emphasis was on a style of life very similar to that of the wealthy, leisured aristocrat of ancient Athens.[133] Exemption from all external control, and the claim that only the gentlemen-aristocrats recognized the standards of right conduct, placed such an elite in a position to exercise power over the vast majority of other people while having no direct power exercised over themselves.

Independence allowed the gentry to undertake important responsibilities in the society at large. For instance, the gentleman of old Virginia was expected to serve several days a month as justice on his county bench, and to do so without pay. He was expected to supply the necessary disinterested leadership in government, and later to help staff the officer corps of the Continental army (paying for his own rations, clothing, and equipment on a rather limited salary). The ideal was to provide disinterested public service and leadership from the classical position of independence and freedom from the marketplace. The British theory of unpaid public service was widely accepted by such gentlemen.[134]

George Washington, for example, performed the public services and held the public offices appropriate to his status as a gentleman: he served as vestryman in his Anglican church, as a member of the House of Burgesses, as trustee of the town of Alexandria, and as justice of the county court. Thomas Jefferson as a young man served as justice of the peace, member of the county court, and in the House of Burgesses, among other posts.[135] The great majority of Virginians—including those 40 percent who were slaves—were viewed as incapable of taking on such important responsibilities.

The English valuation of manly independence was often carried to great heights in late colonial Virginia. "More than love or salvation, fortune or fame," writes Lewis, "young men aspired to independence, so much so it could seem like a state of spiritual grace."[136] In England, it was the ownership of broad acres of land that assured someone of the rank of a gentleman. But in Virginia, land was cheap—and by itself was not enough to guarantee such a status. Thus, land ownership *and* the ownership of vast numbers of slaves were necessary for assuring the desired style of life.

These emergent aristocrats enjoyed a comfortable life-style, with their leisure and authority being taken for granted. Although from an earlier period in the eighteenth century, William Byrd, master of Westover, former burgess and king's councillor, provides an excellent example. His diary describes the activities of a day: "I rose at 5 o'clock this morning and read a chapter in Hebrew and 200 verses in Homer's *Odyssey*. I ate milk for breakfast. I said my prayers. Jenney and Eugene were whipped. I danced my dance. I read law in the morning and Italian in the afternoon. . . ." Lockridge, to whom I am indebted for this quotation, goes on to add: "Daily, Byrd said his prayers, 'danced his dance' for exercise right after breakfast, spoke to his overseers or his wife about disobedient house slaves, perhaps saw the local parson or a client seeking a favor, read in two languages, gave his wife 'a flourish,' and went to bed. Twice a year he rode to Williamsburg to join in the minuet of colonial government."[137] Thus, the life of an aristocratic gentleman.

Just as in Massachusetts, there existed an inner conflict between two cultural coalitions from midcentury on. The Great Awakening, an outburst of religious enthusiasm during the 1740s, reached deeply into Virginia.[138] Established ways of preaching and experiencing religion were challenged by an emphasis on public readings of the Bible, intense devotional exercises, and a concern with individual salvation.

51

Evangelists began to challenge also the hegemony of the elite gentry. Virginians, these evangelists insisted, had fallen into luxurious, corrupt, and sinful ways. In opposition to the extravagant, excessive, individualistic, and independent way of life of the Virginia gentlemen, the evangelists preached plain dress, austere and gentle living, devout prayer, and humility.[139] Men were encouraged to seek their own religious experience and to live simply, without presumption. The simple folk were to be the inheritors of the earth. Lockridge describes them as follows:

> Equality and simplicity in all things became the order of the day. Simple in their speech, in their dress, and in their language, members of reborn communities frowned where gentlemen smiled, walked where gentry rode, and avoided with deliberate passion the cockfights, militia-day punchbowls, and taverns where gentle young bloods displayed their social leadership.[140]

These Virginians saw a severe need for the orderliness and self-restraint called for by Baptist teachings. They criticized and challenged the religious authority of the official Anglican church. But they went beyond this religious challenge and expressed the larger conviction that Virginia was being corrupted by its ties to England. Thus, they also challenged all government, including the county courts and the House of Burgesses. They rejected all hierarchies of authority, including the civil.

In other words, the Baptists and their like had opted out of the hierarchical social system led by rich and leisured Virginia gentlemen. These gentlemen saw that this rejection of authority constituted a threat to their own leadership and claim to rule. The gentry's consensual domination of Virginia society and the traditional conception of authority was fundamentally disturbed. A deep incompatibility was created between the humbling, soul-searching culture of the evangelists and the proud, assertive culture of the gentry and their adherents.[141] Although the cultural war between these two conflicting value systems was papered over during the American Revolution, it was to erupt after independence.


## IV

### The Revolution and Independence

Just as they differed in so many other ways, Massachusetts and Virginia had different experiences leading up to their involvement in the American Revolution. Both came to be committed to their colony's freedom in regard to Britain, but for highly dissimilar reasons. Although historians in the consensus tradition had argued that there was a uniform American experience and that the colonists everywhere fought the British to preserve human rights and representative government, contemporary historians emphasize the ways in which nonpolitical concerns helped shape political ideology.

Beginning in the early 1760s, Massachusetts experienced a continuing controversy with British authorities. Through Crown and Parliament, Britain ruled all the colonies. It ruled them separately, and it ruled them in different ways in accordance with their separate histories and experiences. Whatever colony people lived in, however, all free Americans alike were subject to the British Crown, and all alike claimed the benefit of traditional British liberties.[142]

For the purposes of this study, there is no need to review all the events leading up to the involvement of Massachusetts in the Revolution, but some deserve special mention. In 1763 the British government made the "fateful decision to recoup some of the costs of the colonial defense from the colonists themselves, initiating a sequence of events that culminated in the American Revolution."[143] Linked with this was a criticism of the colonists by the imperial authorities for not having pulled their weight in the Seven Years' War with the French, a criticism that was greatly resented by the colonists.

Boston rapidly became the center of colonial resistance to Britain. Fearing any new tax burdens, Boston merchants created The Society for Encouraging Trade and Commerce, a union of some 150 merchants who opposed any adverse changes in trade policy, customs procedures, or taxes.[144] The main function of the society was to protect the interests of local merchants. Merchants in the ports of Salem, Marblehead, and Plymouth soon formed similar societies.

The following year, the British Parliament passed legislation for the specific purpose of raising money from the colonies for the Crown. This so-called Sugar Act sought to prohibit illicit trade with other nations and threatened strict enforcement of previously ignored and unenforced duties on sugar. At a Boston town meeting on May 14, 1764, James Otis raised the issue of no taxation without representation, and the meeting joined him in denouncing any policy of taxation without representation. The Massachusetts House of Representatives authorized a Committee of Correspondence to contact other provinces to propose a united action by the colonies in protest.[145]

Then, in 1765, the British Parliament passed the Stamp Act, which placed stamp duties on domestic colonial newspapers, legal documents of all types, insurance policies, ships' papers, licenses, almanacs, pamphlets, and broadsides to help finance British military expenses in America. Stamps would be required for all documents and would have to be paid for in gold or silver, which meant a one-way drain of currency out of the colonies.[146] The stamps would also be most penalizing for those people most likely to influence public opinion: printers, lawyers, shop-keepers, and traders.

In response, groups known as the Sons of Liberty were formed in the provincial towns to organize opposition to the Stamp Act. In Massachusetts, as elsewhere, these groups often resorted to violence in order to force stamp agents to resign their posts and Boston merchants to cancel their orders for British goods. At this time, the Sons of Liberty and the merchants' society took the same position at the Boston town meetings.[147]

Following the Stamp Act, other tax acts were passed by the Parliament. New import duties were imposed on glass, lead, paints, paper, and tea in the Townshend Acts of 1767.[148] These, too, were strongly opposed by the colonists. In August 1768, nearly two-thirds of the members of the Boston merchants' society pledged not to import any goods bearing the Townshend duties from 1 January 1769 until the duties were repealed.

The situation rapidly became more serious with the arrival of British troops in Boston in the fall of 1768.[149] As Alan Rogers makes clear, the colonists' first taste of real military government fed their fear of the threat to freedom posed by a standing army.[150] Like all other Englishmen, Boston patriots considered the use of a standing army against civilians in peacetime a major sign of impending tyranny.

In 1771, Samuel Adams, a Boston radical and the cousin of John Adams, revived the Committee of Correspondence in the Massachusetts House. This committee drafted a letter to Parliament asserting that the American colonies were "still united in the main principles of constitutional and natural liberty."[151] Adams then published the "committee's" letter in the *Gazette*. In a continuing series of articles, he revived a number of irritants from the past: the Stamp Act and, after its repeal in 1776, the remaining duty on tea, the presence of the British fleet in Boston Harbor, and several other complaints.

Although the Boston merchants had sided with the radicals in fighting the imposition of new rules on trade in the 1760s, by 1771 they were avoiding any further affiliation with the radicals of the town. Some had lost too much through earlier nonimportation agreements and refused to participate in nonimportation in the future. Nor would they any longer agree to attacks on the provincial administration. The Boston merchants' society was unwilling to risk any part of its members' prosperous trade or to risk further confrontations with the Crown.[152]

Samuel Adams and the other radicals recognized the increasing reluctance of the merchants to cast their lot with them, and had already begun to widen their political base with "the people" and to dissociate themselves from the Boston merchants. Adams said that the merchants had been too long "unconcerned spectators" on the political scene and that they could be depended on only when they believed that their own business interests were directly threatened. It was "the body of the people" who must decide the acceptance or rejection of the parliamentary decisions.[153]

By this time, the Sons of Liberty contained more than 350 members and far outnumbered the members of the merchants' society. Mainly artisans and small tradesmen, these men began to participate more actively in the town meetings. The power and backing once supplied by the Boston merchants had been thoroughly replaced—and magnified a hundredfold—by 1773, not only by "the people" of Boston but by a network of town committees throughout Massachusetts. Samuel Adams had considerable support from those yeoman farmers in the small towns and villages of rural Massachusetts. They were more radically democratic than their city counterparts, and showed great hostility toward royal officials and British loyalists. These rural "locals" were obviously not as concerned about British taxation as were the Boston cosmopolitans, for it was the latter whose position was threatened by taxation. The Massachusetts farmers were more concerned about the power of all aristocracies: British and American alike.

After 1774, most of the merchants deserted the common cause in their concern for their own dignity and power. Having temporarily left the socially conservative camp in search of support from the people, these cautious merchants worried about the radicalism of many of the artisans. Their association with these working-class radicals had helped push the merchants toward an outspoken opposition to further domination by and dependence on Great Britain. But while opposing this *external* authority, these wealthy merchants resisted the surrender of any *internal* authority to the people. Thus even as they shared a radical stand against Great Britain, Boston artisans and merchants were divided on the question of who should rule at home.

Meanwhile in Virginia there were other events that would lead to its participation in the Revolution. These had to do largely with problems faced by the gentry in maintaining their high style of living in the 1760s and 1770s. As I noted earlier, the ideal of being a gentleman involved the expectation of providing disinterested public service and leadership.

The problem was that there were not many Virginia gentry who were capable of living idly off the rents of tenants, as the English landed aristocracy did. Even those with vast landholdings and large numbers of slaves found it difficult to acquire the leisure and security necessary for devoting their time and energies to public service.

This was especially so with the great tidewater planters of mid-eighteenth-century Virginia. Because of the thousands of slaves working the land, there was practically no white laboring class. Even though the smaller farmers were often not very well-off, they perceived a common identity with the wealthy planters. Both were equal, Morgan points out, in not being slaves.[154]

Relations between large and small planters were generally open and relaxed, and were often eased by the willingness of the rich Virginia planters to extend credit to the smaller ones. This easy credit constituted a form of patronage, and was an indication of the rich gentleman's own complete independence and others' dependence on him.

In fact, control of credit was an important basis for dominance by the wealthy in Virginia society. Charles Sydnor shows that the debts owed to a great gentleman by his humble neighbors might constitute a substantial proportion of his total assets.[155] The power inherent in the control of credit helped assure the gentry's ability to secure deference and compliance in colonial Virginia. Paternalistic dominance by the gentry rested very heavily on patronage given and deference returned.

Serious problems arose, however, because of the gentry's own indebtedness to their British agents. In order to sustain their rich life-style, many Virginia gentlemen borrowed far more than they could repay. They were invariably in debt to those merchants who sold their tobacco and managed their affairs, and were almost always short of cash.[156] Even less than Massachusetts did Virginia have sovereignty over its economic system. The British controlled the currency, loan capital, and prices.

As a consequence of the international financial crises during the 1760s and 1770s, the British merchants began to call in long-standing debts from the Virginia planters. Just as the gentry showed leniency in collecting the debts owed them by their poorer neighbors, the British creditors had never previously demanded immediate payment of what was owed to them. It was considered inappropriate to do so, for both the relationships between the rich planters and their poorer neighbors and those between the planters and their British creditors were defined as relationships between friends. A "friend," Rhys Isaac notes, "was a person, whether of high, lower, or equal station, related by the expectation of a mutual exchange of services."[157]

The commercial "friendship" between the rich Virginia planters and the British merchants allowed the planters to market their tobacco in England. The consignment merchants would sell the tobacco and also obtain various luxury goods for the planters that were not available in Virginia. The pattern was for the merchants to extend credit to the planters until such time as a new crop of tobacco was ready or until the to-

bacco was actually sold. These loans or advances enabled the impecuni-
ous planters to maintain their rich life-style.

But when the British merchants themselves came into financial diffi-
culties, they were compelled to demand payment of the outstanding debts.
They not only applied pressure to get the money owed them, but they even
*publicly* called the planters' credit into question. The planters, in turn, were
forced to badger their poorer neighbors to pay what was owed to them.

Seeing themselves as virtuous gentlemen, the planters had expected
their British friends to carry them through bad times. Thus, when the merchants began to call insolvent planters to account, to pressure them to
pay their debts, the planters felt dishonored and betrayed. "In the correspondence with the merchants," writes T. H. Breen, "the planter almost
reflexively associated the demand for payment with a loss of integrity, with
subservience, and when a merchant complained about the state of a Virginian's account, the planter usually protested that he had behaved in an
honorable manner."[158]

Because the Virginia gentry aspired to achieve complete personal independence and freedom from obligations to others, the unwillingness of
the British merchants to continue to extend credit compromised their personal autonomy, and with it their honor, virtue, and integrity. This often
humiliating experience, which threatened the privileged position of the
Virginia gentleman and raised questions about the survival of a traditional
social order, provided the context in which abstractions about independence and "liberty" found meaning. The planters' merchant "friends"
were transformed into British adversaries. And the Virginia planters' hostility came to be focused not only on the British merchants but on the
British government as well.

More specifically, these Virginia gentlemen were increasingly influenced by an important idiom in British opposition politics: radical country
ideology.[159] The Country party's values were rooted in agriculture and ownership of real property; these agrarians disdained the corrupting influence
of commerce and feared all forms of centralized power. Farmers were
praised as the source of social virtue and political independence, and they
were venerated as the protectors of liberty against tyrannical forces.[160]

Virginia's great planters were very receptive to this way of thinking. Aristotle had laid down the axiom that "the best material of democracy is an
agricultural population" and that people engaged in other occupations
had "no room" for the virtues that were necessary to a republic.[161] Thomas
Jefferson echoed those words when he wrote that "those who labour in the
earth are the chosen people of God," that "the proportion which the aggregate of the other classes of citizens bears in any state to that of its husbandmen, is the proportion of its unsound to its healthy parts."[162]

By 1776, at least ten of Virginia's great planters owed five thousand pounds or more to British merchants. Among those owing between one thousand and five thousand pounds were such wealthy planters as George Washington and Thomas Jefferson.[163] It was probably this experience that accounted for what Morgan calls Jefferson's "obsessive aversion" to debt. "The trouble with debt," observes Morgan, "was that it undermined the independence of the debtor. It opened him to pressure from his creditors and thereby limited his freedom and capacity to defend freedom."[164] Jefferson and other Virginia gentlemen wanted to live in a society that was as much under their control as possible. Owing large sums of money placed them in a position of dependency and undermined such control.

Although Virginians made up only 21 percent of the colonies' population in 1776, they owed almost 50 percent of the debts to British citizens.[165] The problem of these old debts to British merchants continued for a quarter of a century after the Revolution, until at last the United States created a fund that paid off at least part of what was owed to the Virginia gentry's former "friends."[166]

As early as 1765, Patrick Henry had acted to transform the individual discontent of the Virginia gentry into a collective issue when he introduced the Stamp Act resolves in the Virginia assembly. Asserting that the right of Virginia to govern its internal affairs had always been recognized by the Crown, he claimed for the province's general assembly the sole power to tax Virginians.[167]

In 1769, Washington, Jefferson, Richard Henry Lee, and other "principal gentlemen" joined Patrick Henry in signing the Virginia Nonimportation Resolution.[168] They agreed not only to cease purchasing any items specifically mentioned in a new Revenue Act but also to halt purchase of the sorts of luxury items (for example, pewter and clocks) that they had heretofore ordered through the British consignment merchants.[169]

In the following years, the Virginia gentry was united by its increasing hostility toward the British government. The Baptists and their like joined them in the attacks on the British Parliament and Anglican pretensions. The Virginia House of Burgesses appointed a committee for intercolonial correspondence, including Patrick Henry, Thomas Jefferson, and Richard Henry Lee in 1773. In 1774, a convention of rich planters endorsed not only the conception of nonimportation but also nonexportation. "At long last," says Breen, "the great Tidewater planters were persuaded to declare their independence from the merchants of Great Britain, and in the context of tobacco America, this meant revolution."[170]

Thus, by 1774, patriots in both Massachusetts and Virginia were ready for conflict with Great Britain. In the summer of 1774, after some twelve years of controversy with the British authorities, men throughout the colonies had reluctantly concluded that their own traditional liberties as British citizens were threatened by the Crown. The only way to get the British authorities to take their complaints seriously, they concluded, was through collective action.

It was in this connection that the First Continental Congress was called in the same year, with the delegates passing ten resolutions setting forth the rights of the colonists. Among these were the rights to "life, liberty and property."[171]

After preparing an address to the king and to the British and American peoples, Congress adjourned on October 26. Its members agreed to meet again a year later if by that date the colonies' grievances had not been redressed. From the beginning of 1775, there occurred various crises in Massachusetts and elsewhere. On May 10, 1775, the Second Continental Congress met. Five days later, Congress resolved to put the colonies in a state of defense and on May 29 adopted an address to the people of Canada asking them as "fellow-sufferers" to join with rather than against the twelve colonies (Georgia was not officially represented at the Congress).[172]

On June 15, Thomas Jefferson nominated George Washington to be commander in chief; John Adams seconded the nomination, and it carried by a unanimous vote. In August, King George III declared a state of rebellion in his American colonies, and in December Parliament stopped all trade with them.[173] By the spring of 1776 there was widespread sentiment for a break with Britain. In June the Continental Congress met again, and a Declaration of Independence drafted by Jefferson (with a few changes by Adams and Franklin) was approved by the Congress and declared on July 4, 1776.[174]

It needs to be emphasized that the colonies had not purposely set out to gain independence, to break off relations, to be totally separate from England. Instead, they demanded recognition of the rights to which American colonists were already entitled. After all, they were British citizens with the traditional rights of all other citizens. And, for the most part, they wished to remain British citizens.

In Massachusetts and Virginia alike, American patriots believed that there were British conspiracies against freedom. John Adams asserted that "somebody or other in Great Britain" had "dedicated for us . . . a direct and formal design . . . to enslave all America." Jefferson wrote that there was "a deliberate and systematic plan of reducing us to slavery." And George Washington believed "beyond the smallest doubt" that the British were "endeavoring by every piece of art and despotism to fix the shackles of slavery upon us."[175]

To a very considerable extent, it was the British themselves—and not the colonists in North America—who created the possibility of an independent America. Few London officials grasped the extent or significance of the enormous regional differences among colonies three thousand miles away. In imposing new patterns of uniformity (taxes, duties, and the like) on these diverse colonies, they treated them as a whole that had no real existence. They reified their concerns into a totality they referred to as "America," and they almost took it for granted that the American colonists would someday demand their independence as a separate political unit.[176] Thus, a national destiny that virtually none of the North American settlers had envisaged before the crisis of 1774–76 was created by British policies that eventually drew the colonies together in opposition to a common enemy.

# THE COMMUNITARIAN IDEAL AND
# THE AMERICAN REALITY

As I NOTED at the beginning of chapter 2, communitarian writers give considerable attention to the prominence of community in the period of America's founding. Many of their claims are based on the work of those historians who emphasize the influence of the republican tradition during the revolutionary and constitutional periods.

Although this is also true for Bellah and his collaborators, there is much in the presentation of *Habits of the Heart* that resembles the descriptions offered by Tocqueville a century later. He stated that equality of condition and a homogeneity of background, values, and habits of the heart were characteristic of the American people from the beginning. These "Anglo-Americans settled in the New World in a state of social equality; the lowborn and the noble were not to be found among them."[1] They all spoke the same language, and all had the same values.[2]

At the time of the American Revolution, Tocqueville writes, people in the thirteen colonies had "the same religion, the same language, the same customs, and almost the same laws."[3] This description still held, he said, some seventy years later when he visited America. "Almost all the inhabitants of the territory of the Union are the descendants of a common stock; they speak the same language; they worship God in the same manner; they are affected by the same physical causes, and they obey the same laws."[4] In addition, they all share "a passion for equality" as well as an actual equality of condition,[5] and "universal suffrage has been adopted in all the states of the Union."[6]

Bellah and his collaborators say that it was Tocqueville who influenced them most profoundly in their thinking about life in early America.[7] In fact, much of the rhetorical power of *Habits of the Heart* comes from its reliance on Tocqueville's observations. These authors speak, for example, of "the homogeneous well-integrated towns Tocqueville described,"[8] the "still-functional covenant concern for the welfare of one's neighbor" in Tocqueville's still-agrarian America,[9] and the anchoring of American citizenship "in the ethos and institutions of the face-to-face community of the town."[10]

It should be obvious from the previous chapter that America in the seventeenth and eighteenth centuries scarcely resembled this idealized communitarian description. One reason for this, I believe, is that the ruling gentry shared a perspective very much akin to a politics of the common good. These men believed that the privileges and obligations in American society were distributed in accordance with the realization of what was ultimately in the interests of everyone. They advocated a hierarchic political order resting on the natural right of the wise to rule the less wise.

We cannot understand American society at the time of the founding without acknowledging agreement among wealthy gentlemen as to the structure of a proper republic. Gordon Wood points out that the distinction between "gentlemen" and others in society had a vital meaning for the revolutionary generation.[11] It was a division of two highly unequal parts: between the small group of independent gentlemen and everyone else.

These gentlemen, as I noted in my discussion of the gentry in Virginia, favored a brand of classical republicanism having its origin in ancient Greece. From this perspective, the citizen body should be dominated by men who have achieved a life of complete freedom or independence—from material want, from manual labor, from dependency on others. A society's leaders require, it was argued, a sufficient level of independence and leisure to be able to devote themselves to promoting the common or public good.

In practice, of course, this meant that the leaders would have to be men of wealth and property. Property was, in fact, the necessary basis for a committed republican citizenry.[12] Such property took the form of the ownership of slaves as well as land and money. The rootless and impoverished were excluded altogether from entry into the sovereign people.[13]

The gentry elite were agreed that the interests of society as a whole were safest in the hands of white, property-owning men like themselves. Along with securing the defense, the common good in the founding period included the increased commercial prosperity of America as a whole and the protection of private property rights by the state. Although they had successfully challenged an existing political order in declaring independence, these wealthy gentlemen continued to identify the republican perspective with the maintenance of the dominant set of institutional arrangements in American society.

Very much like their seventeenth-century ancestors, they viewed society as a system in which the various parts functioned for the good of the whole. And in the same way, they saw the different parts as arranged in a natural hierarchy. They took for granted the "natural" distinctions between the wise and the foolish, the weak and the strong, and the like. Men were not equal by nature, nor should they aspire to equality. "The notion of Levelism," William Cooper, a Congregational clergyman, told his Massachusetts listeners in the mid-eighteenth century, "had little foundation in Nature."[14] One man differed "by nature" from another, wrote John Adams, "almost as much as man from beast." "Was there, or will there ever be," he asked rhetorically, "a nation, whose individuals were all equal, in natural and acquired qualities, in virtues, talents and riches?"[15] It is, thus, not surprising that Adams opposed a bill before the Massachusetts legislature in 1777 to abolish slavery.

In the eyes of the gentry, then, Americans were arranged in a natural hierarchy according to their virtues, talents, and riches and thus their ability to meet society's needs. And only the elite gentlemen were in a position to judge the full nature of society's needs.[16] The different orders or classes were expected to practice their specific talents and defer to the talents of the other orders. As with the standpoint accepted by the early settlers from England, this view of society rested on the model of the patriarchal family, with the father at the head. Leadership and influence flowed from the superior to the inferior levels of this social hierarchy.[17] Personal relations were everywhere mediated through institutional arrangements.

Let me, then, systematically consider the evidence regarding the four characteristics of community in early America. My concern here is with the extent to which sociopolitical reality meets the communitarian ideal of community set out in chapter 1, where a full-fledged community is conceived of as a group of people who live in a common territory, have a common history and shared values, participate together in various activities, and have a high degree of solidarity. To the extent that these characteristics are missing, MacIntyre, Sandel, and Bellah and his associates, as well as other communitarians, are mistaken in their claims about the prevalence of "community" in late eighteenth-century America.[18] For as they themselves argue, a collection of persons does not constitute a genuine community.

I

*The Territorial Dimension*

I begin with the territorial dimension. For eighteenth-century America to have been a community, it at least would have had to have reasonably well-defined geographic boundaries that allowed for recognition and agreement about the extent and identity of the area which constituted that community. This was generally the case. At the national level—at the level of the North American colonies—most Anglo-Americans did indeed share a common territory. But it is mainly a shared territory at the level of the local village or town that communitarians see as having the special power to engender community.

A common locale, they argue, helps assure that most of people's ties to others are unchosen and nonvoluntary. Sharing a common locale, individuals inherit their positions and relate to one another as members of a group with a rich texture of interconnections. What is important about the territorial dimension, according to communitarian scholars, is that people's commitments and responsibilities are a consequence of *where* they find themselves "to begin with."[19]

In both seventeenth- and eighteenth-century America, however, large numbers of people did not stay in the place where they found themselves to begin with. They left the places where they were living and thus created new relationships. Of course, the original migration to America was itself an indication that the continent was to be inhabited by a restless people. "Furthermore," observes Meinig, "a large proportion of those who moved to America had already moved from their native localities. They had left the farms and villages of their youth and were living in or near one of the larger towns, seaports, or capital."[20] They knew what it was to pack up and leave home, and were thus later well prepared for moving on when land was available, opportunity beckoned, or there was a desire to escape from debt, boredom, failure, disappointment, or whatever.

By the time of the Revolution, geographic mobility was widespread throughout the colonies. Although many communitarians emphasize the stability of the colonial town or village, the tendency everywhere—though less, of course, in New England than elsewhere—was toward dispersion. "In the average rural community perhaps 15 percent of the population left in the course of a decade," says Jackson Turner Main, "and even more newcomers arrived. Probably 40 percent of the population or thereabouts moved during a few years time."[21] As a consequence, relationships were formed and broken with a frequency that increasingly made it impossible (had it ever been) for many individuals to take their identity from a fixed place in one particular town or village.

Except in the sense that they all lived on the same continent, then, the sharing of a common territory in the revolutionary period was certainly less than in the versions of America's history set forth by communitarian writers today. For whatever reasons, many people did not accept their inherited membership in the town or village where they found themselves. To the extent that Americans migrated from one locale to another, the inherited membership so critical for genuine community was missing in the founding period.

This lack of fixed territorial settlement was, of course, partly a consequence of the sort of politics of the common good espoused by the rich and comfortable. Although it was not only poor people who were on the move, it was the disproportionate ownership of the decent land by the wealthy gentry that made it so difficult for ordinary men to make a living. The poor and landless had far less opportunity than the better-off to locate permanently in one particular town or village. Territorial stability was, in any case, not encouraged by a societal vision that saw the pursuit of the common good as requiring large inequalities in the ownership of land and property.

## II

### A Common History

Consider now the extent to which a common history and shared values, the second attribute of community, were dominant at the time. In a genuine community, individuals think of themselves primarily in terms of their membership in a particular group and of their values as the values of that group. A community always has a history and so is also "a community of memory," according to Bellah et al. A community of memory does not forget its past. "In order not to forget the past," we are told, "a community is involved in retelling its story, its constitutive narrative, and in so doing, it offers examples of the men and women who have embodied and exemplified the meaning of the community."[22] As they point out, MacIntyre and Sandel also emphasize the importance of a common history.

A common history of membership in a territorially rooted group—with its own specific background of events, activities, successes and failures, victories and defeats—assures consensus about where people have come from and to whom they have rightful commitments and obligations. Common origins and common experiences help provide the sense of connection and attachment crucial to community. A common history underlies those "structures of normality" that provide the most basic framework for people to understand one another.[23] Many of the everyday, taken-for-granted, unquestioned practices of a community's members rest on their common history and these structures of normality. Such a common history, communitarian writers agree, characterized America's founding period.

Their claim is too sweeping, for Americans in the founding period did not all share a common history. Tocqueville says that the people in the thirteen colonies were the descendants of a common stock and had the

CHAPTER 3

same religion. He seems to have taken this description over from John
Jay, who in *The Federalist* No. 2 was concerned with stressing the American people's common heritage. Jay had written of "a people descended
from the same ancestors, speaking the same language, professing the
same religion, attached to the same principles of government, very similar in their manners and customs."[24]

But the reality was otherwise. At the time of the Revolution, the English and the Welsh accounted for about half of the total population,
Scots and Irish for about 14 percent, and Germans for about 7 percent.
People of Dutch, French, and Swedish background accounted for most
of the remaining population of European heritage.[25] Furthermore, of
course, about 20 percent were black slaves of African heritage.

As for religious affiliation, the English predominated as Congrega-
tionalists, the Scotch-Irish were Presbyterians, and the Irish were Catholic. On the eve of the Revolution, the colonies were divided into Congre-
gationalists, Anglicans, Presbyterians, Quakers, Baptists, Catholics, the
German and Dutch ethnic churches, and a small number of Jews.[26]

Just as Britain had been the major force of unity, it was in the revolutionary era about all that the colonies shared. The thirteen colonies
shared no common links other than to Crown and Parliament, and they
had no shared history outside the British context. They did have a language in common. But that, too, pointed back to Britain.

The various colonies differed dramatically from one another in size,
geographical location, population composition, wealth, and historical
experience. In a sense, there were not one but many Americas. Both
among and within the thirteen colonies, there was too much heterogeneity in origins and background, and too regionally and class-differenti-
ated a colonial past, for there to have been a common history arising
from people's experiences on the continent of North America. A large
body of research over the past two or three decades reveals a degree of
diversity in the American experience that was never imagined by earlier
historians.

*Shared Values*

The same holds true with regard to shared values. The word *value* implies a code or standard which has some persistence through time and is
sufficiently important to regulate people's preferences and behavior.
The new communitarians claim that Americans in the founding period
agreed upon several central values relating to everyone's conduct. These
early Americans, according to communitarians writers, all valued individual dignity, respected one another, and were committed to a rough

equality of conditions. There was, in addition, a widespread concern for the public good and the welfare of one's fellows.

Consider, first, the value placed on equality of condition. Contrary to what communitarians suggest, the discourse of the American Revolution in no way rested on assumptions about an egalitarian social order. The founders' interest in equality was in the collective form: equality with Britain. By claiming equal rights and an equal status, J. R. Pole observes, America's leaders did "not thereby make any admission as to the relations among its own members."[27]

As I showed in the previous chapter, the original English settlers saw the social arrangements in society as eternal and unchangeable, reflecting the natural hierarchy of social distinctions. This conception never really changed very much in early America, and during the revolutionary era there continued to be sizable differences in the distribution of wealth, status, and influence at every level: local, colonial, regional, and national. There was everywhere a hierarchy of relations, and a division between the haves and the have-nots. The rough equality of condition, emphasized by Bellah and his associates, simply did not exist.

Alice Hanson Jones estimates that the wealthiest 10 percent of the population owned about 53 percent of the total wealth in the thirteen colonies, and 66 percent in the South.[28] In the northern colonies, according to Main, poor people comprised at least one-third of the total white population. He says that this figure was even higher in the South.[29]

Although America in the late colonial period did not have the extremes of wealth and poverty or the hereditary privileges and exclusions that characterized most Old World societies, there were significant differences in wealth throughout the thirteen colonies.[30] The social and political elite, says Jack Greene, consisted of 3–5 percent of free adult males.[31]

Property and power were everywhere unequally held. But the degree of inequality varied widely in connection with other attributes of the places where people lived. For the three hundred or so villages and towns of Massachusetts around 1775, Cook reports a strong relationship between the type of village or town and the distribution of wealth: the larger the village or town, the more unequal the distribution of property and power.[32]

In farming villages and newly settled towns, the top 10 percent of the taxpayers typically owned between one-quarter and one-third of the property. In "secondary towns," which served as centers in the rural counties, the richest 10 percent owned between a third and a half of the property. These towns also contained a substantial number of landless poor.[33] Power was concentrated in the hands of the more prosperous farmers and tradesmen.

"Major" county towns were more commercially developed, had a more stratified social structure, and had power concentrated in a narrower elite group than in secondary towns. Cook finds that more than 50 percent of the wealth in these towns was in the hands of the wealthiest 10 percent of the taxpayers.[34] As in the secondary towns, there was a visible class of landless poor at the bottom of the status hierarchy. At the top, town leadership comprised no more than 3 percent of the population.

Along with these three hundred villages and towns, there were also the two urban areas discussed earlier: Salem and Boston. These two cities had the highest concentrations of property in the colony. More than 60 percent of the wealth in Boston was concentrated in the hands of the top tenth of the taxpayers, while Salem's top-tenth concentration was about 52 percent.[35] Power in both cities was in the hands of a tiny elite group. Cook estimates that the pool of active leaders in Boston never exceeded 1 percent of the city's population.

Inequality in Boston was reinforced by the fact that the city was collecting a poor population that other towns were unable (or unwilling) to accommodate. By 1771, almost 30 percent of Boston's inhabitants were too poor to be taxed.[36] For the state as a whole, as many as 20–25 percent of the population had little beyond their immediate belongings.[37] Along with these many poor persons, there existed a tiny elite of the rich and powerful.

The distribution of wealth in Virginia was even more unequal than in Massachusetts. Two-fifths of Virginia's people were, observes Morgan, "as poor as it is possible to get."[38] These slaves had virtually no personal property at all. But they were not the only poor people in Virginia. At least 25 percent of the free white population possessed no land and very little personal property.[39] At the other extreme, the rich upper-class elite—consisting of perhaps 5–10 percent of the white heads of household—owned more than half of all the land and property.[40]

Among the elite we find two Virginians whom the authors of *Habits of the Heart* describe as being "exemplary of the republican tradition": George Washington and Thomas Jefferson.[41] Both of these men were at the top of the class hierarchy in old Virginia; Washington was one of the richest. He had vast land and slave holdings, enjoyed a lavish life-style, bred horses, hunted foxes once a week with his fellow aristocrats, maintained his estate, Mount Vernon, with a large court of servants, and entertained lavishly. Jefferson inherited tens of thousands of profitable acres and dozens of slaves from his father.[42] As did Washington, Jefferson became richer still through his wife. Two years after she married

Jefferson, Martha Wayles Skelton inherited more than eleven thousand acres and 135 slaves. Jefferson's great wealth allowed him to indulge his very expensive tastes, to travel widely, and to satisfy his vast intellectual curiosity.

The extent of economic inequality varied, then, from region to region and city to city, and between city and countryside. But it was always inequality rather than equality that was the norm. No student of stratification in eighteenth-century America has claimed the existence of equality of economic condition.[43] Nor are any assertions about such equality to be found in the writings of any historian at the time. The opposite was the case.

"If 'Equality is the soul of a republic,'" asked the New Hampshire historian Jeremy Belknap in 1784, "Where, then is our soul? . . . Where shall we look for an equal division of property? Not in the five southern States, where every white man is the lordly tyrant of an hundred slaves. Not in the great trading towns and cities, where cash in funds yields 13 or 16 per cent, and in trade much more." And certainly not among the "yeomanry of New England," who are "as mean and selfish as any other people, and have as strong a lurch for territory as merchants have for cash."[44]

Consider now the shared concern for the public good and the general welfare, a second value that communitarians see as having been widespread in America's founding period. Again they are mistaken. Rather than there being a shared concern with the public good in the larger republic, or even in the state, town, or village, there were conflicting interests based on differences in region, property, class, gender, race, and religion.

Especially apparent were the internal divisions during the fighting of the revolutionary war itself. From the time of the Declaration of Independence in 1776 until the Articles of Peace in 1783, the war joined many Americans in a common cause. Beginning as a civil war within the British Empire over colonial affairs, the conflict widened. America was joined by France in 1778, Spain in 1779, and the Netherlands in 1780. Yet the war never united all, or even the vast majority, of Americans.

Although revolutionaries had undertaken war on the premise that the people were committed to independence and would voluntarily contribute to its achievement, this did not prove to be the case.[45] Recruiting was to be a great problem throughout the war. The army was consistently short of its voted strength of 75,760 men. The total strength of the Continental army in October 1776 was less than 22,000.[46] There were too few volunteers, states were initially reluctant to conscript men, and not many of those who enlisted were willing to reenlist. Among those who did join, the desertion rate was between 20 and 25 percent.[47] Not only did the public generally refuse to help army detachments apprehend deserters, but they frequently assisted the deserters in escaping arrest.

The ideology of voluntarism did not work for those many men who could manage to avoid serving. After 1777, conscription was widely used by the states, but it was mainly a technique for determining who would hire a substitute to serve in his place. By then it was clear that a long-term army was necessary, and that the American people had given up the pretense that the war would be fought by all citizens.

On July 22, 1776, just four days after the Declaration of Independence was proclaimed in Boston, the Boston Committee of Correspondence ordered the townsmen to appear on the Common for a military draft. "Gentlemen, subject to the draft, bought substitutes when their numbers were drawn by lot to join the army."[48] In practice, it was only some men—usually unmarried, poor men in their late teens and early twenties—who filled the enlisted ranks.[49] As Charles Royster states, "Privateering, farm labor, brief service as a militia substitute all offered more money, food, and physical comfort than regular army duty did."[50]

Not surprisingly, there was a vast difference between these enlisted men and the officers who commanded them. Continental army officers saw themselves as very much superior to the ordinary people around them. The prevailing ideal in the officers' corps, says Royster, was "to make the individual military gentleman and his glory the center of concern."[51] As much as possible, they avoided all contact with their men. These gentlemen-officers were generally inexperienced and lacked the qualities of military leadership. Their demeanor sometimes evoked respect, but resentment, hostility, and revolt were more common reactions to the aristocratic pretensions of these socially ambitious members of the officer corps.

Not only was there friction between enlisted men and officers but also between soldiers and civilians. Throughout the war, the theft and destruction of property was a serious problem. Soldiers damaged the private homes and buildings that were used for their quarters, plundered livestock and grain, burned people's trees and fence rails for firewood, beat people up, and robbed them.[52] Unlike British army plunderers, these soldiers were abusing their own people.

But the misbehavior was not only on the side of the military. Many high officers believed that state governments were too weak in supporting the army and that the public wanted to be free from any obligations of war. General Alexander McDougall, for example, warned that the army could not supply itself "unless the civil authority and Congress will do their duty."[53] He said that soldiers would not allow themselves "to be made Scape Goats of, to bear the Iniquities of the Country, to support them in Ease and Liberty, and to lay a foundation for Riches and opulence for America" while the public indicates little willingness to support their own army.[54]

The determination of many Americans to profit from the war was considerable. The graft and dishonesty of contractors and suppliers did much to hinder the war effort. Royster notes that "Americans repeatedly sold defective food, clothing, gunpowder, and other supplies to their own army." And he goes on to say that "the army received bundles of blankets that when opened, revealed that each blanket was only a fraction of the proper size; gunsmiths cheated the government when hired to repair arms; large quantities of gunpowder were 'bad and not to be depended on.' "[55]

In contrast to the usual celebrations that idealize the American people during the revolutionary war years, more recent research reveals much conduct inconsistent with the emphasis on concern for the public good. The desperate devices to escape military service, the behavior of many soldiers toward civilians, the vulgar ambitions of many gentlemen-officers, the greed of farmers and dealers in manufactured goods, the graft of public officials and contractors, all these served to undercut the supposed virtue and valor of Americans in the founding generation.

Contrary to the claims of communitarian thinkers, the American people were not tied together by shared values in the founding period.[56] This is again not surprising, given the republican vision of the elite gentry. There was certainly no shared value placed on equality of condition. Just the opposite was the case. And the same holds true for the idea of a shared concern for the good of the social whole. It was conspicuous by its absence.

Since it was the ruling elite who defined what was in the interests of society, it is to be expected that there would be enormous differences both in the extent to which different sorts of people were viewed as being important to the functioning of society and in the economic positions of such people. What this meant in practice was that certain social arrangements involving exploitation and oppression were considered necessary for assuring the good of the whole.

# III

## Political Participation

Just as the empirical evidence gives scant support to the existence of a common past and shared values, participation by people in the affairs that concerned them—the third attribute of community—is found to have been very limited. From the perspective of communitarian theo-

71

rists, community grows out of the collective, participatory involvement of people in common talk, common decision making, and common action.[57] There was indeed some participation of this sort. But active involvement of Americans in the affairs that were important to their lives was enjoyed by only a very small group in the late eighteenth century. How could it have been otherwise when the dominant ideology limited participation to that portion of the people who met the property-based, republican standards?

Throughout the thirteen colonies, the franchise was restricted to white men who were able to meet the required property qualifications. In Massachusetts, as in the other colonies during the later colonial era, all "citizens" had certain rights and privileges in common. But not everyone was deemed a citizen. Thinking about political rights at the time was derived from the English idea that the franchise was tied to ownership of land. It was argued that the suffrage ought to be limited to men who held "freehold" to land of a certain specified value which was clear of all charges and deductions.[58]

The requirement in Massachusetts was a freehold with a total value of fifty pounds or an annual income of forty to fifty shillings (which was apparently reckoned to be about the same thing).[59] Citizenship, as symbolized by the right to vote, was limited to those who evidenced a permanent attachment in the form of property.

Property, however, was not the only criterion for the franchise. Even among those who met the prevailing property qualifications, the franchise was denied to roughly half of the adult white population: women. It was also denied to males below the age of twenty-one, nonnaturalized aliens, indentured servants, those who received alms, and often Catholics and Jews as well. Those few blacks (even the free ones) living in Massachusetts were denied the vote until 1781.[60] The essential idea was that the franchise should be extended only to that class which was relatively independent, that is, exempt from external control or support.

Non–property owners, children, those in servitude to others, and people who received alms were not accorded the vote because it was claimed that their votes would be influenced by those on whom they depended. The same went for most women. In addition, women, children, nonwhites, criminals, and the insane were held to be incapable of self-control and thus unable ever to achieve the independence necessary for citizenship in society. Ideas about blacks were changing and many Massachusetts residents were becoming increasingly hostile to slavery, yet blacks were still widely viewed as childlike, ignorant, and irresponsible. Property requirements for voters (and their representatives) were justified, then, by "the stake in society" argument, other exclusionary requirements, and by arguments about people having no self-control or will of their own.[61] The franchise requirements were similar both before and after the Revolution.

Chilton Williamson estimates that as many as 50 to 75 percent of white adult males had the vote at the time of the Revolution.[62] But white adult males constituted only about 20 percent of the total Massachusetts population at the time, and thus the Massachusetts electorate consisted of a very small group.

In Virginia, neither women, the young, nor those without sufficient property could vote. In 1736, the requirement for the franchise in Virginia was fixed at one hundred acres of unimproved land or twenty-five acres with a house and plantation.[63] Only those with such holdings counted as "the constituent members" of the commonwealth.[64] In the founding period, adult males constituted about 20 percent of the white population of Virginia and about 13 percent of the total (black and white) population. One-quarter of white men lacked sufficient land to have the franchise. Women were second-class citizens, while blacks did not count at all. Thus, fewer than 10 percent of the inhabitants of old Virginia had the right to vote.

Despite the restrictions on the right to vote, most of those with the franchise chose not to utilize it. Consider the situation at town meetings in eighteenth-century Massachusetts.[65] These New England town meetings have been celebrated as a unique characteristic of America's past. Tocqueville wrote that "town meetings are to liberty what primary schools are to science; they bring it within the people's reach, they teach men how to use and how to enjoy it."[66] In New England towns, he remarked, "power has been distributed with admirable skill, for the purpose of interesting the greatest possible number of persons in the common weal."[67]

The kind of political experience described by Tocqueville is what the authors of *Habits of the Heart* term "the politics of community." Found, they say, in "the New England township of legend," the politics of community "is a matter of making operative the moral consensus of the community, reached through free face-to-face discussion."[68] Such face-to-face discussion, they believe, occurred at the town meeting.

In her excellent study of attendance at town meetings in New England, Jane Mansbridge notes that no representative data are available on attendance at early town meetings. But the data she has located suggest that in eighteenth-century Massachusetts anywhere from 20 to 60 percent of the potential voters attended town meetings.[69] Although there was a great deal of variation from one town to another and between different time periods,[70] in most towns the majority of those men eligible to attend the town meeting did not do so. Whatever the ideal, these town meetings never involved more than a small minority of the town's inhabitants. Even among those eligible to attend, most did not regularly do so.

It was similar with voting: most men simply did not vote. Although we would expect heavy voting on important issues, that was seldom the case. Robert Brown mentions the vote on a new constitution in Berkshire County in 1778. "The total vote was 5,654 to 2,049 in favor of a new constitution, but the significant point is that this represented less than 15 percent of the qualified voters."[71] And on the question of ratifying the Massachusetts Constitution in 1780, the overwhelming majority of qualified men did not vote. It was not until 1787 that more than 25 percent of the voters of Massachusetts regularly went to the polls.[72]

In Virginia, as in Massachusetts, elections seldom stimulated much interest in voting among those persons who were eligible to do so.[73] An exception was the relatively cohesive, self-conscious, and unified gentry, who participated regularly in the political process and occupied the highest offices in Virginia.[74] Although some ordinary men who exercised the franchise could expect to hold minor offices, the planter elite "offered scant opportunity for a small farmer to cross the watershed that separated ordinary mortals from gentlemen."[75]

To sum up, then, only 10–15 percent of the total population had the right to vote in Massachusetts, and an even smaller percentage in Virginia. Women, of course, made up the largest group excluded from the political domain. It was simply taken for granted (by men at least) that men could represent women in the political sphere. Exclusion from the franchise defined women, of course, as lacking political rights—as less, that is, than full citizens, and as dependent on men. But even so, most of those men with the franchise did not utilize it. Whether because of a lack of perceived difference between candidates or their positions on most issues or because potential voters recognized that the wealthy and powerful usually filled the important offices, elections seldom stimulated much interest in voting among those men who held the franchise in Massachusetts and Virginia. And exactly the same held in all the other colonies (or states).[76]

Along with attendance at town meetings and voting, serving in the offices of the town or village provides a further indication of the extent of political participation. In Massachusetts towns of every size, Cook reports, a small percentage of men filled the major town offices. Comprehensive data from the period 1750–74 shows that the percentage of officeholders varied inversely with the size of the town: in Boston, fewer than 1 percent held office; between 1 and 3 percent held office in most towns with more than 1,000 inhabitants; between 3 and 6 percent in towns of 500–1,000; and more than 6 percent in towns with fewer than 500 inhabitants.[77]

Not only participation in town government but also a man's involvement in provincial politics depended on wealth. As Cook notes, wealth enabled men to "devote time to acquiring the personal contacts and educational polish that were associated with social and political eminence" beyond their village or town, as well as establishing their overall status in town.[78] Most men with high provincial offices (either elective or appointive) were social and political leaders at the local level as well.[79]

With the exception of a brief period after the revolutionary war, when there was increased involvement of men from a less prominent background in the political process, late eighteenth-century office holding was virtually restricted to "the better sort." Although the Sons of Liberty included many men from the lower classes, the officers and committee members were men of some substance, drawn from the middle and upper ranks of society.[80]

It was this "better sort" that later called for a constitutional convention in order to curb the so-called excesses of democracy after the Revolution. But whatever these aristocratic gentlemen might have thought about the democratic excesses of the people, the vast majority of Americans had no access to a political arena in which they could participate and fulfill themselves as public-spirited citizens.

Contrary to MacIntyre's assertion that Americans in the founding period were "assumed to possess equal rights and privileges," to Sandel's claims about an "active public life," and Bellah et al.'s reference to "a self-governing society of relative equals in which all participate," the revolutionary and constitutional periods were characterized by a deep and abiding pattern of political inequality.[81]

## IV

### Social Solidarity

Given the discussion in this and the previous chapter, and what I have already said about the first three attributes of community, my conclusion about the fourth attribute is obvious: there was no strong sense of social solidarity in late eighteenth-century America.

The dimension of social solidarity, I noted earlier, combines two elements found in the conceptions of community advanced by communitarians: social interdependence and the "we sense" of belonging together. Communal solidarity involves obligations that are *special*, in that they hold only within the community in which people share membership; and are *personal*, in that they run not just to the community in a collective sense but also from each member to each other member.

As I have shown, there was neither a widespread sense of social interdependence nor a sense of unity and belonging together in the founding period. Because of enormous diversity and cultural pluralism among the various colonies, there was a general lack of fellow feeling and concern for those living elsewhere. And there was very little sense of sharing membership with others in this, *our* country.

The revolutionary war did, of course, join many Americans in a common cause for a short period, and there was then some sense of "we" and "they." But we must not forget that about 20 percent of the total population sided openly with the Crown, and many more remained politically neutral and uninvolved.[82] Beyond this, as already discussed, there was hostility between officers and enlisted men, and frequent antagonisms between soldiers and civilians. Further, mutual suspicion and distrust intensified as the patriots from different regions came into more frequent contact with each other. There really was no identifiable national community to which Americans felt a special sense of social solidarity and obligation. And there certainly was no notion of personal obligation to all other Americans.

The most conspicuous antagonisms were between the New Englanders and everyone else. Observers from other regions commented frequently on the inability of Yankees to conceal their sense of moral superiority. "We Pennsylvanians act as if we believe that God made of one blood all families of the earth," observed William Maclay, "but the Eastern people seem to think he made none but New England folks."[83] When John Adams passed through New York City in 1774, he heard Yankees castigated as "Goths and Vandalls," infamous for their "Leveling Spirit." In the privacy of his diary, Adams noted the lack of virtue, gentility, and good breeding outside New England.[84] And Abigail Adams expressed to her husband, John, the belief that the "common people of Virginia" were like the uncivilized natives depicted by the British as so characteristic of North America.[85]

For their part, the southerners often looked with disdain upon the Yankees. George Washington's remarks about the numerous New Englanders who failed to enlist or who deserted and his unflattering views about the Massachusetts soldiery under his command in the autumn of 1775 are one example of the low opinion in which many Virginians and other southerners regarded their New England comrades.[86] After being routed by the British at Kip's Bay in 1776, New Englanders endured such taunts of reproach and dishonor as " 'Eastern Prowess' and 'Camp Difficulty,' which also meant diarrhea."[87] Jefferson made no secret of the intensity of his contempt for New Englanders. In a letter to a fellow Virginian, Jefferson noted that "they are marked, like the Jews, with such a perversity of character as to constitute, from that circumstance, the natural division of our parties."[88]

Recriminations by both soldiers and civilians were frequent, with men from the North and the South charging one another with cowardice or misconduct. These antagonisms between the various colonies—and especially between the Republic's self-announced progenitors, Massachusetts and Virginia—continued throughout the period of the War of Independence.

As a consequence, there was never anything like true unity among the colonies. The Continental Congress had increasingly assumed the powers and attributes of an American government. It raised an army and appointed officers and quartermasters. It appointed a committee to negotiate with foreign powers. It imposed requisitions on the various states, based on their population and resources. And it issued money on its own authority. During the eight years of struggle between America and Great Britain, the Congress exercised power on behalf of the thirteen new states. But once victory was achieved, the Americans' strongest motive for unity was removed.

By the 1780s it had become absolutely clear that the experiment in republicanism was in danger of collapsing. The ejection of royal governments in 1776 had released explosive antiaristocratic forces all over America. Almost all the roughly 250 aristocrats who had staffed the royal governments in the former colonies were driven into private life or exile.[89] Resentment of the rich and privileged became widespread, and men of more humble background often came forward to assume positions of authority.

Americans at the time saw the thirteen states that made the Revolution as composed of two distinctive and often hostile regions: the "eastern" or "northern" states of New England, and the "southern" states from the Chesapeake south to Georgia.[90] Few references were made to such middle states as New York, Pennsylvania, and New Jersey.[91]

These major divisions also came to be reflected in both the creation and the ratification of the Constitution. The Constitutional Convention had to deal with two central problems. One was, of course, that of distributing power between the states and the national government. At issue here were questions about the transfer of important powers from the state to the national level, the separation of powers, the location of sovereignty, and the like.

The other was the less formal—but, nevertheless, crucial—problem of distributing power among different regions of the Union. To a considerable extent, argues Drew McCoy, the political history of the postrevolutionary era concerns "the daunting challenge of fashioning political coherence from the recalcitrant materials of a regionally differentiated colonial past."[92]

From the beginning, the Constitutional Convention was characterized by a struggle between the northern and southern states. This was commented on by both James Madison of Virginia and the Massachusetts delegate, Rufus King. Madison spoke of "great" and "essential" differences of interest between the northern and southern states.[93] And King insisted that "the great danger to our general government *is the great southern and northern interests of the continent, being opposed to each other.*"[94]

If the number of representatives for each state in the new Congress was based solely on the number of free persons in that state, the North would overwhelm the South in the new Congress. But if slaves were counted equally with free persons, Virginia would then have more delegates than any other state. It was similar with South Carolina (the state with the second greatest number of slaves), Georgia, and North Carolina: counting slaves equally with free persons would assure them of a larger number of delegates. Thus if slaves were included in the count, the South would outnumber the North in the Congress.

The deliberations of the 1787 convention were guided, then, by a recognition of sectional rivalry within the nation. The deep animosities that developed between some northern and southern delegates make it clear just how opposed their interests were. Because of this, certain compromises were perhaps inevitable, since neither group could get very far on its own.

Among other concessions, the slave states obtained extra representation in Congress through the three-fifths clause. This clause had been offered as a compromise between those who did not want slaves to be counted at all (because they were unfree) and those who wanted to count them fully for purposes of representation. The clause provided for counting three-fifths of all slaves in determining representation in Congress.

Other concessions were the right to import new slaves for at least twenty years through the slave trade clause[95] and the right to have runaway slaves returned through the fugitive slave clause. The northern delegates insisted that they were opposed to slavery and to its continuation. But they were eager for a stronger Union with a national court system and a unified commercial system. To obtain them, the northern delegates were willing to compromise with their southern adversaries. "Although some had expressed concern over the justice or safety of slavery," writes Paul Finkelman, "in the end they were able to justify their compromises and ignore their qualms."[96]

Whatever the extent of opposition to slavery by the northern delegates to the Constitutional Convention, most Americans seem to have been indifferent to it and to have felt no embarrassment about the apparent contradiction between the Declaration of Independence's assertion that "all men are created equal" and the existence of slavery. Even those liberal Americans who were troubled by this institution were seemingly unable to imagine a society in which blacks and whites would live together as fellow citizens.[97]

People were undoubtedly more concerned with what happened where they lived than what was going on elsewhere. But this does not necessarily make for community. As I indicated in my initial discussion of solidarity in chapter 1, one of the features of community is that intensity of concern for other persons is ordered by social distance. The normative ideal of community, I noted, conceives of people's concern as extending all the way to the outermost limit or boundary of the community. Thus, communitarian writers might be willing to acknowledge that community was, just as I say, absent at the national level. But they might still want to claim that it existed at the local level of the state or town.

Again, they would be mistaken. For suspicion, distrust, hostility, and a lack of solidarity characterized many of the relationships not only *between* the different colonies (later states) and regions but also *within* them. I have already mentioned the division between locals and cosmopolitans in Massachusetts and between evangelicals and the elite gentry in Virginia. And I have noted the exclusion of women, nonwhites, and many others from full citizenship.

Exactly the same story could be told for the other colonies at the time. New York and Pennsylvania, for example, were even more divided than Massachusetts and Virginia by different religious groupings, economic interests, and ways of life.[98] In every state, there were the ruling circles and the cultural out-groups. As Greene and Pole observe, "people's status was in great measure determined by the extent to which they could or could not exploit other people."[99]

Even at the level of the village and town, it would be difficult to speak of any widespread sense of social solidarity. While concern for the well-being of others was undoubtedly greater than at the state or national level, there was never a concern for all others. Some people's lives were considered more important than others. It was not simply that people cared more about the welfare of, say, their parents, their children, or their husband or wife than they did for others. Of course they did. But men and women everywhere regularly excluded others from their circle of concern because of the others' race, gender, religion, economic position, or whatever.

The absence of a sense of fellow feeling and mutual concern at the national level is easy to understand. After all, America was not only very large but consisted of people with vastly different experiences, histories, and traditions. And the same might be said about each of the colonies; within each one, there was tremendous diversity. But even at the level of the village and the town, there were cleavages between the rich and the poor classes and between privileged groups of men competing for power and domination.

Once more, because the gentry's brand of classical republicanism emphasized *their* contribution to assuring the common good, there was little room for any sense of mutual obligation or balanced reciprocity. All over America, the rich and wellborn assumed the superiority of the able few and the inadequacy of the ordinary many.

To conclude, then, the sociopolitical reality of late eighteenth-century America bears little resemblance to the idealized depictions of community set forth by communitarian writers. Except perhaps for the territorial dimension, historical evidence fails to support communitarian claims about the founding period. A common history and shared values, widespread political participation, and bonds of social solidarity are conspicuous by their absence. Communitarian writers appeal to the everyday experiences of Americans in the founding period in support of their thesis that community once reigned supreme. Unfortunately, they evoke and celebrate a conception of community that has an ideological rather than an empirical basis.

Some readers will not be surprised by the failure to locate community in America's past. Certainly for many sociologists, the "golden age" of community is considered to have been during the Middle Ages. Durkheim, Tönnies, and other nineteenth-century social theorists contrasted the modern nation-state with what had existed in medieval Europe. They saw Europe in the Middle Ages as made up of a network of communities in which people lived together in fellowship and cooperation, and where individuals were defined by the sum of the connections to family, clan, and village. I turn to the Middle Ages in the following chapter.

# LIFE IN THE MIDDLE AGES:
# AN OVERVIEW

LIKE THE classical polis, writes MacIntyre, the medieval kingdom was a community in which men "in company pursue *the* human good."[1] Medieval society appeals greatly to MacIntyre, for he sees the Middle Ages as a period when morality was in good order in the community. Medieval society also provided a point of reference for many of the major nineteenth-century social theorists. Comte, Weber, Simmel, and Durkheim all contrasted the social structure of the modern nation-state with what existed in the Middle Ages.[2] "The rediscovery of medievalism—its institutions, values, themes, and structures," writes Robert Nisbet, "is one of the significant events in the intellectual history of the nineteenth century."[3]

More than any other nineteenth-century social theorist, it was the German sociologist Ferdinand Tönnies who drew on the Middle Ages as the definitive point of reference. First published in 1887, Tönnies's *Gemeinschaft und Gesellschaft* turned into a best-seller and eventually went through eight editions.[4] This book provided later generations with the most widely used terms for discussing forms of social organization.[5] As Harry Liebersohn notes, it "was the first work to make *Gemeinschaft* a cardinal concept of sociology and to develop a logical and historical dichotomy between it and modern society."[6] Since then, this dichotomy has been widely used in studying social change.

Tönnies distinguished between two opposed and complementary types: gemeinschaft and gesellschaft. Although there are no exact English equivalents of these two terms, they are usually translated as "community" and "society." Tönnies used these terms as ideal types, noting that elements of both are found in most social relationships. But, he emphasized, patterns of relationship differ greatly in the relative strength of these two elements.

Tönnies viewed all social groupings as "willed" creations of their members. When people act completely in terms of what he called their *essential* will—will as naturally grown in and with thought—their actions give rise to gemeinschaft types of social relations. With essential will, rational activity occurs in order to realize desires derived from group sentiments, customs, habits, and relations. Social action is based on relationships of sympathy, friendship, affection, and the like.[7] Tönnies offers family, kinship groups, neighborhoods, and friendship networks as examples of gemeinschaft patterns of group solidarity. In discussing these sorts of relations, Tönnies uses much of the same terminology employed by communitarian writers today. He emphasizes the importance of the group, intimacy, attachment, tradition, understanding, shared memory, common ties, and the common good.[8]

Similarly when he considers gesellschaft relations—dominant here are individualism, isolation, separation, exclusion, exchange, and contract. In gemeinschaft, people are concerned for the common good, but in gesellschaft, "every person strives for that which is to his own advantage and affirms the actions of others only in so far as and as long as they can further his interest."[9]

In the course of history, Tönnies argues, the original collective forms of gemeinschaft have developed into gesellschaft, and folk culture has given rise to the civilization of the state.[10] A period of gemeinschaft in which concord, folkways, mores, and religion were paramount has been replaced by the dominance of gesellschaft characterized by convention, legislation, and public opinion.[11]

Tönnies says that gemeinschaft existed in its purest form in traditional societies and in the precapitalist, preurbanized world of the Middle Ages. Gesellschaft is dominant in modern, capitalist, urban society. This change from gemeinschaft to gesellschaft, writes Tönnies, "reaches its consummation in what is frequently designated as individualism."[12] He clearly regarded community as the natural type of human relationship and regretted its replacement by society (gesellschaft) as the primary form of social organization.[13]

As Nisbet points out, Tönnies "derived all of the substance of his typology of gemeinschaft from medieval village, family, and clan."[14] Drawing heavily on the work of Otto Gierke, Sir Henry Maine, and other historians and cultural anthropologists of the time, he described the Middle Ages as a period dominated by the sorts of natural communities of common will, custom, and sociability that he termed *Gemeinschaften*. I want now to present Tönnies's picture of the Middle Ages in some detail.

## I

In considering community life, Tönnies distinguishes various forms that were found in the Middle Ages: household, village, town, and commonwealth. With regard to the household, Tönnies says that it consisted of three strata grouped in concentric circles. The innermost circle was made up of "the master and mistress of the house and other wives if they [were] all of equal rank."[15] The next circle contained grandparents, children, and other relatives. The servants, male and female, formed the outermost circle. Tönnies says that family life was the general basis of life in the gemeinschaft, and his description of home life is very reminiscent of the Greek *oikos*.[16] Tönnies's defense of servitude sounds much like Aristotle's defense of slavery, and he criticizes that "prejudice as deep as it is thoughtless [which] considers servitude itself as a disgrace of humanity because it violates the principle of the equality of men."[17] The servant, like kin, belongs to the household, though the relationship is "like that of a natural possession."[18]

This family household is depicted by Tönnies as the basic unit of ownership, production, and consumption in the medieval period. He speaks of the community of daily and nightly abode, and emphasizes the importance of cooperation in work and consumption. Labor was divided between the sexes, and the work of the members of the house was separated and divided. The man's responsibility was to obtain and provide the necessities of life, and the woman's was to conserve and prepare them. The man directed his energy toward the outside, fighting and leading the sons, while the woman was confined to the inner circle of home life and was attached to the daughters.[19]

This division of labor was based on innate differences between the sexes. "It is an old truth," says Tönnies, "that women are usually led by feelings, men more by intellect."[20] Men are more clever, and they alone are capable of abstract and logical thinking. Only men possess rational will, and they are much more capable than women of active perception, growth, and development.

Thus, in the household, all work was according to the "natural expression of Gemeinschaft."[21] The place of men was outside, and that of women inside the home. This pattern was adhered to by all those making up this basic unit of community: parents, married children and their spouses, grandchildren, other relatives, and male and female servants. But the household members were "reunited around the table for the necessary distribution of the fruits of their labor."[22] The household was self-sufficient, and barter was contrary to its essential nature.

Somewhat more complex than the household was the village community, which can be considered a large family or clan.[23] The village community in the Middle Ages, says Tönnies, was in its relation to the land like an individual household.[24] In such a community, one finds "the cultivation of the soil practiced in common and the possession of common property in village fields or land held in common by the village."[25] Ancient custom regulated the use of the land and economic relations.[26]

In the village community and surrounding countryside, says Tönnies, people's behavior was regulated by shared folkways, mores, and customary law. Because of the proximity of houses, the communal fields, and the cooperation necessary in common projects, people had frequent contacts with and intimate knowledge of one another.[27] There existed a shared set of moral norms, which were mainly an expression and organ of religious beliefs and community spirit.[28] Everyone in the community was united by this spiritual bond.

A third form of community was the town, the highest and most complex form of social life for Tönnies.[29] In speaking about the town, he writes: "According to the Aristotelian description and in conformity with the idea which underlies its natural phenomena, the town is a self-sufficient household, an organism with a collective life."[30] This was true, says Tönnies, for the Middle Ages.

According to Tönnies, the town was a form of social organization in which people unrelated by blood learned to live together in fellowship and cooperation. Each town was a self-sufficient economic entity, "held together not so much by common objects of nature as by common spirit."[31] The town council, the individual guild, and the church and clergy all concerned themselves with the economic well-being of the community.[32] Describing this spirit of cooperation in the medieval town, Tönnies writes: "Within the town we find as its typical products or fruits the fellowship of work, the guild or corporation, and the fellowship of cult, the fraternity, the religious community. These are together the last and highest expression of which the idea of Gemeinschaft is capable."[33]

In addition to household, village, and town as forms of social organization characterized as gemeinschaft, Tönnies also devotes attention to the commonwealth as another form of collective life.[34] A commonwealth was a regional unity composed of a number of estates, villages, and towns. It was, in general, a unit of self-protection. The highest authority in most commonwealths in the Middle Ages was usually the king or prince. The commonwealth was a system of families, clans, and communities, which the army served as the embodiment of its united will.

The army, Tönnies observes, consisted of men who had a share in the ownership of the land. And when these landowners were involved in fighting, "work in the fields and stock raising [were] left to women and servants."[35] Sometimes in the Middle Ages a warrior caste came into existence, drawn from the ranks of the nobility. When the nobility was unable to live adequately on its own estates, it relied for its support and maintenance on the contributions of neighboring peasants. Such contributions, Tönnies emphasizes, were entirely voluntary. He sees this as another instance of that taken-for-granted cooperation so characteristic of the medieval period.

The commonwealth derived its full dignity, according to Tönnies, from the consensus and cooperation of three different organs: the prince or king, the nobles, and the multitude (the masses). Although one or another of these organs may have become dominant, the commonwealth as a form of community consisted of the united activities of these three organs.[36]

The household, village, town, and commonwealth were all forms of community found in the Middle Ages. Each of these types of community was characterized by concord, folkways, mores, and religion; by shared customs and time-honored understandings; and by relationships of intimacy, trust, and cooperation. With the coming of the city, there occurred an erosion of those features common to gemeinschaft relationships. In the city, people's exchanges, contacts, and contractual relations "only cover up many hostilities and antagonistic interests."[37] Family life decays in the city, as family members are attracted by outside interests and pleasures.[38] As the controls of the gemeinschaft were eliminated, convention and the laws of the state took the place of the folkways, mores, and religious beliefs which theretofore regulated community life.[39]

In an earlier chapter I quoted MacIntyre as saying that "what matters at this stage is the construction of local forms of community within which civilization and the intellectual and moral life can be sustained through the new dark ages which are already upon us."[40] One hundred years ago, Ferdinand Tönnies used strikingly similar language in diagnosing the ills of modern society and in emphasizing the need for community:

> The entire culture has been transformed into a civilization of state and Gesellschaft, and this transformation means the doom of culture itself if none of its scattered seeds remain alive and again bring forth the essence and idea of Gemeinschaft, thus secretly fostering a new culture amidst the decaying one.[41]

Aside from his evaluation of the medieval period, Tönnies's main concern was to analyze and explain the enormous changes that had occurred in European society from the beginning of the Middle Ages up to his own time. He contrasted the growth of capitalist society, as it had developed since the High Middle Ages, with those forms of natural community out of which it grew. According to Tönnies, then, the Middle Ages were predominately gemeinschaft-like, while the modern centuries have become increasingly gesellschaft-like.

Tönnies's typology continues to occupy an important position in many theoretical considerations of community. Nisbet, for example, draws on Tönnies in referring to the absence of a separate, autonomous individual and "the centrality of personal status, of *membership* in society" in the Middle Ages; the existence of family-owned rather than individually owned property; and the prevalence of "the extended family sometimes numbering hundreds of persons."[42]

Before turning to a consideration of medieval community in terms of the evidence made available to us by historians today, I want first to say something about the bases for the claims about community made by nineteenth-century social theorists. Since many social scientists today rely on Tönnies and others from his time for their picture of life in the Middle Ages, it is important to specify the foundation of those nineteenth-century ideas.

## II

Tönnies and other nineteenth-century social theorists drew heavily on the work in social history and cultural anthropology of contemporary scholars who were themselves concerned with family structure, property relations, and variations and changes in social forms. In particular, Tönnies was influenced by J. J. Bachofen's *Das Mutterrecht* (Matrimonial Law), L. H. Morgan's *Ancient Society*, W. E. Hearn's *The Aryan Household*, Sir Henry Maine's *Ancient Law*, G. L. von Maurer's research in medieval agrarian history, E. Laveleye's writing on the origins of property, and O. Gierke's *Genossenschaftsrecht*, which described the riches of communal life.[43] These writings were the source of many of Tönnies's assumptions and ideas about the character of medieval life and historical changes since that time. Although he made no detailed citations of specific studies of the Middle Ages, Tönnies's references to the more theoretical work of the above-named scholars show his debt to them.

Tönnies utilized these writings in arguing that not only the structures of kinship and kin groups but also the social, economic, and political arrangements of human society lead back to the clan and to descent from a common ancestor. He saw the clan as the germ of all social grouping. "The most important social organization or corporate body which originates therefrom and which among all known peoples occurs as the original form of a common life," writes Tönnies, "is the kinship group, the gens, clan, or whatever name is applied to designate this ancient union or unity."[44]

As did Marx and Engels, Tönnies accepted the idea of Germanic kinship based first on matrilineal clans, then developing to patrilineal clans, and, finally, to monogamy. More important than the tracing of relationships through either females (matriliny) or males (patriliny), however, was the assumption that relationships were originally traced through *one* line, that is, were unilineal.

A clan is a group of kinsmen formed on the basis of descent from a common ancestor.[45] Drawing from the historical and anthropological knowledge of his time, Tönnies accepted that clans formed the basic elements of the early Germanic society, gradually disintegrated in the course of the early Middle Ages, and later disappeared altogether. He spoke of the clan as being the family before the family, of the "Gemeinschaft by blood, denoting unity of being," and of the living individuals in the family having been "connected with each other by the presence of past and future generations."[46] Eventually, he says, people came to be more connected to each other by the bonds of field and soil. The gemeinschaft based on common ancestry came to be "developed and differentiated into Gemeinschaft of locality, which is based on a common habitat."[47]

Along with accepting the existence of extensive lineage or clan structure as the prevalent form of kinship among the early Germanic people and its evolution into modern forms of kinship, Tönnies also accepted an evolutionary account of the development of property. This account was connected with the ideas of kinship development just considered. Both were major ingredients in the nineteenth-century conception of societal development advanced by Tönnies and other social theorists.

Ownership of property was thought to have been originally collective or communal. Among the Germanic peoples, it was argued, property went through three stages: the original collective state, the familial stage, and then an increasingly individual stage as a result of the confrontation with Roman law. The main source of this claim was the work of Laveleye, Bachofen, von Maurer, and Morgan, mentioned earlier.

Given the assumed existence of lineal ties of kinship and the absence of private property, Tönnies concluded—as did Marx and Engels—that early society was egalitarian and nonexploitative. In speaking of the clan, the neighborhood, and the village as different epochs of gemeinschaft, Tönnies states that "in Gemeinschaften property is considered as participation in the common ownership."[48] Even today, Alexander Murray notes, the dominant nineteenth-century ideas of kinship development and the development of private property have remained deeply rooted in the literature.[49]

The ideas about community held by Tönnies and other nineteenth-century German scholars were also undoubtedly influenced by the strong tradition of nationalist and romantic Germanic historiography. The *true* German society was viewed as one of egalitarian harmony where all things fit together and where there was a common concern for the mutual good. It was thought to have had its origin in ancient clans, to have survived in the local community during the Middle Ages, and to have continued to a certain extent in German towns right up to the nineteenth century.

An ideal of community that was different from and truer than existing society was emphasized, and there existed a widespread hostility in orthodox German political and social thinking toward the workings of the national state.[50] A ubiquitous yearning for organic wholeness was a dominant theme of intellectual life at the time, and its influence on Tönnies, Marx, and other thinkers was considerable.

Earlier in the nineteenth century, and even in the eighteenth century, various German scholars had written about the separateness, stability, and integrity that distinguished community from society. In 1721, Christian Wolff published a book on what might be termed legal sociology. This book was divided into two parts, titled "On the Essential Community" and "On the Societies of Men."[51] And writing in 1855, Riehl spoke of the division between *Gemeinde* and gesellschaft.[52] "A whole parade of German scholars after the 1850s," Mack Walker points out, struggled with distinguishing between forms of social life.[53] Thus, the distinction between two general forms of social organization was already assumed to be valid and had become a major part of social thought in Tönnies's own day. It was in reference to this ongoing concern that Tönnies elaborated "the distinction, social and historical at once, between *Gemeinschaft* and gesellschaft."[54] Tönnies's preference was clearly for the former.[55]

There is, of course, much more evidence about the Middle Ages available today than was the case a century ago.[56] A number of recent developments, including the discovery of large quantities of documents and other records, allow for a reexamination of those earlier claims about the prevalence of community in the medieval period, while providing a more detailed and accurate picture of life in that time.[57]

## III

The Middle Ages are variously defined but are usually taken to have set in about A.D. 500 and lasted one thousand years. This is obviously an extremely long time, and patterns of life in the later periods were different from those in the earlier ones. My focus here will be on the evidence regarding community in that period of the Middle Ages described by nineteenth-century social theorists and referred to by MacIntyre in *After Virtue*: what is usually termed the High Middle Ages. This was a period extending from the twelfth century and lasting for some two or three hundred years. It is specifically this period that MacIntyre refers to in his discussion of medieval community and morality. And the same goes for Tönnies and those other nineteenth-century theorists who contrasted modern life with medieval society.

Most of the nineteenth-century historians and anthropologists whose work Tönnies used saw the change from *Gemeinschaft* to gesellschaft as coming much later than the Middle Ages. This means that the picture of community sketched out by Tönnies as characteristic of the Middle Ages—prior to the decay brought about by the development of the city and the state—should certainly be found in the period I am going to examine here.

Tönnies viewed the Middle Ages as made up of a network of communities in which people lived together in peace and harmony, and where man was defined as the sum of his connections to family, clan, and village. These tightly knit organic communities are described as being characterized by a peasant-household economic system, collective rather than individual ownership of property, production for immediate use, the dominance of the multigenerational family, early marriage, high fertility, and an absence of geographic mobility. Many other theorists have held a similar view. But, say these scholars, one or another new and irresistible force—the Reformation, the Puritan ethic, the rise of capitalism, or some other influence—destroyed these once dominant forms of community.[58]

I will describe a few important characteristics of the High Middle Ages in order to set the stage for my examination of Tönnies's claims in terms of more recent research. During the High Middle Ages, England, Germany, France, Italy, the Iberian peninsula, and the Low Countries were strongly permeated by Christianity, united in the Roman faith and church organization. Lay society was everywhere Christian. Perhaps most significant for my concerns here, historians today seem to agree that these countries or realms were generally quite similar to one another with regard to economic system, class structure, and political organization.[59]

Of considerable influence at the time was a doctrine very similar to the communitarian idea of a politics of the common good. Basically, it was held that society was composed of three orders—three stable, strictly defined, social categories: those who fought, those who prayed, and those who worked. According to this doctrine of the three orders, each of the different segments had its own God-given function. "Since the Creation, God had assigned specific tasks among men," writes Georges Duby. "Some were commissioned to pray for the salvation of all, others were pledged to fight to protect the mass of the people; it was up to members of the third order, by far the most numerous, to provide for the men of religion and men of war by their labour."[60] The essential class division was between noble warriors and clerics, on the one hand, and peasants, on the other.[61]

Following this divine plan, each order had its own station and its own duties. In spite of their plurality, the three orders formed one body. Each, therefore, had to play its assigned part in maintaining the status quo in a world which was ordered by God and was consequently unalterable. These ideas were transmitted to medieval peasants through innumerable sermons about the duties and expectations of the various orders of society. Attending to their own work and remaining where God had assigned them, the peasants were told, would help assure social harmony. Let us now look more closely at the different layers of medieval society.

Relationships between nobles and peasants are often portrayed by historians in terms of their feudal character.[62] But, as Susan Reynolds points out, the concept of "feudalism" is a modern invention. For contemporary historians, she argues, words like vassal and knight, and fealty and homage, have a much more precise connotation than did words like *feudom* and *feodum*, or *vassus* and *vavassor*, for people in the Middle Ages.[63]

The term *noble* was also rather vague, since the privileges and obligations of nobility were nowhere legally defined. Some were men with inherited property or benefices, that is, an elite by birth, while others were men who acquired wealth and status as businessmen or in the field of combat, where they fought alongside the noble knights. Thus, the criterion of elite by birth was modified by the acquisition of wealth and status by accomplishment.[64] The term *peasant* is also rather ambiguous, since it is not always possible to distinguish between free and unfree, *liberi* and *servi*.[65]

What was important was that privileges and duties were more strongly dependent on wealth and status than they were on any formal, legal, rigidly defined hierarchical positions. Thus, the idea of the three orders—nobles, clergy, and peasants—is useful in characterizing societal divisions in the Middle Ages, so long as it is recognized that the terms *noble* and *peasant* are being used rather loosely. Whatever terms are used to distinguish between the lower and higher orders, the essential division was between those who enjoyed wealth and prosperity and those who did not.

The specialists in warfare constituted the actual ruling class.[66] These noblemen were the most powerful of the three orders, and their position and behavior guided the economic structure throughout the late Middle Ages. They were at the top of the political hierarchy as well. They held the land, often lived in idleness and spent lavishly upon themselves, and controlled the important lay positions in society. Many noblemen were warrior-horsemen who underwent the ceremony of initiation into knighthood. Knighthood served as a common denominator in the different strata of the nobility in most countries during the Middle Ages.

The higher church authorities—bishops, monastic heads, abbots, and the like—were born in roughly the same privileged circumstances as the lay aristocracy. Monks and higher dignitaries came from noble families and enjoyed a style of life similar to their wealthy brothers or cousins. Many of them lived with women, and it was not at all unusual for them to father children.

Among the nobility, Murray indicates, probably one child in four entered ecclesiastical life in the central and late Middle Ages.[67] A younger son without lands could be placed in a wealthy chapter or monastery without loss of the comfort and respect to which his noble birth had accustomed him. A son or brother in a high clerical position could help assure a cooperative relationship between church and nobility. The sons of wealthy families, then, often exchanged one form of noble life for another, if usually a somewhat more circumscribed one. And the same went for daughters. "An unmarriageable daughter," writes Murray, "might find congenial company and curriculum in a noble religious house."[68]

The third order, the peasantry, constituted the vast bulk of the population. They were, of course, the ultimate source of labor throughout the Middle Ages. Particular arrangements about the position of peasants and the use of land varied according to local circumstances. But generally the peasants were "bound to the soil." This soil was found on one or another nobleman's landed estate. His estate was the site of his hall and his home-farm, as well as the holdings that he often let out to peasant tenants.[69] The nobleman received rent from his tenants, and they were frequently required to give him a portion of the produce from the fields as well.[70] It was the dependent status of the peasants that was the most important social characteristic of this arrangement.

For his part, the wealthy landowning nobleman owed the peasants protection and the administration of justice. The manor often functioned as a sort of local police authority and saw to the enforcement of the law. These functions necessitated regular court sessions and convocations of juries. It was through these manors that large inequalities in wealth and power most clearly expressed themselves.[71] The ruling class was supported, in other words, by this manorial system. The agricultural base constituted by the manorial system also helped support the clergy, which itself held a great deal of land.

Advances in agriculture from the eleventh century on began to lead to a loosening of the rigid arrangements between individual peasants and wealthy landowners. For example, fields appropriate to new plowing techniques were too large to be held and cultivated by a single peasant household, and thus they were often taken care of by several households working together.

Agricultural innovations and improvements also led to increased wealth and new demands on the part of noblemen. To satisfy these demands, says Duby, "groups of specialists, masons, vinedressers, craftsmen and merchants emerged from the mass of peasants."[72] The emergence of these new sorts of specialists, and the consequent quickening of the exchange of goods and money, helped encourage the growth of towns. An agricultural surplus provided sufficient food to support these towns. Not only the specialists but also ordinary peasants were sometimes able to go off to the new towns.

Those craftsmen and merchants who lived in the towns wished to be free of the power of wealthy noblemen, to assume control over their own economic activities, and to assure some means of keeping the peace. Thus they struggled to govern the towns themselves, free from the interference of nearby nobles. Many towns emancipated themselves almost completely and established themselves as small, self-governing republics. Others became virtually independent city-states, and some received charters of liberties from the king that allowed them to establish their own town governments and officials.

By the end of the eleventh century it was common for peasants to earn personal freedom and to hold their own lands in return for an annual payment to the lord. As a large number of manorial estates became too far removed from his physical presence and direct management, the lord also came to prefer such an arrangement. Thus, the peasants became increasingly free and able to move about freely. It became more difficult for a nobleman to hold his peasants in a dependent status when other peasants were often free in adjacent towns. Nevertheless, rich noblemen continued to own most of the land, and most peasants continued to owe duties and fees to these men.

## IV

The above is a very abbreviated outline of some of the main social and economic arrangements in the High Middle Ages. As I move now to examine the existence of community in this period, I will fill in some of the details about conditions at that time. My main focus, however, will be on those forms of community that Tönnies distinguished as dominant in the medieval period: the household, village, town, and commonwealth.

### The Household

Like many others, Tönnies saw the family as the model for an ideal community. According to what he writes, the household was made up of the extended family and their servants. This household "community," he said, was the basic unit of ownership, production, and consumption. People within the household worked cooperatively, and there existed a division of labor with the women working inside and the men working outside. In contrast to the extreme individualism of the small modern family, the medieval family had strong feelings of responsibility toward those many others living in the same household. How accurate, I am asking, is Tönnies's portrait of the medieval household?

To begin with, it is now widely recognized that it was the nuclear family—husband, wife, and children—that actually constituted most households in the High Middle Ages.[73] The kind of multigenerational family with three or more generations under the same roof was apparently never the norm in medieval Europe. As Jack Goody writes:

> It is not only for England that we need to abandon the myth of the "extended family"—as the term is often understood. In one form or another this myth has haunted historical and comparative studies since the time of Maine and Fustel de Coulanges, whether the work has been undertaken by historians, sociologists or anthropologists. Whatever the shape of the kin groups of earlier societies, none were undifferentiated communes of the kind beloved by nineteenth century theorists, Marxist and non-Marxist alike.[74]

To understand this absence of the large, extended family in the Middle Ages, it is useful to look at recent evidence concerning life at the time. I will begin with marriage, which was arranged by the families among all classes in medieval society. Marriage was a matter of negotiation involving the elders of the family.[75]

Contrary to many myths, people in the High Middle Ages did not marry when they were young adolescents. The most common medieval pattern was for men to delay marriage until their middle or late twenties, while most women married before their twentieth year.[76] When young brides married mature males, the wives were likely to be widowed when still relatively young. Since there was an abundance of women over men, many of these medieval widows never remarried. As David Herlihy points out, "they were effectively freed from the risk of pregnancy, while still biologically capable of bearing children."[77]

Given the average age at marriage and the long birth intervals of more than two years for peasant women who suckled their children, it is unlikely that a woman would have given birth to more than eight children by the end of her fertile period. Because of the extremely high infant mortality rate and the frequent death of young children, most families contained not more than three or four children.[78] Furthermore, perhaps as many as one-third of the families were childless. So the number of children in the typical peasant household was rather small.

Life expectancy was, of course, low. For example, the average *further* life expectancy at age twenty at the end of the thirteenth century was found to be twenty years in one study and twenty-five to twenty-eight years in another.[79] Since only a fraction of the population surived long enough to begin this period of "further" life expectancy, the overall average life span would obviously have been much lower than forty-odd years. Consequently, the typical peasant household was unlikely to contain relatives other than the nuclear family itself. In Montaillou, for instance, there was sometimes a grandmother living in the household but never more than one married couple.[80] And obviously, most peasant households contained no servants. The average household in the High Middle Ages thus probably contained about five persons.[81]

Noble households were also made up of few family members. Husbands were often absent for long periods of time on crusades, or at war to serve the king or seigneur.[82] Many from the warrior class met a violent death in tournaments, on crusades, and by execution during civil wars. Thus, noble households often had no husband or father present at all. And certainly few men were likely to have lived long enough to become grandfathers. When households were large, this was due mainly to the presence of many servants.

The point I am making here is that neither the extended family nor a large number of persons made up the household community in the High Middle Ages. With the exception of the households of the nobles, which contained several servants, households in the medieval period were generally quite small. In some towns, journeymen and apprentices lived in people's homes. But it was not the case that the dominant family form in preindustrial times was the large family community in which several generations lived together.[83]

Nor is it true, as traditional historiography has assumed, that the clan was ever the germ of all social grouping. There is no evidence at all for extensive lineage or clan structure among the population of either antiquity or the Middle Ages. Thus, Tönnies and other nineteenth-century social theorists, as well as Nisbet and others who today refer to literally hundreds of relatives in the Middle Ages, are mistaken.

Even as great a scholar as Marc Bloch, Murray points out, believed that there was a gradual disintegration of the clan and unilinealism during the Middle Ages.[84] But rather than clans and lineages—which are based on ancestor focus—being the basis of relationships, the universal group of the Middle Ages was the bilateral kindred. The members of a bilateral kinship group did not share descent from a common ancestor but were defined by their relationship on the paternal or maternal side. Despite the assertions of nineteenth-century scholars and some scholars today, the idea that clan and lineage were the constituent kinship groups in the early Middle Ages is now seen as without foundation. "On a theoretical level, it rests upon outmoded assumptions as to the nature of kinship forms and the developments of human societies," concludes Murray, "and the evidence cited in its support fails to confirm any of its major tenets."[85]

Let me now consider Tönnies's statement that the household community tradition established that the man's place was always outside and the woman's inside. Earlier historical material concluded that the peasant woman was indeed responsible for household work and the kitchen garden alone, while the man was responsible for field and pasture labor. And certainly the difference in age between the husband and wife, as well as his frequent absences, meant that the mother spent much more time with the children. It was probably through her that a significant part of the cultural inheritance was passed on to the children. But it is now agreed by medieval historians that if this sort of division of labor existed in the Middle Ages, it existed only for men. They did, in fact, no work within the house at all.

Medieval women, on the other hand, did both household work and many auxiliary chores. With regard to the former, Shulamith Shahar writes:

> The household chores and work in the kitchen garden included cleaning, cooking, drawing water and bringing it home, stoking the hearth, bringing wheat to the nearest mill for milling, cheese-making, tending animals and work in the vegetable plot by the house. Ale was brewed by women not only for home consumption but also for sale. Spinning and weaving were also among the female chores.[86]

In addition to their numerous household chores, peasant women worked in the fields weeding, hoeing, sowing, and harvesting. They took part in the vintage in wine-producing areas. They tended the animals, worked in the dairies, and brought surplus agricultural produce to the fairs and markets.[87] In other words, Tönnies exaggerated the extent to which peasant households in the Middle Ages were characterized by a division of labor by sex.

It was not only peasant women who worked outside the household. The same was true in the towns, where women were engaged in a variety of occupations. As was the case with peasant women, women in the towns also had sole responsibility for the work in their own households. Many women were busy in family workshops as the wives and daughters of craftsmen, and others were members of the guilds. Although there were bans and restrictions on women in certain guilds, some married women and spinsters were members of guilds, and there were even guilds (in which women themselves drew up the statutes) composed exclusively of women.[88] Shahar cites research showing that women worked in eighty of one hundred occupations in Paris in the thirteenth century. Another six occupations were exclusively female, all of them connected with clothing.[89] So many women earned a living by spinning in the High Middle Ages that the unmarried woman acquired the title "spinster."[90]

Women also worked as barbers, as goldsmiths, as crystal workers, and as makers of pins and needles.[91] Many women, either working alone or helping their husbands, "rented out houses, managed hotels and taverns, and in particular engaged in commerce in foodstuffs both in shops and stalls, in the markets and at weekly or seasonable fairs."[92]

The above pertains mainly to women of the laboring class in the towns. Although they usually worked from necessity, their opportunities to find work in a variety of occupations were far greater than for the wives of rich burghers. These burghers were essentially men engaged in business and commerce—activities they did not entrust to their wives. Very few of the wives of rich burghers worked during their husbands' lifetime, and most were responsible solely for the management of their households. Here is one of the few instances where we can find a clear division of labor between men and women in the High Middle Ages.

Noblewomen, on the other hand, fulfilled many of the functions performed by their husbands. In the long periods when medieval noblemen were away from home, their wives saw to the economic management of the estates. This included such activities as leasing land, supervising the work of peasants, receiving reports from the bailiffs, collecting rents, and sending surplus crops to market.[93] Even when her husband was at home, the noblewoman carried on many of the economic tasks of the manor. The nobleman was, after all, first and foremost a soldier. So he was often undoubtedly quite content to have his wife take responsibility for economic affairs. Besides those "outside" activities which she performed, the noblewoman carried out the supervision of the numerous tasks involved in running a large household.

Since Tönnies believed that by nature women are led by feelings rather than intellect, and are incapable of abstract and logical thinking, he would have been amazed at the responsibilities and power apparently exercised by these noblewomen in the Middle Ages. Not only was there little in the way of a distinct division of labor between the sexes, but many women of the ruling class enjoyed a status that was to be unparalleled for centuries to come.[94]

So far, I have been concerned with two elements that are central to the beliefs of Tönnies and other nineteenth-century theorists about the household as a form of community in the medieval period: the presence of several generations in the large family community, and a division of labor by sex. Neither of these elements, I have shown, was much in evidence in the High Middle Ages.

It should also be obvious from what I have said about the sorts of work done by men and women that the family unit was not generally self-sufficient. Of course, there were individual households capable of growing most of the food they needed. But even they usually obtained some commodities by purchase: salt, ale, pitch, tar, articles made of iron, and earthenware, for example.[95] Rather than all households being self-sufficient, many occupied holdings too small to provide adequate food for a family. They thus had to earn wages elsewhere so as to be able to purchase the necessities.[96]

Nor is it true, as asserted by Tönnies and other nineteenth-century theorists, that ownership was communal, with the original collective state being followed by a stage of family property. Since it is now clear that there is no evidence for extensive clan structure, there obviously were no clan holdings. No trace is to be found of extensive corporate groups involved in landholding, inheritance, or legal procedures. With the relationship of inheritance to kinship, for example, it was not corporate groups but individual kinsmen who were called to take up the property of deceased relatives.[97] Contrary to the idea of collective property, there were many variations in the freedom of disposition enjoyed by the holder of property.[98] Beyond this, barter and trade were common to the family experience.[99] Without going into greater detail about these matters, it seems clear that the evidence casts strong doubt on Tönnies's portrayal of the household community in the Middle Ages.

### The Village

It was not, however, the household as a form of community that most interested social theorists in the previous century or that is most appealing to some communitarian thinkers today. For them, it is the more complex forms of community seen as representative of the medieval world which serve as the ultimate standard of comparison. Let me, then, turn from the family household to that form of community viewed by Tönnies as a sort of large family: the village.

Medieval villages generally contained anywhere from one hundred to six hundred inhabitants.[100] Sometimes a village was bound to an estate or lordship, and sometimes not. Some villages were tied up with a parish, though this was not always the case. In many instances, a village seemed to consist of people living in scattered settlements rather than in direct proximity to their neighbors. It should *not* be thought, Reynolds says, that the bulk of the rural population lived in the typical medieval village of the textbooks: "a firmly nucleated settlement with its own church and single manor-house in the middle, and its open fields and common pastures spread round about."[101]

Most villages possessed by customary right pasture, heaths, forests, water supply, and fishing rights, all of which were essential to people's livelihood.[102] There apparently was some sense of the village having common property, although it might have to be shared with the local lord.[103] Among those using the land there were systems of common rotation, common grazing, and other types of cooperative activities.[104] Disputes frequently arose, however, between neighboring villages over woods, pastures, and the like.

An essential attribute of any collectivity that was perceived as a definable group, says Reynolds, was the right to participate in its own government.[105] That is, it was a social and administrative unit. The larger village community consisted of a variety of formal and informal bodies which watched over and enforced local customs and laws. Members of a village community had the right to be tried within it. Thus villagers were often allowed to settle many of their disputes among themselves.

Those who were entitled to participate in decision making selected the officials responsible for performing various functions in the village community.[106] In making their decisions, the concern was how best to combine the needs of justice and order.

Villagers often lived and worked in close proximity to one another. Although their emotional lives were centered primarily within the nuclear family, villagers were forced to rely on an ever shifting group of neighbors and acquaintances to provide them with protection against thieves and thugs, with assistance in economic activities when the need arose, and with support in times of sickness and need.

"Just as the protection of his men was the duty of any lord," writes Reynolds, "so protection of its members was the duty of any community."[107] People had the need to be protected, individually and collectively, not only against crime but also against oppression. To consider now Tönnies's idea of the typical medieval village, he appears to have been mistaken in thinking that the village community was usually identified with a great family or clan—although there was sometimes, just as he said, a vaguely articulated myth of common descent.[108] It was not the case, however, that the village was filled with kin as a result of limited geographical mobility.

Villages were not cut off from the outside world, as was claimed by many medieval historians of Tönnies's day. Peasants went to market, visited nearby towns, made pilgrimages, often traveled great distances in seeking work, and served in armies. Thus, they were not tied to the village in the way that Tönnies suggests. And villages were certainly not self-sufficient communities.[109] After all, in addition to what might be termed agricultural villages, there were fishing and seafaring villages, and others which specialized in particular products. Trade and exchange between villages was, therefore, often necessary in the High Middle Ages.[110]

Tönnies was correct, however, in stressing the readiness of village people to act collectively and to cooperate in a variety of activities. While many of the hamlets and individual farmsteads were not large enough to require collective controls or collective activities, Reynolds notes that such cooperation was required in the twelfth-century village. Whether the fields were those of a manor, of a more or less autonomous village, or of some other small group within either, there were systems of common rotation, common grazing, and other types of cooperative activity among those using the land.[111]

But these collective activities were not the result simply of a spontaneous and affective spirit or a shared concern for the common good. Instead, people cooperated when it was to their mutual benefit to do so. There was never one sort of group that acted collectively. To the contrary, says Reynolds, "people seem to have been ready to act collectively in any group that had common interests in the matter at hand."[112] This was a matter of expediency and necessity.

### The Town

As noted earlier, Tönnies considered the town to be the most complex form of natural community. He described it as a form of social organization in which people unrelated by blood lived together in fellowship and cooperation. Each medieval town was a self-sufficient economic entity. Like the village, it was a political community held together by a "common spirit."[113] Everyone, he said, was concerned with the well-being of the community.

Towns were not in great abundance anywhere in Europe in the ninth century. Those that did exist were usually small and rather weak. But from the tenth century, archaeological evidence shows, larger and more for-tified towns began to appear throughout Europe. They then multiplied and grew very rapidly in the eleventh, twelfth, and thirteenth centuries.

The reasons for their rise were manifold: protection, trade, their status as otherwise important sites (for example, as the locations of lordships or mother churches), and their geographic advantages seem to have been the most important. Whatever the relative significance of the various reasons, it appears that almost all medieval towns were located around a market or a fair. The markets themselves often began outside a castle or abbey, which provided protection, or by a river or harbor, which supplied a means of transport.

Market towns allowed peasants, craftsmen, merchants, and others to buy and sell together in one large marketplace. The weekly markets attracted sufficient customers to encourage townsmen to concentrate on special crafts and to leave the bulk of agricultural work to the farmers.[114] As these medieval towns grew and prospered, they turned to manufacturing and the importing and exporting of various goods.

Towns often came to specialize in the production of a particular product: leather, enamelware, paper, cloth, or whatever. These were mostly small-scale industries carried on in small workshops. Textile towns were especially numerous in the High Middle Ages, with there being hundreds, large and small, all over Europe.[115] "But the determining characteristic of a town," writes Lester Little, was "the presence there of people engaged in many other specialized kinds of work: industrial workers, merchants who dealt in long-distance travel and travelled to fairs and to market towns, petty traders who retailed in local shops and markets, lawyers and notaries, school masters, entertainers, government officials, servants, waiters, porters, butchers, and bakers."[116]

"Whatever their origins," write Julius Kirshner and Karl Morrison, "medieval townsmen were united in seeking personal liberty, security, and autonomy in managing their own commercial, political, fiscal, and judicial affairs."[117] In much of Europe, towns eventually received their charters of liberties from a king or from the powerful lords on whose lands they happened to be situated. The charters often deemed the householders in medieval towns to be personally free and allowed them free title to their land.[118] In return for these privileges, the townsmen agreed to supply their lords with badly needed revenue. The towns themselves eventually acquired fiscal autonomy; that is, they were free from interference and control by royal or feudal agents. During the twelfth century some older towns acquired a formal recognition of their independence, and many newer towns were granted independence from their founding.[119]

In the earlier Middle Ages, most medieval towns were dominated by a lay or ecclesiastical ruler who was the immediate source of authority and law. Although he was often beholden to an overlord, he controlled the town and its inhabitants. As a town grew more prosperous, it usually happened that the richer members began to chafe against the control of the court, king, bishop, or whoever was effectively exercising control, and to fight for increased independence.

The scope of a medieval town government's activities was determined by the scope of its liberties. This, as Reynolds makes clear, varied enormously throughout Europe in the High Middle Ages.[120] But since every town had the function of supplying goods and services to the countryside around it, all towns were centers of trade and industry. One responsibility of every town, then, was the regulation of markets, inspection of weights and measures, fixing and collecting tools, setting wages, regulating and controlling the conditions of work and the quality of goods, and regulating prices. In addition to those tasks connected with the economy, the town government had responsibility for public health and public works, hospitals, schools, and the construction and upkeep of buildings.

A man's right to participate in a town's political activities and collective decision making was highly dependent on his location in the stratification hierarchy. In the end, it was usually the richer (male) citizens who ran medieval towns. Everywhere in Europe it was the same sort of people who had the franchise and exercised governmental authority. Speaking about thirteenth-century Siena, Judith Hook writes that the town government consisted of traders, merchants, manufacturers, and bankers, "a highly selected citizen-elite, whose leaders differed scarcely at all in wealth, economic interest or power from the nobility they professed to despise and with whom, in fact, they customarily inter-married and conducted their business."[121]

Consider, for example, the town assembly. It seems likely that even those men outside the franchise could go to the big open meetings and there shout with the rest. But in the assembly, the fundamental institution of town government, it was everywhere the rich elites who took the lead. And, notes Reynolds, they "had probably done so long before towns became autonomous."[122]

Although these open assemblies were the ultimate source of authority when town governments were set up, they were not intended to embody a group of equal individuals. In fact, very complex systems of indirect elections were instituted all over Europe so as to assure that the "right sort" would be elected to run the town governments. What was to be avoided was the kind of open meetings described as taking place in London in the middle of the thirteenth century which included "the sons of divers mothers, many of them born outside the city and many of servile condition," who shouted "ya, ya," or "nay, nay" in response to the proposals put to them.[123] Domination by these sorts of "mobs" and by demagogues was to be avoided by choosing from among the wealthier and more powerful of a town's citizens.

By the thirteenth century, open assemblies were being superseded by councils in many medieval towns. These councils undertook the planning of much of civic public life: the building of the town hall and churches, the provision of schools and universities, the running of hospitals, almshouses, and old people's homes, and a variety of other services and activities.[124]

In truth, life must have been miserable for the great majority of town dwellers. To see this, let me touch very briefly on the "texture of life" in the typical town of the High Middle Ages. The bulk of the population lived in what were little more than hovels. Behind these hovels were gardens cluttered with outbuildings, many of which sheltered cattle, pigs, and other animals. The narrow, often sunless alleys, the piles of garbage, the excrement from the animals, and the open sewers together lend a sober dimension to the view of the medieval town advanced by many nineteenth-century social theorists. Standards of hygiene were low, and life expectancy was short.

Time was regulated by the church, seasonally through the spacing of the various Christian feasts throughout the year, and daily by the chime of church bells. Work hours were, of course, geared to the seasons. They were usually regulated by the bell from city hall and generally ran from sunrise to sunset, with an hour off for the midday meal.[125] In winter, when there was little sun in most of Europe, the shortest workday was seven hours; in summer, it ran to thirteen. Due to the absence of street lighting, all towns had a strictly enforced curfew. This was imposed at dusk, after which it was forbidden to walk about the town except with special permission.

The curfew was often associated with the fire watch, for most houses were built of wood, and medieval towns were full of stables, stalls, and stores of grain and hay. Even the smallest fire might therefore spread with alarming rapidity. The curfew was also a precaution against crime. Criminals wanting to use the darkness to cloak their movements found it more difficult to escape detection when there was always a nightly patrol or guard.[126]

### The Commonwealth

Thus far, I have considered three of the forms of natural community in the Middle Ages described by Tönnies: the household, the village, and the town. I turn now to the commonwealth, the last form of collective life that he discusses. Tönnies viewed the commonwealth, it may be recalled, as a regional unity composed of estates, villages, and towns. Like the other forms of community he describes, the commonwealth in his view was characterized by shared norms and customs, time-honored understandings, and relationships of intimacy, trust, and cooperation. It derived its dignity from the united activities of three different organs: the prince or king, the nobles, and the masses. In most commonwealths of the Middle Ages, says Tönnies, the prince or the king was the highest authority.

But it needs to be emphasized that Tönnies's use of the word *commonwealth* was not a translation of any medieval expression. Because of his failure to look at the actual political ideas or arrangements of the Middle Ages—or to utilize the work of scholars who had made such an examination—Tönnies used a term that is less appropriate than would be such words as *duchy, county, state,* or *kingdom. Commonwealth* is a term of evaluation, and it serves to indicate how Tönnies so often confused analysis with evaluation.

In her detailed discussion titled "The Community of the Realm" in the Middle Ages, Reynolds gives systematic attention to what Tönnies termed the commonwealth: the *kingdom.*[127] Kingdoms, she says, seem to have been perceived as the ideal type of political unit in the High Middle Ages, just as kings were seen as the ideal types of rulers. A kingdom was never thought of as simply the territory that a king ruled. Instead, it "comprised and corresponded to a 'people' (*gens, natio, populus*), which was assumed to be a natural, inherited community of tradition, custom, law, and descent."[128]

In medieval terms, argues Reynolds, a people, or a *populus,* was thought of as a community of custom, descent, and government. By the tenth century, a people or a kingdom almost always meant the permanent, settled inhabitants of a reasonably well-defined territory. Whatever the extent of their actual power and influence, kingdoms were generally perceived as the political norm.

The subjects of a kingdom often claimed that they were all of common origin or shared the same ancestry, that they all had the same history and customs, and sometimes that they all spoke a common language as well.[129] Whether it was France, England, or another kingdom, people obviously had loyalties besides those that Reynolds terms "regnal" ones. But there were times when their loyalties to family, village, town, or lordship were less important than their loyalty to the kingdom. Especially when threatened by external danger, people forgot such divisions and united in support of the kingdom.

Any kingdom which survived, Reynolds observes, did so because the people felt that they owed it their loyalty.[130] Local law and custom always, of course, exercised a strong day-to-day influence on people's actions. Nevertheless, whenever contact with the central government was maintained, there were ties of loyalty to the kingdom that paralleled local and provincial ties. Government consisted of layers of authority, and loyalties were attached to each layer accordingly. Kingdoms, then, were units of government which were perceived as peoples.

# THE COMMUNITARIAN IDEAL AND
# THE MEDIEVAL REALITY

HAVING considered the social structure in medieval Europe at some length in the previous chapter, I can be brief in discussing the extent of community as regards the elements in the communitarians' normative ideal: a common territory, a common history and shared values, political participation, and a high degree of social solidarity. My focus will continue to be on the High Middle Ages.

Given the doctrine of the three orders discussed earlier, it cannot be expected that an accurate picture of medieval Europe will closely resemble the description set forth by Tönnies and apparently still accepted by many social scientists. We saw earlier that it was up to the peasants to provide for the men of war and the men of religion. These two groups, meeting man's temporal and spiritual needs, shared the government of the Christian world.

In the view of the church and government, the peasants' duty was to support these two orders and not to involve themselves in affairs beyond their understanding. Peasants or workers, the doctrine held, could contribute most to the good of society by concentrating on what they could do best. By supporting those men in whose hands the destiny of society rested and otherwise confining themselves within their own designated realm, they would best be able to perform their God-given functions. The doctrine was especially propagated by those who had the most to gain from it: the nobles and the clergy. This conception of Christian society was used to justify a great deal of exploitation and social repression.

## I

### *The Territorial Dimension*

As with my examination of community in the founding period of America, I begin with the territorial dimension. Certainly at the level of kingdom or commonwealth, people shared a common territory. In fact, as I pointed out earlier, a kingdom meant the permanent, settled inhabitants of a reasonably well-defined territory. And people also, of course, shared a common territory at the level of the family household.

With regard to the village and town, there was a great deal of geographic movement at the time. Detailed studies of town populations in that period show that anywhere from one-third to one-half of a town's population consisted of people who had immigrated from the country.[1] Although the geographic movement to and from villages was undoubtedly much less, Duby says that outsiders made up at least 16 percent of the recorded population in various villages in the eleventh century.[2] This probably increased in later years.

In his study of Halesowen, Zvi Razi finds constant migrations from one village to another in the period between 1270 and 1348. Like other researchers, he reports a considerable intensification of geographic mobility in the postplague period. He says that outsiders constituted almost 20 percent of the total village population) for the period 1391–95.[3]

Whatever the extent to which people in the Middle Ages stayed put, it was certainly less than in the versions of medieval life accepted by Tönnies and many other nineteenth-century social theorists. They viewed people's permanent location in a town or village as creating strong ties and connections with one another. Contemporary communitarian writers, as I showed in chapter 1, also see shared locality or place as having a unique community-engendering power. A common locale helps assure that people's ties to others are largely unwilled and nonvoluntary.

The fact that there was so much geographic mobility in the High Middle Ages does not by itself indicate that those moving were not content to accept their "natural" inherited membership in a town or village. People may have preferred to stay where they were, had they not had to leave for economic reasons. But Duby speaks of men moving "to break the bonds tying them to their lords," and settling elsewhere where they might be exploited less harshly.[4] He also refers to craftsmen drifting away from aristocratic households and moving to towns.[5] For it was mainly in towns where there were opportunities for improving their economic situation. Other men left to escape conflict, or in search of adventure.

In short, there was sufficient geographic mobility to cast doubt as to the extent that towns and villages were communities in the full-blooded sense advanced by many communitarian theorists. And much of this movement, it appears, was a direct result of the exploitation and oppression associated with the doctrine of the three orders.

## II

### Shared History and Values

Movement from one village to another and from village to town meant also that people shared less in the way of a common history and similar values than would have been the case if everyone in a given place had spent his or her entire life there. Whatever the actual amount of movement between different areas, it is difficult to judge the extent to which people considered themselves to be united by a common history and values.

As I noted earlier, Reynolds's research indicates that the subjects of a kingdom did often accept the idea that they were united by a common history and shared values. The church and government in the High Middle Ages promoted the mythology that a kingdom's subjects had a common origin or the same ancestry, as well as emphasizing the doctrine of the three orders. And certainly those in a position to do so stressed submission to lay and religious authority, as well as the essential harmony of people's interests. Reynolds indicates that many people at least gave the appearance of accepting the official ideology in village, town, and kingdom alike.

The village as a community, according to Tönnies, was a self-contained and self-sufficient economic and social unit, with common ownership, shared values and customs, a deep attachment to the community (as a consequence of being born and dying in the same village), a concern for the common good, and the regulation of life by what Gierke termed "community decision."[6] Tönnies claims that class differences were relatively small in the village community. Too much inequality in wealth and status, he believed, were incompatible with gemeinschaft.[7] In his view, there was a shared value as to the importance of relative equality among a village's inhabitants.

Yet within a medieval village, there was obvious economic and social differentiation. Hierarchy was a fundamental fact of life. Aside from the large differential in wealth and power between most people and the lord of the manor, and between merchants and peasants, there were often inequalities in the economic well-being of peasant families. In Montaillou, LeRoy Ladurie estimates that the richest family in the village was fifty times wealthier than the poorest families.[8] And he says that perhaps 20 to 25 percent of the local population was poor.[9]

The richer man possessed more money, more land, a greater number of sheep, of oxen, and so forth. "Such differences did not prevent social intercommunication," says LeRoy Ladurie, "but they did sometimes turn it rather sour, even when there was no real class struggle."[10] It is no wonder, then, that Montaillou was strongly divided by various village clans, each with its own values and interests.[11] Because these rustic hamlets were relentlessly intimate, there was no way for people to avoid those they feared or disliked. Consequently, medieval villages were riddled with petty conflicts, and hatred, fear, and violence were endemic.

Along with quarrels among the peasants themselves, there was frequently conflict between peasants and the lords. This was inherent in the underlying structure of village society. Reynolds speaks of the peasants in a village "acting in groups over against their lords, whether because the lord was granting them privileges or otherwise ordering their activities, or because they were in conflict with him."[12] Conflicts arose over a variety of issues: the level of rents and dues, the lord's right over labor services, various taxes due to the lord, and so forth. In many if not most instances, of course, peasants found it safer to silently accept their exploited situation rather than risk penalty or punishment. When there was conflict, the poor generally came off badly. Crimes committed by the rich often went unpunished.

With regard to the activities of local government in the village, Reynolds writes that "although undemocratically organized for inegalitarian ends, [these collective arrangements] probably seemed right and reasonable to most of them, provided they conformed with custom."[13] It was certainly the intent of the doctrine of the three orders to assure that people would accept such arrangements as in the very nature of things.

Yet, in Montaillou at least, people did not accept customary arrangements as right and reasonable. Just as in the society as a whole, says LeRoy Ladurie, the village was characterized by unending conflict.[14] Loyalty was to house rather than village, and thus "militated against the growth of a civic sense of community."[15] Contrary to what Tönnies claims, then, a sense of shared membership was not usually present in the medieval village. Villages appear, then, not to have been united by shared values and a spiritual bond.

The same was true for the town. All towns were highly stratified, with a relatively small number of men controlling most of the land and wealth and the activities of others. Differences in the economic situation of those variously located in the social hierarchy were considerable. And they were reflected in differences in power and the ability of the well-placed to direct the lives of ordinary men and women. Towns were the location for commercial activities, the headquarters of important lordships, and the centers of opportunity for people on the move. Despite the existence of a social hierarchy there as elsewhere, the town presented the best chance for improving one's lot.

As I indicated in the previous chapter, Tönnies was mistaken in his claim that there was a strict division of labor between men and women in the Middle Ages. Contrary to what he said, women were involved in a great variety of types of work. Nevertheless, relations between men and women were characterized by great inequality. This was true whether the women lived in a village or a town. Women were, in one sense, considered to be citizens of towns if they were married to men who were citizens, held property through inheritance, or were members of a guild. But they enjoyed only part of the town's privileges. By law, a woman had no share whatever in the government of a town; she could not participate in any institution of government, whether it be councils or assemblies.[16] Women lacked a wide variety of legal and civil rights available to men. The restriction of a woman's rights was justified in secular law by her limited intelligence, her light-mindedness, her wiliness, and her avarice.[17]

Whatever assets a woman brought with her to a marriage, the wife had no legal power to sell, pawn, or transfer any property without her husband's consent. She was under the guardianship of her husband, and could not draw up a contract or take a loan without his consent. In the High Middle Ages, "the dumb, the deaf, the insane and the female [could] draw up a contract, neither alone nor through a representative, since they [were] subservient to the authority of others."[18] In theory, and usually in practice, women occupied a very disadvantaged position in the High Middle Ages. Woman was seen as an inferior sort of creature. This conception of women was represented everywhere in law and custom.

No more in the town than in the village did people live together in fellowship and cooperation. Quarrels, intrigues, violence, and crime were commonplace in the medieval town. We ought not forget that these were days when everyone carried a knife for cutting food, when many people carried a dagger, when gentlemen carried a sword at all times, and when barroom brawls and street fighting and bloodshed were everyday occurrences.

Although it is obviously difficult to estimate the level of violence in the Middle Ages, T. R. Gurr has recently compared data for homicides in England between 1250 and 1800. These data reveal that the homicide rate in the thirteenth century was more than twice as high as it was in the sixteenth and early seventeenth centuries, and that the latter rate was five times higher than it is today.[19]

Gurr concludes that "these early estimates of homicide rates . . . sketch a society in which men were easily provoked to violent anger, and were unrestrained in the brutality with which they attacked their opponents. Interpersonal violence was a recurring fact of rural and urban life."[20] Given the frequency of violence, it is not surprising that in twelfth- and thirteenth-century Siena, for instance, popular disturbances and riots led to a strict night curfew and to the creation of a large police force, with about one law-enforcement officer for every 145 inhabitants.[21]

In addition, as we know, towns were very much at the mercy of catastrophes of various kinds: flood, famine, and disease, along with fire.

Without the considerable immigration of people from the countryside, the medieval town would never have grown. The death rate was so high that the town population never reproduced itself. In this regard, Mark Girouard writes:

> Death and destruction by act of God were supplemented by death or mutilation by act of man, the result of feuds within the ruling families, plots against the city government, sack and pillage from outside . . . struggles between artisans and merchants, massacres of Jews or burnings of heretics combined with frequent public executions for murder, theft or fraud, and public mutilations or flogging for other offences.[22]

Trial by ordeal was widespread from 800 to 1200. Especially common were the trials by fire and water: holding onto or walking on hot iron, immersing the hand in boiling water, or complete immersion in a pool or stream. With the first of these, for example, a man accused of a crime or seeking to defend his rights would be required to pick up a hot iron, walk three paces, and put it down. His hand would then be bandaged and sealed and, after three days, inspected. If it was healing without discoloration or suppuration, the man was declared innocent or vindicated. If the wound was unclean, however, he was guilty. These ordeals were used for a wide range of offenses, including murder, theft, witchcraft, and forgery. They were employed only when other ways of discovering the truth were not available.[23] Ordeals were deemed especially appropriate in deciding charges of sexual misconduct. If a woman's husband accused her of adultery, then she might be required to clear herself with the hot iron.

Although the ordeal was sometimes applied against free men, it was used mainly against the servile classes. Unless their lord had made special arrangements to stand for them, the unfree were not allowed to enter fully the legal world of oath swearing, presenting written testimony, and calling witnesses.[24] The point of the ordeals was that they provided a chance to assert a claim or vindicate innocence in a dramatic public spectacle. With the ordeal procedure, the assumption was that the issue was placed in God's hands. But since the courts were run by ecclesiastics, royal officials, and lords, it was these men who actually decided the fate of the accused.

Many acts of cruelty were carried out in public in the Middle Ages as warnings to all malefactors. Men condemned to be executed were generally put to death by hanging; nobles were decapitated with an axe. Burning at the stake was reserved for the very worst crimes, although in Italy, Germany, and Brabant, women were almost always burned at the stake or buried alive when they committed serious crimes.[25]

As part of the violence and cruelty so rife in medieval towns, there was considerable violence toward women. They frequently complained of injury inflicted by males in the street, the market, at fairs, and elsewhere.[26] Women often pressed charges against men for rape. Though a crime throughout Europe in the High Middle Ages, it was not everywhere treated with the same severity.

In England or France a rapist might be blinded, castrated, or even put to death, while in Germany, on the other hand, the penalty was flogging, with the victim apparently helping to carry it out.[27] In thirteenth-century England, however, a judge could dismiss a charge of rape if the woman conceived as a result. According to a prevalent medieval conception of woman's sexual and physiological nature, she had to secrete a certain seed in order to be able to conceive, and this happened only when she achieved sexual satisfaction. Pregnancy, therefore, served as evidence that the woman had enjoyed the experience and thus had no right to press charges.[28] We can only guess at the extent of "domestic violence" in so violent a place as the medieval town. In any case, the right of a husband to beat his wife "within limits" was widely recognized.[29]

All of this points to the absence of the shared value of social and economic equality emphasized by Tönnies, as well as the absence of the kinds of affective ties that he believed were so prevalent at the time. At the level of the kingdom or commonwealth as well, there existed much less in the sense of shared values than is often claimed. Tönnies described the commonwealth as resting on the "consensus and cooperation" of the king, the church, the nobles, and the masses. But discord and opposition were not unusual. Although the idea of Christian society being composed of "orders" was intended to assure submission to lay and religious authority, conflict on both the individual and the group level was a regular part of everyday life.

Aside from the conflicts already mentioned, there were frequent disagreements about rights of ownership. To a large extent, "ownership" of property was based on social relationships defined in terms of relative strength and power. The dominant relationship between lord and tenant had serious consequences for subsequent generations in this regard.

For example, the heir was often defined by primogeniture. But, in recognizing the authority of the lord by doing homage, he also paid a relief for inheriting the tenure. Thus, the tenant's heir had no actual right in the land; he had merely a claim to succeed his ancestor in assuming control of the land belonging to the ruler. Consequently, there was, in Michael Saltman's words, a "conflict between rights of inheritance on the one hand and the reversionary rights of rulers on the other."[30] This conflict led to widespread litigation in the courts of local lords in England. But since the judges in these courts were recruited primarily from among the landlords, they favored their own interests, and complaints about injustice became increasingly frequent. At the very least, we witness a plurality of norms and values about property, with tenants striving for heritable rights over land, local rulers for landowner status, and the central government for maximal control over land.

Now it is possible, of course, that everyone truly accepted the doctrine of the three orders and believed deeply that this unity of hierarchy and order was indeed in the interests of the common or public good. Were this the case, then the inequalities, conflicts, and disputes that I have cataloged should be viewed as minor annoyances or irritations arising from the imperfect functioning of the doctrine of the three orders.

Just as with any other doctrine similar to a politics of the common good, what appear to be disagreements about conflicting social values should perhaps be viewed as differences in how to interpret and act on a basic value shared by everyone: performing one's duties in accordance with God's plan.

But the evidence shows that not everyone accepted what was in the interests of the privileged and well-situated. That is to say, it is obvious that at least some portion of the peasantry held values other than what were espoused by the doctrine of the three orders. The same was true for some in the warrior and religious orders as well.

In other words, there were conflicting views about what was a tolerable or acceptable amount of economic inequality; about what ought to be designated as a "crime"; about what arrangements were "right and reasonable"; about the way struggles between artisans and merchants, or peasants and lords, ought to be settled; about competing claims to control over land.

## III

### Political Participation

Evidence of the existence of community is not particularly strong in regard to the third characteristic in the normative ideal either. Civil participation and involvement in collective decision making were not widespread in the Middle Ages. They most certainly did not involve the poorest peasants or workers in any active way.

Not everyone in the village was entitled to participate in decision making. The men occupying the highest positions were often referred to simply as so many "good men," and sometimes as "the better and older" or "better and more discreet."[31] Women, children, unfree peasants, and living-in servants were generally excluded from any sort of involvement in decision making in the community.[32]

Those men who did have the right to participate were dominated by the wealthier citizens. Even in a peasant village, Razi reports, the poor were never elected to fill any public offices. In Halesowen in the period 1270–1348, middling peasants filled only the secondary offices, and all the important positions were held by the rich peasants.[33] And in the postplague era, he says, the "major public offices in Halesowen were filled by a small group of families which dominated and led the village community for generations."[34]

A lack of active participation by the majority of village inhabitants, the dominance of a small group of wealthier peasant families, and a system of class justice enabled the richer peasants and their families to maintain their ascendancy for a period of several generations. LeRoy Ladurie reports a similar pattern for Montaillou.[35]

The same thing occurred in the towns, some of which were quite large by 1300. At that time, northern Italy was the most urbanized region of Europe. Venice and Florence each had a population of between 90,000 and 100,000, and several other towns had populations of 10,000 to 30,000. Paris, northern Europe's greatest city, had already achieved a population of about 80,000 by 1328.[36]

Town liberties were normally granted to all the citizens of the town. Those who obtained such liberties were referred to as the citizens, the burgesses, or the men.[37] These different words all apparently came to the same thing: only a portion of the population enjoyed the privilege of the franchise. Just as in the village, women, children, servants, and many of the townsmen were excluded from participation in government or collective decision making. Yet, Reynolds points out, the question of what were the *qualifications* for the franchise has never received very much attention.[38]

It seems to have been assumed in the Middle Ages, says Reynolds, that the rule about a year and a day's residence applied to all resident householders (or at least to all adult males).[39] This rule concerned an immigrant's right to become a burgess or citizen of a town after such a length of residence there.

But Reynolds argues that there were actually further restrictions on citizenship. These restrictions were not based so much on consistent policies as they were on responses to particular problems in differing circumstances. So in thirteenth-century Siena, for instance, extensive geographic mobility gave rise to the creation of several categories of citizenship according to the length of time that people or their forebears had been there.[40]

In England at the same time, the franchise was extended in London to those who had served a seven-year apprenticeship under a citizen. Other English towns also linked citizenship with apprenticeship and membership in a craft. Such restrictions were obviously associated with a considerable amount of geographic movement, as Reynolds suggests: "Perhaps in an age of high immigration apprenticeship was specified because it was a convenient way of measuring the length of residence, especially for an aspirant to the enjoyment of trading privileges."[41]

Among those who did participate in the town assembly or court, the leisured rich were prominent. As noted earlier, they occupied all the important posts in the medieval town. The same came to be true with councils. Some historians have seen the establishment of councils as a ploy by the rich and powerful to entrench their position by closing the system to poor citizens.[42] But Reynolds draws on documentary evidence to suggest that assemblies were replaced by councils for other reasons as well. In addition to what might be termed avoidance of mob rule, she points to another important reason. These councils of twenty or twenty-four members, usually elected by some indirect method or by the retiring councillors, were simply far more practical than large assemblies as regards regular meetings.

Further, of course, they were much more likely to assure that the best and most responsible of a town's citizens were directly involved in running the town. "It was accepted as in everyone's interest," writes Reynolds, "to get the rich and prominent to do most: the better, more discreet, and more powerful citizens or burgesses were those who, in medieval terms, had the duty as well as the right to take the lead in running their communities."[43] Such rich and well-established citizens were likely to be men of leisure who were not themselves required ever to engage in any very demanding work with their own hands.[44] Not unexpectedly, a similar pattern held true in regard to participation in the wider lordship or kingdom. Only those who were rich and free enough to attend courts and perform duties at some distance from home participated actively in the decision-making process.[45]

Now, of course, it was part of the doctrine of the three orders that people belonging to each of the strictly defined social categories would best contribute to the good of Christian society by performing their assigned tasks. One aspect of this ideology was that only the "right sort" were in a position to participate intelligently in political activities and decision making. Very much as we saw in my consideration of America's founding period earlier, the idea was that those few men who had the leisure and freedom to participate politically did so for the common or public good. This doctrine required the exclusion of ordinary people from participation.

There was, of course, no way that the ruling lords and clergy could have extended the franchise to all adults or even to all adult males. For this would have been inconsistent with the intention behind the doctrine of the three orders: to keep lowborn people in their places when they were trying to climb out.[46] Duby argues that the very design of the doctrine of the three orders was intended to persuade the peasants or workers of their duty to supply the lords and clergy, "thereby sanctioning social inequalities and all forms of economic exploitation."[47]

## IV

### Social Solidarity

I come now to the last ingredient in the communitarian ideal: social solidarity. This, it may be recalled, concerns the extent and direction of fellow feeling and mutual concern for others in the household, village, town, and kingdom. According to Tönnies, Durkheim, and some communitarian writers today, morality in the Middle Ages consisted in being solidary with all others in the collectivity. The taken-for-granted guiding moral principle was for people to act so as to preserve and enhance the well-being of the group.

MacIntyre speaks of the medieval kingdom as a community "in which men in company pursue[d] *the* human good and not merely as—what the modern liberal state takes itself to be—providing the arena in which each individual [sought] his or her own private good."[48] The demands and concerns of the community, he says, took precedence over those of the individual.

There does seem to have been a rather high degree of commitment and loyalty to one's own place of residence among many male citizens. The fact that one was a citizen of *this* particular village or town appears to have led to a sense of pride and concern for its well-being.[49] Whether or not the bulk of inhabitants who were not citizens felt that way is not known. Further, of course, feelings of concern and loyalty for the community did not mean that men agreed about what was required to assure the common good.

And even when people (or at least male citizens) were concerned with the welfare of their community as a collective whole, they seem to have been much less concerned with the well-being of the individual members taken separately. At the level of the commonwealth or kingdom, this is easy to understand. After all, a kingdom was not only very large but also often made up of people with differing backgrounds, experiences, and interests. But even at the level of the village and town, there were cleavages and conflicts between the rich and poor classes and between privileged groups competing for dominance.

People obviously evidenced a considerable amount of social interdependence. The question is whether it reflected a true sense of social solidarity and the conception of morality attributed to the medieval period by some communitarian theorists. Throughout much of the Middle Ages, the powerful men were expected to defend the vast bulk of the population.[50] This also concerned the sick and needy.

There was an enormous amount of poverty in the medieval period. Michael Mollat estimates that anywhere from 25 to 40 percent of the population in the thirteenth century can be classified as poor. He observes that the wealth was very unevenly distributed and suggests that "the number of people living in a modest, vulnerable, insecure or indigent condition exceeded the number who were comfortable or wealthy."[51] The poor included "the starving, the blind, the infirm, the leprous, the orphans, and the aged, as well as the dependent, the ignoble, and the contemptible."[52]

Everywhere, the condition of the poor and sick depended on the rich and well-placed. Oftentimes, this dependence was phrased in religious terms during the Middle Ages. Care of the poor was a Christian duty.[53] One criterion of assistance was residence; the poor within the area constituting a village or town were the charges of the rich in that area. But it was not entirely Christian charity and feelings of solidarity that led to care for the poor. Charitable giving also helped to assure, in the case of the peasant village, that people survived through the winter months so as to be able to help with the work in the spring. Such charity also was probably viewed as keeping the poor from rebelling and as preventing crime. Whatever the reasons, collective charitable systems developed in the village and especially in the towns all over western Europe in the late Middle Ages.

But because of their dependency, it appears that the poor and needy actually encouraged their own separation from those rich persons who were responsible for helping them. Even though the level of maintenance for the poor and needy was never very high, the division between the rich and the poor was made more visible by the dependence and vulnerability of the poor in relation to their wealthy religious or secular benefactors. The rich, the powerful, the poor, and the weak all had a place in society, where it was seen as proper that they should remain. Thus, the very same charitable activities that serve as evidence of concern for the disadvantaged in the medieval village or town also serve to reflect mechanisms that worked against a deeper sense of community cohesion and solidarity.

Whatever the existence of charitable giving may say about the presence of a sense of fellow feeling or mutual concern in the medieval community, other relevant evidence needs to be mentioned here. Consider the realm of the law. Writers like Laurence Tribe and Jerold Auerbach see a genuine community as characterized by an absence of fixed rules and an absence of litigation.[54]

In his book *Justice without Law*, Auerbach contrasts the relation between conflict resolution in traditional communities, on the one hand, and contemporary state-centered mechanisms of individuated justice, on the other. Auerbach seems to accept all those stereotypes about community common to Tönnies and most other communitarian writers. The price paid for state-centered law, he says, is the loss of community concern among people who settle their differences by their own standards in their own way.

America, according to Auerbach, chose to substitute formal standards of adjudication for more informal, local standards of conflict resolution. This is in contrast to the situation in traditional societies, where a sense of solidarity allowed the community to resolve its internal conflicts without recourse to the law. Communities characterized by intimacy, care, and feelings of mutual obligation, Auerbach argues, will be nonlitigious. One reason that Americans are so litigious, he says, is that community has been allowed to disappear.[55]

In the medieval village, where the individualism so often attacked by communitarian scholars was supposedly absent, one would expect a resort to legal machinery to be antithetical to the ties of community. Contrary to this expectation, however, the law courts in the Middle Ages constantly had to deal with a variety of disputes where individuals brought others to court for one or another complaint. Had there been a sufficient level of consensus about right and wrong, misconduct would have been uncommon. And had people been able to resolve conflicts on the basis of informal customs and local standards, there would have seldom been recourse to the courts. But this was not the case.

We can get some idea about conflict and the significance of courts by looking at Razi's research on the village of Halesowen for the period 1270–1348. In his attempt to investigate and understand people's conduct in this village during the later Middle Ages, Razi made wide use of manorial court rolls from the time. Consider now his description of what these courts actually did:

Manorial courts dealt with land conveyances and transactions; disputes about inheritances, roads and boundaries; trespasses against the lord and neighbours; failures to render services, rents and other exactions; disturbances of the public order; infringement of village by-laws and the assize of ale and bread; and the election of jurymen, reeves and other village officials. In addition, the court recorded deaths, marriages and pregnancies out of wedlock of bondswomen; entries into tithing groups; and the departures of villeins from the manor with and without permission. *The range of these activities is so wide that it is hard to conceive how a villager could have avoided appearing before the court from time to time.*[56]

The considerable litigation found by Razi in the manorial court rolls belies the ideal of a shared sense of solidarity. The Halesowen villagers are reported as regularly suing fellow villagers for failing to pay back a quarter-bushel of oats, for not paying the price agreed on, for not remitting a debt on time, for trespassing on a neighbor's land, and for various other offenses. Given the number of times that the villagers appeared in court, Halesowen was certainly not characterized by strong attachments of people to others in the village or by adequate nonlegal mechanisms for resolving differences among them.[57]

We have no idea, of course, as to how representative Helesowen is of medieval villages at the time. But other studies about life in medieval towns also suggest the absence of strong feelings of solidarity with fellow villagers, townspeople, or inhabitants of the kingdom.[58] Or, at the very least, they show that possible *feelings* of solidarity did not assure the absence of conflicts. People probably did feel more concerned about local residents that they saw every day than they did about people living elsewhere. But they also had more conflicts with them.

This brings me to the significance of guilds in the medieval towns as a source of solidarity. Tönnies, Durkheim, and other nineteenth-century social theorists placed heavy emphasis on the warmth and sociability offered by guilds. Gierke (from whom Tönnies drew his view of the medieval guilds) thought that the medieval craft guild was a distinctive type of social entity, intermediate between family and state, that "embraced the whole man" and "united its members with one another like brothers."[59] And Durkheim viewed the medieval guild as the kind of occupational group which provided a *milieu moral* for its members and attached them to it more thoroughly than could the family, the church, or the state. By inculcating a sentiment of common solidarity, this ideal type of organizational form filled the moral gap between the individual and the wider society. Like Tönnies and Durkheim, many social scientists and historians today see these medieval associations as characterized by brotherhood and friendship.

As Reynolds makes clear, however, most scholars have failed to distinguish between two different types of associations, both of which have been referred to as "guilds" in the literature. Essentially, the distinction is between the voluntary club or fraternity, which in some places in medieval Europe was called a guild, and an association of craftsmen, which is often referred to as a craft guild.

The guild or fraternity was a voluntary association of men who—while not actually blood brothers—used the analogy of brotherhood to express their solidarity. Members would swear allegiance, drink together, and provide various kinds of mutual help and protection for one another: insurance against flood and fire, support for poor members, and burial funds for deceased members. Of course, a guild formed for one purpose could later come to serve a different one. As towns grew, the members of some fraternities or guilds became connected with particular crafts. This is what has led some historians to see "craft guilds" as the quintessential form of guild.[60] They have assumed that the primary purpose of a guild was to regulate its craft and that most guilds were concerned with particular crafts. These are mistaken assumptions.[61]

Since every town government was considered to have the right and duty to regulate economic matters, craft associations were normally regulated by the rulers of the town. This was usually done through the delegation of authority and detailed supervision to the leading members of the crafts. Regulations pertaining to hours of work, standards of craftsmanship, and the like were made by delegation from the town government, not by voluntary associations of craftsmen. Some of the resulting craft organizations came to have convivial or charitable functions, but many did not. Within these craft organizations, authority was exercised by those with greater experience and higher standing. The organizations were in no way characterized by ideals of equality and fraternity.

The important point here is that Tönnies and many others have confused the convivial and charitable functions of guilds or fraternities with the public function of economic control exercised by craft organizations. They have followed nineteenth-century historians in seeing "gildsman" as a synonym for craftsman.[62] It is now clear, however, that these were two different forms of social organization. In the absence of evidence to the contrary, then, it cannot be assumed that any particular guild or association of craftsmen had *both* convivial and economic functions.

In any case, a fraternity or guild was often used by its members to help further their economic interests. But this was never its primary concern. "Guilds proliferated in towns," writes Reynolds, "partly because so many people there were uprooted from their homes and families of origin and needed the warmth and sociability they offered."[63]

This emphasis on the warmth and sociability offered by guilds may seem to support the claims of Tönnies and Durkheim, so long as we are careful to distinguish guilds from craft associations. The medieval guild or fraternity, as already noted, was a type of social entity that united its members as brothers. Ties within the guild were often deep and extensive, and members were obliged to give one another mutual aid as friends or brothers. Guilds probably played a more important part in many men's lives in the Middle Ages than at any other time in history.

But the contrast between the medieval and the modern situation should not be exaggerated. Nineteenth-century writers assumed that membership in a guild created a genuine community in which men shared the same norms and values, and shared feelings of attachment and solidarity with one another. In fact, the guild was in many ways like a private club or fraternal organization today. For some members, relations within such a voluntary organization are deep and extensive, feelings of obligation are strong, and loyalty to the organization may outweigh many other loyalties. Many other members, however, will not share these feelings and sentiments.

The same was surely true for the medieval guild or fraternity. Leaving aside the fact that they confused the guild with the craft organization, Gierke and Durkheim exaggerated in thinking that the guild "embraced the whole man" or attached its members more thoroughly than did the family. The depth and extent of individual members' involvement and commitment to the guild depended partly on the degree of each individual's piety, greed, and ambition, and partly on the availability of a wife and other family members. For those guild members with no family members or close friendship ties in the town, the guild undoubtedly played a very significant role. But it seems likely that for most members of the medieval guild, shared feelings and convictions never constituted a common state of mind, and their loyalty to their fellow members never outweighed their ties to family, kin, and friends.[64] While there was undoubtedly more solidarity among guild members than among people more generally in medieval Europe, solidarity itself was certainly not widespread anywhere at the time.

All in all, then, there is very little support for the claims of communitarian writers about the so-called organic unity of the medieval community. The communal foundations of medieval society emphasized by Tönnies and many others are not to be found in more recent evidence for the period. And MacIntyre's emphasis on the significance of membership in the community and a shared framework of detailed agreement on human and divine justice in the Middle Ages is revealed to be misleading by recent research based on medieval sources.

If community and its associated morality is to be evoked as an alternative to the individualism and abstract formalism attributed by MacIntyre,

Sandel, Taylor, and Bellah and his collaborators to life in liberal society, it will have to be found elsewhere than in the medieval period. As far as the High Middle Ages are concerned, the conception of community advanced by various nineteenth-century social theorists and by some communitarian scholars today is largely a historical illusion. Their version of community in medieval society rests on nostalgia for what never was.

# COMMUNITY AND THE GOOD LIFE
# IN CLASSICAL ATHENS

FOR SOME communitarian scholars today, the classical tradition as represented by Aristotle is important as *the* mode of moral thought opposed to modern liberalism. This is especially the case for Alasdair MacIntyre. While modern liberalism can be characterized by the thesis that questions about the good life of man are undecidable, says MacIntyre, Aristotelian thought is explicitly concerned with the *good of life for man*.[1] Like other communitarian writers, MacIntyre sees liberalism as characteristic of modernity more generally. "If a premodern view of morals and politics is to be vindicated against modernity," he writes, "it will be in *something like* Aristotelian terms or not at all."[2]

In classical Athens, says MacIntyre, the Athenian acquired his understanding of the virtues from his membership in the community. But MacIntyre warns against speaking too easily of "the" Greek or Athenian view of the virtues. He discusses four different views in *After Virtue*: those of the sophists, of Plato, of Aristotle, and of the tragedians. However, he gives special attention to Aristotle's account. In fact, MacIntyre remarks that Aristotle "is *the* protagonist against whom I have matched the voices of liberal modernity."[3] I am, therefore, following MacIntyre here in focusing on Aristotle as the most appropriate representative of that tradition which MacIntyre himself advocates. Just as with early America and the Middle Ages, my main concern is with historical evidence about the everyday life of ordinary people. But because Aristotle is often taken as a source of insight into the actual lives of people in Athens, I consider what he says before turning to an examination of other historical sources.

I

Like the other Athenian standpoints considered by MacIntyre, Aristotle assumed that the virtues have their place within the polis. His aim, MacIntyre tells us, was to provide "an account of the good which is at once local and particular—located in and partially defined by the characteristics of the *polis*—and yet also cosmic and universal."[4] For Aristotle, the Greek polis, or political community, was the paradigmatic form of community required for securing the common good of its members. The point of this complete and self-sufficient form of community was the realization of the personal development of every individual in the community.

In *The Politics*, Aristotle attempts a complete and coherent account of the ideal organization of society. But he not only considers this ideal; he also offers many normative judgments about the beliefs and practices of his own time.

The first sentence of Aristotle's *Politics* tells us that every state is an association.[5] Book I of *The Politics* describes a graded series of associations rising from the household to the polis, with the polis itself being characterized by self-sufficiency and a degree of economic and military competence. This self-sufficiency is moral in quality; it means that the political community has ideal goals which transcend the goals of particular individuals or groups.

Aristotle suggests that individuals from different families and villages initially come together out of mutual need. Everyone is better off if there is cooperation among different families and among people from various villages. This allows for a division of labor among individuals, for specialization, and for a more developed level of production and marketing. The family remains the basic unit for psychological and material support, but its members flourish more fully if they enter into a network of association with their neighbors.

While individuals come together out of mutual need, Aristotle argues that they continue living together for the sake of securing the *good* life. The family, the clan, the village—all constitute communities brought together by the need for realizing the common good. In Aristotle's words:

a state's purpose is not merely to provide a living but to make a life that is good. . . . A state's purpose is also to provide something more than a military pact of protection against injustice, or to facilitate mutual acquaintance and the exchange of goods . . . all who are anxious to ensure government under good laws make it their business to have an eye to the virtue and vice of the citizens. It thus becomes evident that which is genuinely and not just nominally called a state must concern itself with virtue. . . . It is clear therefore that the state is not an association of people dwelling in the same place, established to prevent its members from committing injustice against each other, and to promote transactions. Certainly all these features must be present if there is to be a state; but even the presence of every one of them does not make a state *ipso facto*. The state is an association intended to enable its members, in their households and the kinships, to live *well*; its purpose is a perfect and self-sufficient life.[6]

The polis, then, is a particular kind of community (*koinonis*). It consists of families, clans, and neighborhoods living together with the object of achieving the good life according to the human virtues.

Whether it be the clan, village, neighborhood, town, or city-state, MacIntyre says that every form of community needs to establish hierarchies among various people's claims in order to make final decisions.[7] These hierarchies may rest on age, sex, wealth, free birth, military prowess, talent, and so on. In a prepolitical community like the family or the household it is the hierarchy of age that usually proves decisive, and the same generally holds for the neighborhood and the village.

But what about the polis, the political community? Aristotle recognizes that the claim to participate and to share political power can rest on a variety of criteria. In defining the political community, he says that it is synonymous with the whole of the *citizenry*. And the citizenry, in Aristotle's definition, consists of those who participate in legislative and judicial deliberations. The most basic distinction, we see, is between those who are citizens and those who are not. The question here, then, is, What are the bases of citizenship?

To begin with, Aristotle assumes that everything which exists can be seen as existing for a reason or an end. To understand this reason or end, it is necessary to identify the thing's *function*. Its survival, he believes, is evidence that the thing is performing its function well. Aristotle says that all things derive their essential character from their function and their capacity, and that we ought not to say that they are still the "same" things when they are no longer able to discharge their functions.[8]

Just as the individual parts of the body have a function, so do human beings have a function: to develop their special talent or excellence. To ascertain what the function of man is, Aristotle states, we must find what it is that distinguishes human beings from the lower members on the scale of being.[9] Aristotle concludes that what distinguishes man is his *reason*. The function of human beings is the exercise of their capacity for reason.

In emphasizing that only human beings are able to exercise reason, Aristotle makes it clear that not all are able to do so equally. That is, not all humans qua humans have reason and share in the ability to be rational. Because of this natural difference among groups of human beings, some classes of human beings are by nature more fit for citizenship and rule than are others. That some should rule and others be ruled is, in fact, one of the requirements of the polis: "those which are incapable of existing without each other must be united as a pair . . . of natural ruler and ruled, for the purpose of preservation."[10] Not only are animals inferior to human beings because of their lack of reason and consequent ineligibility to rule, but some classes of human beings are themselves inferior to others and, therefore, also ineligible to rule.

The ground for the inferior and subordinate status of some classes of human beings is, according to Aristotle, to be located in the soul. Fortunately, "an immediate indication of this is afforded by the soul."[11] There are, we are told, two parts of the soul, the rational and the irrational, and it is "natural" for the rational to rule over the irrational.[12] Just as one part of the soul rules the other, so one class of human beings ought to rule the other. That is, the class of beings for whom the rational part of the soul *rules* the irrational part is to have authority over those classes for whom the rational part of the soul does *not* rule the irrational part. The constitution of the soul is used, then, to justify Aristotle's view that certain classes of human beings are by nature to rule over other classes.

Specifically, Aristotle argues that it is only among *adult men* that the rational part of the soul rules the irrational, while in the case of women, slaves, and children, it is the irrational part of the soul that dominates. This means that men are to rule women, masters are to rule slaves, and fathers are to rule children.[13]

In excluding women, slaves, and children from the life of reason, Aristotle poses the problem as follows:

> About slaves, the first question to be asked is whether in addition to their virtues as tools and servants they have another and more valuable one. Can they possess restraint, courage, justice, and every other condition of that kind, or have they in fact nothing but the serviceable quality of their persons? The question may be answered in either of two ways, but both present a difficulty. If we say that slaves have these virtues, how then will they differ from free men? If we say they have not, the position is anomalous, since they are human beings and share in reason. Roughly the same question can be put in relation to wife and child.[14]

Aristotle's solution to the problem, of course, is to argue that the relationship between the rational and irrational parts of the soul is different among women, slaves, and children than among men. "Thus, the deliberative faculty in the soul is not present at all in a slave; in a female it is present but ineffective; in a child present but undeveloped."[15]

Aristotle claims, moreover, that the inequalities between the natural rulers and the ruled are to the benefit of both parties. This is because the qualities of women, slaves, and children consist of knowing how to perform their allotted tasks. Aristotle defines the goodness of each thing according to its function: "let it be assumed as to goodness," he says, "that it is the best disposition or state or faculty of each class of things that have some use or work."[16] The slave's function is the provision of his master's daily needs of subsistence, while the female's primary function is reproduction. With regard to the slave, Aristotle asserts that the condition of slavery is both beneficial and just for him, that his relationship with his master is for the preservation of both, and that the two of them have "an interest in common."[17] Similarly, he also claims that husband and wife have a mutually beneficial relationship. They not only "satisfy one another's needs by contributing each his own to the common store,"[18] but the woman is the beneficiary and the man the benefactor of their relationship.[19]

The existence of such so-called mutual benefits is not, however, consistently maintained by Aristotle. It obviously could not be in face of the hierarchical structure of his world. For, in his view, "wherever there is a combination of elements, continuous or discontinuous, and a common unity is the result, in all such cases the ruler-ruled relationship appears."[20]

Given this view, it is not surprising that Aristotle regards women and slaves as "naturally" inferior to men and "naturally" ruled by them. He sees slaves as basically a form of property: "So any piece of property can be regarded as a tool enabling a man to live, and his property is an assemblage of such tools; a slave is a sort of living piece of property, and like any other servant is a tool in charge of other tools."[21] The life of a slave has no other purpose than to enable the master to pursue a life of virtue among the other male citizens of the polis.

The life of a woman is similarly functional: to produce heirs and provide necessities for the male citizen. Despite her contribution to reproduction, the woman is regarded by Aristotle as clearly inferior. "For the male is more fitted to rule than the female."[22] In fact, Aristotle remarks that "we should look on the female as being as it were a deformity, though one which occurs in the ordinary course of nature."[23]

Since Aristotle's outlook is entirely teleological, he holds that the majority of human beings are intended by nature to be the instruments for assuring that the few will realize their highest good. Indeed, only a small minority of the dominant male sex is able to realize the highest good and achieve happiness. In *The Politics* Aristotle discusses the *areté* [virtue] of the ruler, the free man, the woman, the child, and the slave.[24]

His concern is with the qualities in virtue of which each member of these categories may be termed *agathos*: good of his or her kind. Each should possess as much of the relevant *areté* as is necessary for performing his or her function properly. Thus, there is always a set of qualities in virtue of which a woman is a good woman, a slave a good slave, and so on. A good woman must have, for example, such qualities as quietness, modesty, and a capacity for silence that would be totally undesirable in a man. On the other hand, she must not possess those qualities that are required of a good man, such as strength or cleverness. "A man would seem a coward if he had only the courage of a woman, a woman a chatterbox if she were only as discreet as a good man."[25]

The *areté* which holds the highest place is that which is found among only a tiny proportion of the population; only they possess the virtue necessary for serving the state and realizing the highest level of happiness. Only those who rule over others have a full complement of reason. Only they, says Aristotle, must have practical wisdom.[26] While such practical wisdom is necessary for rulers, nothing more than "correct opinion" is required of women, slaves, and others who are permanently ruled. Although the presence of these latter persons is necessary for the existence of the state, Aristotle holds, they are, of course, not citizens at all and have no share in political life.

In considering the ideal state, Aristotle makes it clear that it will consist both of citizens (who are the only "genuine" parts of the state) and of women, slaves, foreigners, and so on, who simply occupy the same territory and are in the service of the citizens. "A state," he writes, "is an association of similar persons whose aim is the best life possible."[27]

As to what *is* the best life possible, Aristotle states: "What is best is happiness, and to be happy is an active exercise of virtue and a complete enjoyment of it. It so happens that some can get a share of happiness, while others can get little or none."[28] Because of these differences in people's capacity for realizing happiness, says Aristotle, we find different sorts of arrangements in different states.

But all states have certain functions that must be performed if they are to exist at all. These include the provision of goods, skills (crafts), arms (weapons), money, religion, and most essential of all, "a method of arriving at decisions about matters of expedience and justice between one person and another."[29] It is essential in setting up a state, says Aristotle, to make provision for all these necessary functions. He concludes in this regard: "So a number of agricultural workers will be needed to supply food; and skilled workmen will be required, and fighting men, and wealthy men, and priests, and judges of what is necessary and expedient."[30]

The state needs its inhabitants to perform all these functions, but in the ideal state not all inhabitants are citizens, "for being happy must occur in conjunction with virtue, and in pronouncing a state happy we must have regard not to part of it but to all its citizens."[31] And, as already noted, citizenship must be confined to those who are capable of realizing the highest virtue, that is, a limited number of adult Greek males.

Most people, then, lack the characteristics of the citizen in Aristotle's ideal state. He makes it clear that the citizen may not be a shopkeeper, a craftsman, a farmer, a skilled worker, or a hired laborer.[32] Those who *are* citizens, says Aristotle, may be divided into two groups: the military and the deliberative.[33] The roles of soldier and of judge and statesman are, however, to be discharged by the same people. When young, the citizen has the strength necessary for war; when older, he has the practical wisdom necessary for responsible deliberation.[34]

The ideal state requires that its citizens possess not only reason if they are to live the good life but also, says Aristotle, certain external goods as well. For the good life, he observes, needs sufficient material resources and a large quantity of leisure. This overriding necessity for leisure excludes the citizens of Aristotle's ideal state from all forms of work. Their leisure is assured by the possession of ample property, which is to be farmed for them by slaves or non-Greeks.[35]

For Aristotle, a man's economic position is the decisive external factor qualifying him for citizenship. Although the principal division is between citizens and noncitizens, there are divisions based on ownership of property even among those who *are* citizens. Aristotle says that in every polis—he is speaking here only of the *citizen* population—there are three economic groups: the very rich, the poor (who need not be completely without property), and those in between.[36]

Neither of the two extreme "classes" (a term not used, of course, by Aristotle himself) is willing to be obedient to reason. The very rich incline to arrogance and wish neither to submit to rule nor to understand how to do so, while the poor are too subservient and do not know how to rule.[37] The middle group of citizens, however, suffers from none of these disadvantages.[38] "Where the middle element is large, there least of all arise factions and divisions among the citizens."[39] Thus, the greater the proportion of this middle-class group, the better governed the state will be.

Aristotle suggests at one point that perhaps the mass of the people ought to be sovereign, rather than the best few citizens.[40] He considers the necessity for the whole body of citizens to be given political power, at least to the extent of allowing them to elect officials and scrutinize their conduct.[41] His reasoning is that "each individual will indeed be a worse judge than the experts, but collectively they will be better, or at any rate no worse."[42]

This apparent willingness to concede some degree of *areté* to the ordinary citizen is not, however, maintained by Aristotle. He fears that the poor might use their numerical superiority to outvote the propertied class and to confiscate the property of the rich.[43] Here, as in much of his discussion of property and economic position, Aristotle ignores the middle class and speaks only of the rich and the poor, propertied and propertyless, and he always seems to assume that the propertied and the nonpropertied are naturally opposed groups whose interests cannot be reconciled.[44] Although he seeks the ideal state in which conflict would be transcended in the interests of the good life for all, Aristotle insists that no state has ever approached that ideal.

It is because of these antagonistic interests, and the numerical superiority of the poor, that Aristotle suggests that the propertied class of citizens must in some way or another be given extra weight so as to compensate for its small numbers. Among the possibilities he offers are to fine the rich for nonattendance in the courts and at the same time to pay a certain number of the poor for attending,[45] or to reserve the right to share in the constitution for those who are wealthy enough to afford to carry arms and to furnish themselves with military equipment.[46]

The point here is that citizenship in the polis—itself restricted to a limited number of adult Greek males—does not assure equality among the citizenry or an absence of conflict. After all, Aristotle views the state as an arena for conflicting interests.

Aristotle believes that when the propertied class can rule, they do, and that the same holds for those citizens who are poor. Rule by the few who are rich is described by Aristotle as oligarchy, while government by the poor is defined as democracy. Neither extreme is totally acceptable to Aristotle, though it is apparent that he wants to assure that the inevitable conflict of interests between the rich and the poor citizens ought not to be resolved in favor of the latter group. Aristotle's preference is for a polis in which the best citizens rule and are ruled in turn.

## II

Where, we might ask, did Aristotle acquire his knowledge about the supposed characteristics and capabilities of various classes of people? How did he know what sorts of social and economic arrangements were possible, and on what basis did he speculate about the consequences of other sorts of arrangements? From what sources did Aristotle acquire his competence as an authority on the political life of the polis? To all these questions, the answer is essentially the same: he paid very close attention to actual historical processes, social and economic arrangements, and the behavior of various sorts of people.[47]

To begin with, the Greek city-states were agrarian societies, and the bulk of the population was overwhelmingly rural. It was on the backs of the peasantry (as well as slaves) that, in de Ste. Croix's words, rested "the burden of the whole vast edifice of Greek civilization."[48] These peasants lived not on isolated farm homesteads but in hamlets and villages. Many of them owned those small portions of land on which they struggled to survive and yet were still constantly in danger of falling below the subsistence level, at which margin they lived.

Most were illiterate and probably spoke Greek either not at all or at best imperfectly. Nonetheless, these peasants were usually citizens and had certain specified rights. In fact, the great majority of citizens in the classical world were involved in agricultural production. Alongside them frequently worked slaves. The cities and towns were economically parasitic on the countryside, and the fundamental relationship between them was one of exploitation.[49]

In addition to the rural poor, there were the many poor in the towns: largely self-employed artisans and shopkeepers. Though poor, they were distinguished from the paupers, the beggars, and the idlers. Collectively, the peasants, artisans, and shopkeepers were the demos—the common people—and they formed the great bulk of the citizen population in the Greek polis. Not much is known about the urban poor, but at least some were literate. They mixed with the rich and more educated, and it is suggested that they shared the wealthy citizens' outlook and system of values to a very considerable extent.[50]

The wealthy classes (Aristotle's "rich") resided in or near the towns, living comfortably on the labors of others. These rich men spoke Greek, shared in Greek culture, and lived the good life; that is, they lived a life devoted to those pursuits deemed proper to a gentleman: politics, intellectual or artistic pursuits, hunting or athletics.

Education, at least above the most elementary level, was restricted to a small elite. Only they were able to read. And although the ancient Greek world was predominately an oral culture, the elite literate minority must have profited from their ability to read. When basic documents concerning such important subjects as the law and the will of the gods are accessible only to an elite for study and reflection, the rest of society is highly dependent on their interpretations. This, says M. I. Finley, was the situation in antiquity, and it "strengthened acceptance of the elite and its claim to dominate."[51]

Not everyone, of course, had the benefits of citizenship. Estimates of the percentage of the total population who were citizens around the end of the fifth century B.C. range from a low of about 10 percent to a maximum of 20 percent.[52] All citizens were, of course, adult males. Normally, it was birth alone that determined whether or not a man was a citizen. And usually it was only citizens who were entitled to own land, although noncitizens were sometimes granted the right to own land within the territory of the polis.[53] Without this essential right of property, as de Ste. Croix points out, the individual would have been unable to own the one form of wealth upon which economic life mainly depended.[54]

The ownership of land and the power to exact unfree labor (from slaves and others) were concentrated in the hands of the wealthy. Such a propertied class was able to enjoy vast leisure without spending any time at all in burdensome toil. As examples of those sorts of men who belonged to the propertied class, de Ste. Croix mentions the owner of a large or even medium-size farm worked by slaves; the proprietor of a workshop of twenty to fifty slaves; the owner of several merchant ships; and the owner of a fair amount of money capital, who lent it out at high interest. But the ruling classes of all the Greek city-states were primarily landowners.[55]

Their position was in marked contrast to that of most citizens and of the vast majority of the total population. Although free peasants, artisans, and shopkeepers often worked for themselves, they would normally have had to work very long hours in order to live even at the subsistence level.[56] Most citizens, in fact, owned little property and held no slaves. And slaves, of course, cannot be considered to have been working for themselves at all.

Only the upper classes who owned land and exercised command over the labor of others were able to live the good life. Such persons required sufficient property to allow them to live what Aristotle termed the life of leisure.[57] In this regard, de Ste. Croix calls attention to the comments of Heracleides Ponticus, a contemporary of Aristotle, who in his treatise *On Pleasure* declared that "pleasure and luxury, which relieve and reinforce the mind, are characteristics of free men," while labor is for slaves and humble men, whose minds accordingly become shrunken.[58] Liberated from toil, the rich property owners were parasitic upon the vast majority of men (and women).[59]

Finley notes that as substitutes for "the rich," Greek writers employed words that meant literally "the useful" or "worthy," "the best," "the well-born," "the notable," and "the powerful;" while for "the poor," they said "the many," "the mean," "the knaves," and "the mob."[60]

It was apparently widely accepted by most Greeks that slave labor was absolutely essential to their way of life.[61] In fact, Aristotle remarks that a complete household consists of "the free and the slaves," and describes the household as consisting of "master and slave, husband and wife, father and children."[62] The master enjoyed unlimited control over the activities of the slave, and he alone decided how the slave was to be treated.[63] Being totally *without rights*, the slave had no recourse to the courts or to the law.

Although the ancient city-state had no formal police organization, it had a relatively small number of publicly owned slaves at the disposal of the different magistrates. There was no army available for large-scale police duties. This is not surprising, since the ancient city-state army was a citizen militia composed of a wealthy elite. Both calvary and infantry were required to equip themselves, and that obviously reduced the rest of the citizenry to marginal service. The man of wealth and leisure was urgently needed to perform important military functions.

In classical Athens and other city-states, there existed a system of laws concerning, among other things, land ownership and debts. All city-states acknowledged that their citizens were, at least in principle, equal before the law. Athens best exemplified this proposition. There, an equality among all citizens in their political rights had its source in a constitution. This equality meant the right to vote, to hold office, and to participate in policy making in the council and the assembly.

The Council of Five Hundred (the boule) in Athens consisted of men who were selected by lot on the basis of a system by which each of the demes (parishes or neighborhoods) was represented in proportion to its population. Any citizen over the age of thirty could let his name go forward for selection. The term of office was one year, and a man could serve only twice in his lifetime. Council members spent time daily throughout the year on its activities, and for a tenth of the year served full-time. That is, because a Council of Five Hundred was so unwieldy, a standing committee was instituted consisting of fifty members at a time. They were paid a modest per diem for their services. The Council of Five Hundred was occupied with the whole range of administration, especially with preparing business for the assembly (the "ecclesia").[64]

While the councillors were chosen by lot, meetings of the assembly were open to any citizen who chose to attend. In Aristotle's day, the assembly normally met on forty days evenly spaced throughout the year. At its meetings, citizens could initiate, debate, and vote openly on proposals. Those proposals drafted by the council were voted on in the assembly. Mass meetings of the assembly often involved several thousand men, listening to speakers and voting by a show of hands.[65]

In addition to the council and the assembly, there were a number of official positions occupied by eligible citizens. The most prestigious offices in Athens were the ten *strategoi*—elected by vote, not chosen by lot. They could be elected to terms without limit. Their roster in the fifth century B.C. included the best-known political leaders of the time, many of whom were elected because of their known military skill. The actual political leadership in Athens, observes Finley, was thus monopolized by a relatively small stratum. Nevertheless, he says, the Athenian demos displayed much good discrimination in their election of the *strategoi*.[66]

Also prominent in Athens were the mass jury courts. To be a juror, a man had to be aged thirty or more and in possession of full citizenship rights. From those who volunteered for such duty, six thousand were chosen by lot as jurors for the year. The juries for the various courts were made up from this list of six thousand. In some cases, a jury might contain several hundred men. Decisions were made by majority vote, and the number of jurors was always odd (for example, 201 or 401) to avoid a tie.

Jury pay, raised from two to three obols per day in the 420s, was apparently intended to obtain some representation of the poorer classes. Three obols were sufficient to support a small family at the time. Still, Douglas MacDowell indicates that a disproportionate number of the volunteers were old men no longer fit for ordinary work who could not earn money by other means.[67]

Part of the theory behind the mass jury in the law courts was that such a jury was difficult to bribe. Bribery was, in fact, a serious problem in Athenian public life.[68] Obviously, it would have been difficult to bribe a large number of jurors. But the bribery of witnesses remained a possibility, and there were very heavy penalties for such an action. Rotations in the boule also worked against dishonesty; a transient councillor—especially one of the fifty men who were presiding for one-tenth of the year—did not exercise power long enough to be worth bribing.

The existence of a legal system, equality before the law, and participation by citizens in the council and the assembly should not mask the fact that there was continual conflict between rich and poor citizens. Aristotle's remarks about the propertied class and the poor having their own interests at heart were surely based on his own observations.

Aristotle, like other Greek political thinkers, saw the state as an arena for conflicting class interests. As already noted, access to citizenship was severely restricted, women and aliens were excluded from direct participation in political and governmental activity, and slaves counted for nothing. Beyond this, there was often open class conflict—especially between landed aristocratic creditors and peasant debtors. The gap between rich and poor was often enormous, and there was, as emphasized by Aristotle, virtually no middle class.

But since the poor were in the vast majority, why did they not seize the power from the rich? As I noted earlier, Aristotle expressed fear about such a possibility. Why, then, did the poor act with such restraint toward

133

the rich minority? The answer seems to be that the Athenian democracy involved a compromise of interests between the rich and the poor classes. On the one hand, the assembly and the council gave the poor a considerable degree of protection against overt oppression by the rich and powerful. On the other, "the people elected rich men to magistracies, and they as magistrates contributed freely to the public services under their charge."[69]

The burden of "liturgies"—expensive personal contributions to such things as public entertainment and the purchase of military equipment—fell on the very rich. Whether at state behest or voluntarily, these liturgies included most famously the *Khorégia* and the trierarchy. A *khorégos* met the cost of preparing a chorus for an important public event, while the trierarchy involved the maintenance of a large warship (trireme) and its equipment for a period of one year.

In performing these liturgies, the rich men can be seen as following Aristotle's suggestion that displays of generosity by rich magistrates may lead the people to acquiesce in their exclusion from high office. The most supreme offices, he writes, "should have public services associated with them. This will reconcile people to having no share in office, and make them think the more kindly of officials who pay heavily for their position."[70] A requirement that magistrates perform liturgies was, of course, an adroit expedient by the wealthy to keep the poor citizens out of high office.

The rich in reality had great power in Athens. As I have indicated, using their wealth and position beneficiently and performing important services was not simply a matter of philanthropy or obedience to the law. It was also a means for maintaining their status as generous and concerned citizens, and for achieving public recognition. In addition, the liturgy was a form of insurance which assured that the liturgy performer would be remembered in time of need. And it has been noted that such service gave an important advantage to wealthy litigants in court cases.[71]

Finley refers to the liturgies as a sort of "community patronage." This differed from the usual man-to-man, patron-client relationship, although it too was a reciprocal relationship between unequals in which there was a genuine exchange of goods or services. Finley describes such community patronage as "large-scale private expenditure, whether compulsory or voluntary, for communal purposes—temples and other public works, theatres and gladiatorial shows, festivals and feasts—in return for public approval; often . . . for popular support in the advancement of political careers."[72] What gave the aristocracy its hold over the common people, then, was their wealth (and what they could do with it). Through community patronage, this wealth was consciously deployed in support of the power structure.[73] Finley suggests that the deme was the base from which local patronage launched the political careers of the rich.

Let us consider what this might mean for popular participation in the council and assembly. The poor, we must not forget, often lived at a bare subsistence level. At the same time, they did have a share in political decision making. Since the members of the council were chosen by lot, it would seem that direct control over them by patrons would have been minimal. In the assembly, however, citizens could vote for or against a particular policy and could support one leader against another.

It is here—as well as in the jury courts—that the influence of patronage would more often be revealed. Except for those issues that directly concerned their own interests, it is unlikely that the mass of Athenian citizens cared much about the results of the voting on many issues. In such instances, there was apt to be a strong tendency to lend support to their patrons. Thus, A. H. M. Jones mentions "a tacit convention, whereby the people elected rich men to magistracies, and they as magistracies contributed freely to the public services under their charge."[74]

In any case, the formal equality between the rich and the poor in political decision making was less than total. This is perhaps most obvious with regard to freedom of speech in the Athenian assembly. The herald opened debates in the assembly with the words "What man has good advice to give the *polis* and wishes to make it known?"[75] In principle, anyone could make his voice known, since all citizens had the right of *isegoris*: the right to speak out in the assembly.

But not all, of course, were considered to possess an equal share of political wisdom. It was the rich, and the rich alone, who were thought to possess a high level of the "virtue" of political wisdom. Beyond this, the rich man had inherited such advantages as confidence in himself, the expectation of deference by the poor, and often a formal training in techniques of public speaking as well. The common man did not, then, really participate as an equal. "The evidence strongly suggests," writes Finley, "that even in Athens few exercised their right of *isegoria*."[76]

Overall, the Athenian democracy was remarkably indulgent to the rich. The kind of community patronage referred to above, and the kind of dependency that it created, helped to legitimate the right of the rich to greater wealth, social standing, and political authority. While the poor had a share in political decision making, the important and influential positions in the power structure were held by the rich. In advocating the exclusion of the poor from high positions, Aristotle commented that "the poor are generally content enough, even if they do not share in honours, provided only that they are not liable to be ill-treated or deprived of any of their possessions."[77] Such appears to have been the case in Athens.

It was his own awareness of the enormous discrepancy in wealth and power between the rich aristocrats and the mass of the poor citizens, and the consequences of such differences for political participation and decision making, that was responsible for Aristotle's views about the "natural opposition" between the rich and the poor. This opposition had to be recognized, he said, in considering any constitution.

When he discusses the "constitution," that is, the fundamental laws and customs governing political life, Aristotle remarks that the constitution *is*, in effect, the ruler or rulers. The constitution may, he says, be the one, the few, or the many, each of whom ought to rule with an eye to "the common good."[78] But he remarks several times that one must expect in practice that the rulers will inevitably rule in light of their own interests.[79] Thus Aristotle assumed that what had actually occurred in Greek history was likely always to be the case. Because there had been frequent struggles between the rich and the common people to control the state, Aristotle assumed that such a struggle was characteristic of life in every community. Although we might regard these struggles as muted, they were obviously a source of great concern to Aristotle.

Despite living in Athens (though as a foreigner) and being closely acquainted with democracy there, Aristotle did not regard it as the ideal form of political organization. In *The Politics*, he insists that political authority should be exercised in the interests of the ruled and ruler alike: "whenever authority in the *state* is constituted on the basis of equality and similarity between citizens, they take turns in exercising it." The statesman is expected "during tenure of office to look after the interests of someone else, who then does the same for him."[80]

It might appear that the Athenians had achieved this state of affairs most completely, since the demos—all the citizens—were equals and peers, and ruled and were ruled in turn. But Aristotle rejects this sort of democratic procedure. In his view, it rests on a false, arithmetical conception of equality: the mere counting of heads.

Such a conception of equality, claims Aristotle, puts control into the hands of demagogues. Although the term *demagogues* was originally a neutral term meaning "leaders of the demos," it was soon used most frequently in a disparaging sense.[81] This is the way Aristotle uses the term. He writes: "when states are democratically governed according to law, there are no demagogues, and the best citizens are securely in the saddle; but where the laws are not sovereign, there you find demagogues. The people become a monarch, one person composed of many, for the many are sovereign, not as individuals, but as an aggregate."[82] This is, according to Aristotle, the worst possible condition: rule by men, not by laws. And when laws do not rule, he held, there is no constitution.[83]

Aristotle was concerned, of course, that the "best citizens" should be "securely in the saddle." He believed that the demos contained too many people who were not among the best. The best people, as Greek gentlemen liked to call themselves, were those who had been *trained* to rule and had the leisure to devote themselves thoroughly to it. Thus, Aristotle warns, "If we are to take justice to be what is decided by a numerical majority, they will act unjustly, confiscating the property of the rich and less numerous."[84]

Aristotle seemed to regard the Athenian constitution, then, as a form of "extreme democracy," in which there was room for the overriding of laws by decrees passed by the demos in the assembly. But we ought not to forget just how exclusive the demos in Athens actually was. For it was a very narrow minority that excluded slaves, women, and members of the subject states in the empire.

With regard to slaves, de Ste. Croix argues that it was just because Athens *was* a democracy, and the poorer citizens were to some extent protected against the rich and powerful, that the very most had to be made from the slaves. Greek democracy depended, he says, "to a considerable extent on the exploitation of slave labour, which, in the conditions obtaining in the ancient world, was if anything even more essential for the maintenance of a democracy than of any more restricted form of constitution."[85] This helps explain the paradox, noted by Finley, that freedom and slavery advanced hand in hand in the ancient Greek world.[86] The same was true, of course, for white men in eighteenth-century Virginia.

Most of the slaves in Greek cities were imported "barbarians," coming from areas as far apart as Thrace, South Russia, Egypt, Libya, and Sicily, and sharing no common language or culture.[87] A great deal of this slave labor was employed in agriculture, the most important sector of the ancient economy. Many slaves also worked in mining and domestic service. Even households that could not afford male slaves always had a few female slaves. As a conservative estimate, there were some sixty thousand slaves in Athens at the end of the fifth century B.C. This figure represents about 30 percent of the total population at the time.[88] It is no wonder, then, that the permanent work force was composed largely of slaves.

The slave was without rights, and the master had the right to use him (or her) at his pleasure, having the power of life and death over the slave. Male and female slaves alike were unrestrictedly available for sexual relations with rich men. There was the widespread habit of addressing, or referring to, male slaves of any age as "boy" in Greek.[89] Flogging was taken for granted as normal.[90] Slaves could survive only by compromise and accommodation. To the extent that a slave was treated with some compassion, it was because he or she was human capital and represented an investment by the master.

Consistent with the slave's actual position and treatment, Aristotle regards the slave as essentially an "inanimate tool."[91] "The use made of slaves hardly differs at all from that of tame animals," writes Aristotle; "they both help with their bodies to supply our essential needs."[92] And in Book VII of *The Politics*, where he presents the characteristics of his ideal state, Aristotle specifies that the land of its propertied citizens must be tilled by slaves: "As for those who are to till the land, the best thing (if we are to describe the ideal) is that they should be slaves."[93]

It is interesting to see that he immediately follows this statement with the sentence: "They should not be all of one stock nor men of spirit; this will ensure that they will be useful workers and no danger as potential rebels."[94] It is apparent that Aristotle recognizes that even those who are "naturally inferior" are not always willing to accept their position without protest. Making sure that they are not of a single ethnic stock nor possessed of too much spirit is one means of preventing revolts. Thus, the absence of revolts by slaves in classical Greece in no way suggests that they were mildly treated or in some way reconciled to their station. It was rather that there was little chance for them to revolt, even had they considered it. Again, the resemblance with early Virginia is striking.

Just as he based his accounts of political arrangements in the ideal state on what he had observed and heard about, and derived his viewpoint about the capacities of slaves by observing the dominant practices in Greek society, Aristotle did the same with regard to women. He seemed to suppose that the actual roles performed by women were the only ones they were capable of performing.[95]

Young girls were ideally married at age fourteen to men of age thirty. Men married late because of their duty to serve as soldiers for ten years.[96] There was an average of 4.3 births per woman, with 2.7 infants surviving beyond childhood. "Motherhood at an early age, combined with a life spent indoors," writes Sarah Pomeroy, "was disadvantageous to the health of Athenian women."[97] Consequently, the life expectancy was shorter for women than for men: 36.2 years for the former and 45.0 for the latter.[98]

Athenian women in the fifth and fourth centuries B.C. had no effective rights at all.[99] They were not only deprived of the most elementary political rights; they were also allowed only very inferior property rights. In

Athens at least, a woman could not own land. And in Athenian law, a woman could own no property other than her clothing and jewelry. There was never joint (husband-wife) ownership of anything. Property, according to the dominant concept of ownership in Athenian law, belonged to the household. By virtue of his position within the home, the male head of the family controlled all the household property. The head was called the *kyrios* of his wife and children, just as he was the *kyrios* of his lands. So long as she remained married, the wife's dowry belonged to her husband. Her trousseau belonged to him permanently, however, and did not revert to the wife even in the case of divorce.[100]

Greek law assured that control of property would be in the hands of the *kyrios*. The transactions of other family members were valid only with his approval. And throughout her life, the woman remained under control of one or another *kyrios*. At a woman's birth, her father was her *kyrios*. When he died, her brothers assumed the position. If she married, her husband became the *kyrios*. When he retired or died, the woman's sons became her *kyrios*.

A woman had no right of inheritance so long as there existed an equally close male relative. Only in the absence of sons would a daughter inherit; a sister would inherit only in the absence of brothers; and an aunt only in the absence of uncles. In reality, only those women without brothers could ever expect to inherit anything at all. Even when a woman did inherit, her *kyrios* became *kyrios* of the inheritance as well. He was not only responsible for managing it but could dispose of it as he saw fit. Thus, a man was always the legal owner.

With regard to marriage itself, a woman's marriage was entirely at the will of her *kyrios* (normally her father). In at least some Greek city-states, her *kyrios* could also withdraw her from marriage and give her to another husband. If the woman was divorced or widowed, it was the duty of the *kyrios* to marry her off again.

In general, women were excluded from transacting business. According to Athenian law, a child was not capable of performing a transaction and neither was a woman if the transaction was beyond the value of a *medimnus* of barley. A *medimnus* was a dry measure equivalent to about 52½ liters. This was about a six-days food supply for an ordinary family. As David Schaps points out, "the law, then, appears intended to permit the woman to do her week's marketing, while preventing her from spending large amounts of a family fortune."[101] There were some few tradeswomen in Athens, but they were mostly in those poorer trades in which transactions were unlikely to involve more than the value of a *medimnus* of barley.

Although all women in the Greek city-state were disadvantaged as compared to men, there were obvious differences related to class and citizenship. The wives of the wealthy were expected to produce children (especially sons), provide the necessities, and supervise the household. Many of these household tasks were, of course, performed by slave women. But the wife of a rich man would herself be virtually destitute of property rights, and her class position would be greatly inferior to his.

The wives of poorer citizens (i.e., the vast majority of citizens) performed much the same functions as the wives of the rich, although they were likely to have less help from slave women. But because the wives of poorer men often worked alongside their husbands in agricultural activities, they were less inferior to their husbands than were the wives of rich men. In addition, some of these poorer women did nursing and midwifery or engaged in spinning and weaving as an economic activity. Slave women and the wives of noncitizens performed the most menial of tasks for the households of citizens. Their position, de Ste. Croix suggests, might have been "virtually identical with that of a male prostitute or any other non-citizen provider of services in the city."[102]

Since women were so thoroughly oppressed and exploited in Athenian society, it is no wonder that Aristotle regarded women as by nature inferior to men and suited only to doing the sorts of things they had done in the past. Aristotle shared with Athenian men the presumption that males were more intelligent and more worthy than females. But while the Athenian men rarely bothered to state this presumption directly, Aristotle was clear about his view that "as between male and female the former is by nature superior and ruler, the latter inferior and subject."[103]

As with the general division between citizens and noncitizens, rich and poor, and slaves and masters, Aristotle's argument about men and women is essentially circular. He claims that by nature citizens ought to rule noncitizens, the rich rule the poor, masters rule slaves, and men rule women. How does he know that these relations are indeed intended "by nature"?

His evidence seems to be simply that it can be observed that citizens *do* rule noncitizens, men rule women, and so forth. Although Aristotle is often thought to have derived his views about the natural authority of men over women, masters over slaves, and so on from his metaphysical biology and nature's intentions, it is evident that he was very much influenced by the social and political practices that he himself observed. In general, he seemed to accept that the status quo in the social realm is what nature intends and is indeed the best way for things to be.

## III

What, then, can be said about the Greek city-state, and Athens in particular, as a community? In answering this, I will first consider Athens in the fifth century B.C. and will then turn my attention to Aristotle's ideal state. It may be recalled that MacIntyre gives special place to Aristotle and to the Athenian polis in his book. He is, of course, not the only theorist today emphasizing an Aristotelian approach. But MacIntyre's *After Virtue* is the most systematic, sustained, and ambitious attempt to develop an Aristotelian moral philosophy that has appeared in recent years. For that reason, I will continue to focus on his work.

Although there were a number of Athenian views, says MacIntyre, all took it for granted "that the milieu in which the virtues are to be exercised and in terms of which they are to be defined is the *polis*."[104] The virtues have their place, that is, within the context of the polis, or city-state. "To be a good man will on every Greek view," MacIntyre writes, "be at least closely allied to being a good citizen."[105]

Part of being a good citizen, we are told, was to participate in those contests that were so important in uniting men within the city-state.[106] Among those contests were the debates in the assemblies and law courts of Greek democracy, and those involving philosophical disputes. The political, philosophical, and dramatic contests, according to MacIntyre, were much more intimately related in ancient Athens than in our world today. In his words:

> Politics and philosophy were shaped by dramatic form, the preoccupations of drama were philosophical and political, philosophy had to make its claims in the arena of the political and the dramatic. At Athens the audience for each was potentially largely and actually to some degree one and the same; and the audience itself was a collective actor. The producer of drama was a holder of political office; the philosopher risked comic portrayal and political punishment. The Athenians had not insulated, as we have by a set of institutional devices, the pursuit of political ends from dramatic representation or the asking of philosophical questions from either.[107]

Thus, "the Athenians," claims MacIntyre, had a public, shared communal mode for participating in political and philosophical contests and debate.

As MacIntyre tells it, then, participation in the assembly and the law courts involved dramatic presentation and philosophical argumentation, and the audience for dramatic plays understood the political and philosophical significance of what was contained in the performances. The good life in the classical polis involved the citizen in discussion that was continuous, intense, and public. My question here, of course, is about the extent to which the ancient Athenian polis constituted a community in terms of the communitarian conception that I have excavated in chapter 1.

Aristotle insisted that the Greek polis was the paradigmatic form of complete and self-sufficient community for securing the good of its members. What kind of community was, in fact, found in fifth-century Athens? To begin with, the polis or community *did* share a common locale or territory. It was in this environment that the citizen interacted with others to develop his political self and social being. The majority of the inhabitants of ancient Greece were, of course, not citizens. So when I discuss the polis here I am concerned solely with citizens.

In the Athenian polis no fundamental distinction was made between those citizens who lived in or near the urban center of the polis and those who lived outside or in the countryside. Although it is difficult to be precise about the exact population of Athens at the time, various figures provided by Finley lead me to conclude that it was about 200,000 at the end of the fifth century B.C. In his book on ancient slavery, Finley says that the 60,000 slaves at that time constituted about 30 percent of the total population.[108] That would make the total population 200,000. In a more recent book, Finley writes of there being 35,000–40,000 "citizens" at the time.[109] If we take the higher figure, we arrive at the following distribution: 40,000 citizens, 60,000 slaves, and 100,000 other noncitizens. This means that the citizens constituted 20 percent of the total population living in ancient Athens. It is this group of citizens living in the Athenian polis that concerns me here.

Although my concern is with the citizens, I must also consider very briefly the situation of the *population* (and not just the citizens) of Athens in regard to community. It is self-evident, I believe, that Athens as such was definitely *not* a community. The only characteristic of community found there was the territorial one: people did live in the same locale.

But they did not have a common history and shared values. The fact that 30 percent of the population consisted of slaves who were imported "barbarians" by itself testifies to how little was shared. Nor did the bulk of the population participate together in political and other activities. And there was, if anything, a total absence of solidarity, in the sense of concern and responsibility for other people living there.

In fact, the politics of the common good favored by Aristotle (and evident in the institutional arrangements of ancient Athens) required the sort of subordination and exploitation that we have seen above. A whole/part model of society was assumed, at least by the rich and power-ful. That is, society was viewed as an organism whose parts exercised specific functions for the common good of the whole. The individual was perceived as an agent or extension of the state and was evaluated on the basis of his or her contribution to the good of society.

Just as in Aristotle's ideal state, Athenians distinguished between those parts of the organism that assured the good of the whole and those other elements that, though indispensable, were not parts in the strict sense. Only citizens were genuinely parts of the state, while slaves, women, craftsmen, traders, and foreigners were mere sine qua non. Together, however, these two categories were seen to be essential to achievement of the common good in Athenian society.

In the organic, inegalitarian ideal, it was those wealthy men liberated from toil who contributed most to the welfare of the community. These elite citizens were excluded from all forms of work, not only from farm-ing and work as artisans and the like, but also from trade and commerce. Those many people who were engaged in domestic and other manual work lacked the leisure and independence required for responsible citi-zenship and statesmanship. As Susan Moller Okin notes, all those who participated in the performance of "those necessary but inferior func-tions such as domestic management, child rearing, and the production of daily necessities" were unable to achieve a life of excellence.[110] Conse-quently, such persons were denied the privileges of citizenship. Achieve-ment of the common good demanded, then, that the vast majority of the inhabitants of ancient Athens devote themselves to supporting a tiny portion of the population: men of wealth and leisure.

There was, then, practically nothing in Athenian society—taken as a whole—that resembled community. This is surely no surprise to most readers and merits mention here only because of the unspecified claims made by some writers about community in Athens. If there was commu-nity in ancient Athens, it was restricted to that small minority of the pop-ulation who were citizens. Thus, I turn now to consider them.

Since Athenian citizenship was normally acquired by birth only, these men certainly had a common history and shared many values in com-mon. Speaking of what they shared in this regard, Finley says that nearly all Athenian citizens

> would have accepted as premises, one might say as axioms, that the good life was possible only in a *polis*, that the good man was more or less synonymous with the good citizen, that slaves, women, and bar-barians were inferior by nature and so excluded from all discussion; that therefore correct political judgments, the choice between *polis*

143

regimes or between conflicting policies within a particular *polis*, should be determined by which alternative helped advance the good life. The main divergences were in practical judgments, not in the premises.[111]

As far as I can see, the evidence supports Finley's remarks about these shared values. His remarks do, however, tend to conceal the extent to which there was something like a class struggle between the very rich elite minority (within that minority who were citizens) and the demos, or common people, who formed the great bulk of the citizen population. But because every citizen had a vote in the sovereign assembly in fifth-century Athens—both in its deliberative and legislative capacity and in its judicial capacity—we might want to regard the struggles between the rich and poor citizens as what Finley terms divergences in "political judgments." In any case, the fact that the democracy was firm and unshakable during the period lends support to the conclusion that the members of the community were indeed bound together by a common history and shared values.

With regard to the first two characteristics of community, then, the Athenian polis was a community for its citizens. What about the third characteristic: that the members participate together in common activities, in collective decision making, and in the exercise of power? The idea with this ingredient is that virtue evolves through active civic participation, that men learn civic morality in the polis, where their actions are public and where speech and conversation are open and direct.

The evidence shows that there was a good deal of regularized, often face-to-face contact among Athenian citizens. One reason for this was that it was a Mediterranean society in which people spent a great deal of time out-of-doors: visiting, gossiping, and passing time near the harbor and in the town square. More importantly, as far as community is concerned, there were wide opportunities for participation in the political life of Athens.

I have already discussed the rights of citizens in the Athenian city-state, the existence of the Council of Five Hundred, the assembly, and the selection of officials. With regard to participation in the assembly, for example, all citizens could take time off to attend its sessions if they so wished. And the fact that people were paid (though very little) for sitting in the jury courts and on the council meant that even the poorer citizens could, in principle, play an active role in the political life of Athens if they so desired.

Aside from the considerable opportunities for political participation, there seems to have been a fair measure of actual participation. The evidence, some of it archaeological, indicates that attendance at the assembly in fifth-century Athens was sometimes as high as six thousand persons.[112] If there were some forty thousand citizens (as I estimated earlier), then the maximal percentage attending the assembly at any one time was about 15 percent. But presumably very few citizens attended every single session of the assembly, so that the percentage who attended at one time or another was probably much higher than 15 percent.

A perhaps more accurate estimate of the extent of political participation is provided by Finley with regard to the Council of Five Hundred. He cites evidence indicating that "in any decade, something between a fourth and a third of the total citizenry over thirty would have been Council members, serving daily (in principle) throughout the year and for a tenth of the year on full duty."[113] In addition to this, says Finley, we must add the thousands who had court experience as well as those hundreds who served in one or another official capacity, and those many citizens who served abroad in the army and the navy.

It is, of course, very difficult to assess the significance of these figures. Lacking a more precise term to describe the extent of political participation among citizens in the Athenian polis, I have above used the words "a fair measure." There is, in any case, no support for the claim by some scholars that actually very few citizens attended meetings of the assembly and that most citizens were concerned only with the struggle for existence.[114] Nor is it true, to take the other extreme, that fifth-century Athens was characterized by widespread and active participation in civic affairs by practically everyone.

Despite the suggestions to the contrary by MacIntyre and other communitarians, it seems likely that only a minority of citizens regularly exercised their minds with political concerns. As P. J. Rhodes notes, even the most conscientious members probably did not attend all the meetings of the boule (council). And not every member was conscientious.[115] With the "ecclesia" (assembly), attendance was low except in times of crises, although there was probably a "reasonable nucleus of politically-minded Athenians."[116] Furthermore, the boule may have been somewhat biased toward the wealthy. A surviving list of members of the boule from a period in the fifth century B.C. seems to show that wealthy families were overrepresented.[117]

Whatever term one uses to indicate the amount of participation in the council, assembly, and other political affairs in Athens, there is the separate issue of the "quality" of the participation. As mentioned earlier, it seems that political leadership in Athens was long monopolized by a fairly small circle of the rich elite, and the demos never produced spokesmen in the assembly from their own ranks. Nevertheless, the presence of several thousand men at a meeting of the assembly, with the presentation of views by various speakers and voting by a show of hands, all indicate that people were deeply involved in the making and unmaking of policies for the governing of Athens. Their participation, it seems safe to say, was very "real" indeed. With regard to the requirement of participation, then, Athens was apparently a community for a large portion of its citizens. At the very least, such participation was far more common in the Athenian world than in the Middle Ages, early America, or in our Western world today.

I turn now to the last characteristic in my working definition of community: solidarity. At issue here is the extent and direction of fellow feeling and mutual concern among Athenian citizens. To what extent were they concerned with the welfare of the polis itself, and to what extent was there reciprocity, sharing, and looking after the members of the community?

Consider, first, the concern of Athenian citizens for the polis. I earlier quoted Finley as saying that nearly all citizens would have agreed that the good life was possible only in a polis. Beyond that, they seem to have felt that the basic social structure and the value system were fundamentally the right ones for them. This "feeling," Finley notes, was an unreflective, habitual judgment about the legitimacy of the vast inequalities between the rich and the poor.[118] Athenian citizens appear to have been highly patriotic and very much concerned with the national interest. The Athenian polis was able to command sustained allegiance from its citizens.

While they were concerned with the community as a collective whole, Athenian citizens were hardly concerned with the well-being of all the individual citizens who made up the community. As I noted earlier, there existed a system of community patronage in which the wealthy citizens provided for temples, festivals, feasts, and other facilities and activities that were used for common purposes. Even though the assimilation of liturgies to magistracies served to maintain the status and influence of the rich and keep the poorer citizens out of office, the prevalence of this community patronage does seem to indicate some concern on the part of the rich for the mass of poor citizens.

This sort of "ritualized affirmation of inequality," as Barrington Moore terms it, obviously allows the rich to display their wealth and munificence.[119] But it can also be advantageous to the poor under certain conditions. Moore suggests that such displays are not only acceptable but desired under two conditions: first, that the masses believe that the elites whose display they enjoy are serving a purpose that they themselves approve, and second, that "people perceive the display as a manifestation of the greatness and achievement of *their* society."[120] Both of these conditions were fulfilled, I believe, in the Athenian polis.

In addition to community patronage as an indicator of solidarity and mutual concern, there were also what might be regarded as certain "welfare state" benefits in the Athenian city-state. In Athens there was, for example, massive economic support for poor citizens through large-scale employment in the navy. There was also, as mentioned earlier, pay for office, which Finley says was a "form of permanent, governmental 'subsistence crisis insurance.' " He then adds: "Nothing else in classical institutions so enraged anti-democratic publicists."[121] On the other hand, there is nowhere a suggestion that public works were ever undertaken to provide employment for the urban poor in Athens.[122] It seems to me that Michael Walzer's conclusion about welfare provisions in fifth-century Athens is essentially correct: "they did distribute public funds to balance somewhat the inequalities of Athenian society."[123]

As I indicated in chapter 1, to ask whether there is a high degree of solidarity is to ask whether the communal obligations and responsibilities are both special and personal. The obligations of fifth-century Athenian citizens were certainly special: they extended only to other citizens of the polis. In other words, feelings of social interdependence and responsibility involved solely that 20 percent of the population who were fellow citizens.

We cannot, however, consider people's obligations and responsibilities as really being personal, that is , as running from each member of the community to each of the other members. Given the division between rich and poor within the citizen ranks as well as the size of Athens, the primary bonds were to others of the same class standing and not to all other community members. Certainly for the rich, their own lives were viewed as far more important and mutually involved with one another than was their concern for the poor citizens. At the level of relationships among individuals, then, attitudes of mutual concern do not seem to have been very strong in fifth-century Athens.

Still, compared with the situation in revolutionary America and in the Middle Ages, the Athenian polis very much resembles a full-fledged community. Its citizens occupied a common territory, had a common history and many shared values, participated together in political and other activities, and showed some degree of solidarity.

Recall, however, how exclusive this Athenian community was: it excluded slaves, women, and members of the subject states in the empire. I estimated earlier that it was made up of maximally 20 percent of the total population, that is, solely of male citizens. And yet Aristotle, as noted, claimed that the Athenian polis was not exclusive enough. For he opposed the equality found in Athens, where every citizen had an equal vote. His fear, as he demonstrated in several passages concerning the ideal state, was that the minority of rich property owners would have their property confiscated by the numerical majority of poor citizens.

Thus, it is difficult to accept MacIntyre's many claims about the community as depicted by Aristotle. MacIntyre writes of a "community whose shared aim is the realisation of the human good," and acknowledges that this presupposes agreement "in that community on goods and virtues."[124] He goes on to say that a shared recognition of and pursuit of a good "is essential and primary to the constitution of any form of community, whether that of a household or that of a city."[125] This notion of community, MacIntyre emphasizes, is alien to the modern liberal individualistic world. We have no conception of community as a common project "concerned as Aristotle says the polis is concerned, with the whole of life, not with this or that good, but with man's good as such."[126]

But that is just the problem; Aristotle never specifies "man's good as such." More important, he is actually more concerned with the good of man than he is with the good of human beings. Okin points out that "although the Aristotelian tradition, as presented by MacIntyre, is supposedly aimed at the human good, only those whose productive, reproductive, and daily needs are fully taken care of by others, and who are therefore free to engage in the highest goods—political activity and intellectual life—are regarded as fully human."[127] If, as MacIntyre holds, the realization of community presupposes agreement about the human good, then he must recognize what is entailed in appealing to the sort of Athenian polis where the human good as such is that attainable only by a minority of rich males.

Since morality for MacIntyre is mainly a matter of the virtues, he seems to intend that the virtues are intrinsic goods. But no more than Aristotle does he specify *which* virtues are intrinsically good for everyone. Thus, we are left uninformed as to how the Aristotelian tradition can assist us in trying to construct "local forms of community within which civility and the intellectual and moral life can be sustained through the dark ages which are already upon us."[128]

# LEARNING FROM HISTORY

MOST THINKING about community, as Thomas Bender points out, assumes a rather simple and direct relationship between past and present. "In the past, there was community; in the present it has been (or is being) lost."[1] As noted earlier, community has been an important topic in sociology from its beginning. Nineteenth-century social theorists often compared those communal forms of association that they saw as characteristic of the past with their absence in the modern world. Continuing to the present, the disappearance of community has been a central theme in sociology. More recently, of course, moral philosophers, political theorists, and scholars from other disciplines have come to mourn the demise of community. For communitarian thinkers and ordinary people alike, social change has come to mean the destruction of community.

But the evidence presented in earlier chapters questions the usefulness of the community/society dichotomy. For we have seen that community was *not* prominent in the periods so often celebrated by these communitarians: classical Athens, medieval Europe, or the founding period of America. In those times and places, community existed only among that 20 percent of the Athenian population made up of privileged, property-owning male citizens. Given the general absence of community, we must question whether this typological approach really captures the differences between the past and the present.

The work of both nineteenth-century social theorists and various communitarian thinkers today distinguishes traditional or premodern from modern societies. They all refer to a change from a past world characterized by localism, continuity, tradition, and harmony to a modern world dominated by displacement, interruption, novelty, and conflict. Those features associated with an integrated past have been replaced by features connected with a disintegrated present. Rapid social change is described as being responsible for the demise of community. But if the sort of community depicted by communitarian thinkers did not exist in the past, then it obviously cannot be said to have given way to the forces of modernization.

This is not to deny, of course, that life in classical Athens, medieval Europe, early America, and in other times and places in the past was different than it is in most places today. Of course it was. The point is that life in those periods does not seem to have had much in common with the idealized depictions presented by social theorists of the last century and communitarian thinkers today. The historical prevalence of the kind of community they describe is a fiction. It rests on a myth that looks to the past for reassurance and guidance.

Myths are often important, of course, in providing people with shared meanings and agreements about their social and spiritual world. But myths are not only beliefs *about* something. Myths are also beliefs *in* something. With regard to community, these are beliefs in people being linked to one another by continuity in time and space; being united by common traditions and shared values; being committed to the common good, and so forth. Communitarians have a conception of community in which its various components are represented as a seamless web. This is a myth of fundamentalism. As much as possible, it wants to animate those aspects of community that (it is believed) bind people together and provide for peace and harmony.

But along with their belief in community, those taking the communitarian perspective believe that this sort of community was actually prevalent in the past. How, then, can we explain these various scholars being so mistaken in their beliefs about community? What were the bases for the claims about community set forth by Tönnies and other nineteenth-century social theorists? What evidence does MacIntyre call upon in speaking of people in earlier periods sharing membership in one or another community? What underlies Sandel's assertion that a politics of the common good, mutual concern, social solidarity, and a shared understanding united Americans in the founding period? What is the foundation for the claims in *Habits of the Heart* that the founding generation consisted of a self-governing group of relative equals who participated together in open discussion and decision making? I want to consider this matter of their misconceptions before moving on, later in this chapter, to discuss the preconditions and consequences of community, and the failure of a politics of the common good.

I

It seems to me that there are several factors involved in the communitarians' mistaken beliefs about the past. To begin with, criticism of the various shortcomings of their own society may have led some communitarian thinkers to nostalgic and unrealistic views about earlier historical periods. Positing an ideal social order as having once existed not only helped explain how change came about and oriented them to the present but undoubtedly led to an idealization of the past. Thus Weber, in contrasting modern fragmentation to the unity of classical Athens, spoke of the "full and beautiful humanity" of earlier eras.[2] Other nineteenth-century theorists also reacted to the conditions of their day by conceiving of the past as being characterized by a full and beautiful humanity. The same is true for MacIntyre, Sandel, the authors of *Habits of the Heart*, and other communitarian thinkers today. Their emphasis on the fragmentation, dissolution, and emptiness of modern society seems to make it difficult for them to see the past other than through rose-colored glasses.[3] Pessimism, despair, and anger about modern society become associated with an idealized portrait of community in the past.

Related to this, communitarian theorists give surprisingly little attention to what might be termed the historical record. This is certainly the case with MacIntyre and Sandel, and with Bellah and his associates to a lesser extent. They refer to the prevalence of community in the past while using only a small number of historical sources. Empirical studies in local history are almost totally ignored, and research in social history more generally is given little attention. In other words, these contemporary communitarians make insufficient use of current historical scholarship.[4]

This does not, however, explain the many mistaken claims by nineteenth-century social theorists about community in the Middle Ages, some of which are accepted by sociologists today. Scholars like Durkheim, Weber, and Tönnies were extremely well-read in fields outside their own. They closely followed the work of their contemporaries in social history and cultural anthropology, especially as it pertained to questions of family structure, property relations, and variations and changes in forms of social organization. But, as I observed in chapter 4, there is now far more complete and reliable evidence about these matters than existed a century ago. Thus, another factor accounting for erroneous views about community in the past is the inadequacy of much traditional historiography. A good deal of what constituted the received wisdom of a hundred years ago is now considered to be without foundation.

An idealization of the past as a reaction to what are seen as the ills of modern society, insufficient attention to relevant historical research, and a reliance on inadequate evidence, then, are three factors that help explain the mistaken historical claims of communitarian scholars. But the most important factor explaining their mistaken view is perhaps their tendency to see the effects of culture as monolithic within a collectivity. Culture is assumed not only to penetrate all aspects of social life but to do so in the same way for everyone.

Durkheim, for example, spoke of "collective representations": the cognitive classifications, shared meanings, and ordering frameworks provided by the group and internalized by the individual. Emphasizing the crucial influence of these collective representations, he said that "if men did not agree upon these essential ideas at every moment, if they did not have the same conception of time, space, cause, number, etc., all contact between their minds would be impossible, and with that, all life together."[5]

Durkheim argued that different societies have different habits of thought, interpretations of reality, ways of experiencing their worlds, beliefs about external objects or forces, and the like. He recognized, of course, that each individual probably experiences the world slightly differently from every other individual. But by reifying society, Durkheim gave very little scope to individual reason. Thus, he accepted that everyone in a particular society shared the same way of thinking.

Tönnies had a similar conception about the Middle Ages. Thus, he seemed to assume that medieval Europe was a single, undifferentiated, closed society in which everyone had the same habits of thought. Assuming a homogeneity in thought, Tönnies emphasized what there was in common among the prince or king, the wealthy noble, and the peasant who tilled the noble's fields. It is no wonder that Tönnies saw the gemeinschaft as being characterized by common folkways and mores, shared customs, time-honored understandings, and relationships of intimacy, trust, and cooperation.

The positions of Durkheim and Tönnies had much in common with research this century in the history of mentalities.[6] There, too, the emphasis is on shared habits of thought, implicit assumptions, belief systems, daily routines, collective mentalities, and frameworks of life.[7] Consequently, the results of research on one or another narrow stratum of a society are extended by implication to the rest of that society. A homogeneous culture common to peasants, urban artisans, merchants, and noblemen in preindustrial Europe is often taken for granted.

As Susan Reynolds points out, however, some references to mentalities seem to assume—rather than argue—a homogeneity of thought.[8] It has long been assumed, for example, that no one in the Middle Ages was capable of atheism or skepticism. Reynolds observes in this connection that the belief that religious skepticism was foreign to the Middle Ages seems to be shared by "French *Annalistes* and British empiricists, Marxists and non-Marxists, catholics, protestants, and agnostics, historians of politics, of the economy, and of culture and thought."[9] This itself, notes Reynolds, might strike some persons as a perfect example of the kind of shared assumption that is an indicator of a prevailing "mentality." But, she points out, not *all* historians share this assumption. Some scholars have produced convincing evidence of impiety, skepticism, and even atheism in the Middle Ages.[10] In other words, what was thought to be beyond people's capacity to call into doubt *was* doubted by at least some persons. Even so, many historians continue to view medieval Europe as a single, homogeneous, closed society with a common mentality.[11]

Nineteenth-century social theorists and contemporary historians of mentalities are not the only ones to reach unwarranted conclusions because of their holistic approach. Some historians of America's founding period also assume that people in those days uniformly shared the same perspective on the world. Robert Brown and Forrest McDonald, for example, have strongly attacked the arguments of "Progressive" historians like Carl Becker and Charles Beard,[12] who challenged the idea that the Revolution was a movement of a united people. They call into question the diversity emphasized by these earlier historians and emphasize instead the extent to which revolutionary Americans were a unified and undifferentiated people.[13]

But it is the influential analyses of republican ideology by Bernard Bailyn, J.G.A. Pocock, and Gordon Wood, with their claim that the whole revolutionary generation shared a universe of political discourse, that have had the most impact as far as conceptions of community in the founding period are concerned. Bailyn and the others have surveyed vast bodies of writings—pamphlets, letters, essays, songs, broadsheets— in their quest to determine the impact of republican thinking on the founding generation.

According to the "republican synthesis," the political language that the Americans inherited shaped their hopes, their discontents, and the way they saw the world. The shared assumptions of speakers, writers, and their audiences were all-important. Both Sandel and the authors of *Habits of the Heart* draw on these republican revisionist historians to support their claim that republican ideology was dominant in America's founding period and was then supplanted by liberalism.

But those historians advocating the republican synthesis have been severely criticized by many of their fellow historians. For one thing, they have been accused of leaving too little room for the contributions of individual thinkers. Ralph Lerner observes that the founders are portrayed as "enmeshed in a net of meanings, intentions, and significations largely not of [their] making and largely beyond [their] control."[14] Bailyn, for example, speaks of a "structured universe of classical thought" that served "as the intellectual medium through which Americans perceived the political world."[15] Historians in the republican tradition, Lerner points out, are more concerned with "discursive communities" than with the possible contributions of individual thinkers. Meanings are, in their view, not in the mind but in the world. Habits of thought are viewed as all-determining.[16] Like Durkheim, Bloch, and members of the *Annales* school, they underemphasize the ability of individuals to go beyond dominant conventions and ideologies.

Joyce Appleby, a persistent critic of republican revisionism, suggests that these historians have uncritically accepted ideas from Clifford Geertz's cultural anthropology and Thomas Kuhn's work in the history of science. "Neither seventeenth-century England," where classical republicanism had its source, "nor eighteenth-century America was in any way comparable to the small, closed, cohesive communities described by Geertz and Kuhn. Instead, both countries were intellectually as well as culturally pluralistic."[17] In emphasizing what the revolutionary generation supposedly shared, those many elements that set people apart— class, region, gender, religion—are given insufficient attention.[18]

Although the authors of *Habits of the Heart* base their analysis of America's founding period partly on the writings of historians who advance the republican synthesis, they never claim that the republican ideology was all-determining. Instead, they argue that the civic republican tradition existed alongside a biblical tradition in early America. Today, they believe, the moral vocabulary of individualism has almost completely supplanted the languages of the civic republican and biblical traditions in the United States.

Since Bellah and his associates include the biblical along with the republican tradition, they make more allowance for ideological pluralism than do those historians who emphasize solely the republican ideology. Nevertheless, Bellah and his associates also assume a somewhat reductive and deterministic account of political and moral language. Like others with a communitarian leaning, they emphasize the importance of what is shared: traditions, practices, ideology, discourse, values, symbols, meanings, and understandings. In fact, what distinguishes the "Bellah school" from most other sociological approaches is just this stress on the crucial significance of culture.[19]

*Habits of the Heart* is, in a sense, a celebration of the community-forming power of culture. Although their argument about the existence of both biblical and republican strands in America's founding period might seem to suggest that those speaking one language were estranged from those speaking the other, Bellah and his associates avoid this conclusion by noting that "in much of American history, the republican tradition has been closely linked to the biblical tradition."[20]

In the founding period, they argue, community in America rested on the shared moral and political languages of the biblical and republican traditions, and on other elements of a common culture. But I believe that they have a far too restricted reading of America's past. By focusing so exclusively on aspects of a shared culture, they fail to recognize the extent to which America's founding period was experienced by different kinds of Americans—farmers, artisans, wealthy northern merchants, the southern gentry, women, blacks—in different ways. Conflict, upheaval, exploitation, oppression, and suffering are largely ignored.

In fact, Bellah and his associates believe that a shared culture was dominant even in the nineteenth century. They note that Tocqueville had pointed to the importance of mores (*moeurs*) for American society in the 1830s, having defined them "variously as 'habits of the heart': notions, opinions and ideas that 'shape mental habits'; and 'the sum of moral and intellectual dispositions of men in society.' "[21] They then go on to observe that the mores which Tocqueville emphasized continued to be dominant throughout the nineteenth century. "Concern for economic betterment was widespread," they write, "but it operated within the context of a still-functional concern for the welfare of one's neighbor." "In the towns," add the authors of *Habits of the Heart*, "the competitive individualism stirred by commerce was balanced and humanized by the restraining influences of a fundamentally egalitarian ethics of community responsibility."[22]

As I showed in chapter 3, however, Tocqueville was too sweeping in his remarks about the background and values of early Americans.[23] In conceptualizing *his* America, Tocqueville generally ignored divisions and categories that would detract from his homogeneous portrait of the American people. In fact, he even projected his description of equality and homogeneity into America's future: "The time will . . . come when one hundred and fifty million men will be living in North America, equal in condition, all belonging to one family, owing their origin to the same cause, and preserving the same civilization, the same language, the same religion, the same habits, the same manners, and imbued with the same opinions, propagated under the same forms."[24]

Tocqueville must certainly have observed enduring inequalities of condition in the America of the 1830s. He was clear in distinguishing what he termed "the three races" from one another, he knew there were Catholics and Jews, and he considered the position of women in some detail. But by describing each race as having its own "destiny apart," by exaggerating the extent to which everyone was of English ancestry, and by complimenting Americans for "carefully dividing the duties of man from those of woman in order that the great work of society may be the better carried on,"[25] Tocqueville could maintain his basic contention about the equality of condition and homogeneity of the American people. As Stephen Frederick Schneck points out, the rhetorical idea of Tocqueville's America required such equality and such homogeneity.[26] Exactly the same seems to be true for the more recent *Habits of the Heart*.

155

Sandel and MacIntyre also argue that individuals in the past were totally absorbed in community and unreflectively accepted the expectations imposed on them by reason of their social positions. Absolute harmony, a convergence of values, and a shared conception of the common good are seen as having characterized earlier periods in our history. People then were historically situated in the dominant traditions of their own particular communities, while we today suffer a fragmented and alienated existence as a result of the absence of community in our lives. Whatever the extent to which community may have existed in the past, a culturally homogeneous, consensus model of society is obviously Sandel's ideal, and pluralism the enemy. The same holds for MacIntyre.

But communitarian thinkers are simply wrong about people ever having actually been epistemologically locked into experiencing reality in exactly the same way as everyone else in their society. Even when the members of a particular collectivity do have many beliefs in common, not everyone believes equally. And some persons may not believe at all. The same goes for all the other aspects of communal life: values, interests, ideas, understandings, and so on. Many people within a particular group may share them, but others may not.

Beyond this, as William Galston points out, people may disagree in their interpretations of even the same core principles, various principles and commitments may contradict one another, and there may be conflicts between specific principles and social practices.[27] These kinds of disagreements and contradictions are inevitable in every society, he observes, because of the clash of interests among different groups, classes, regions, and sectors; because "the sheer diversity of individual types guarantees differences of outlook"; and because reasonable individuals arrive at different conclusions in judging common problems.[28]

In any case, communitarians are simply mistaken in their assumptions about everyone in a group or society sharing a uniform version of the world. It is this assumption more than anything else, I have been suggesting, that explains their many mistaken claims about community in the past.

## II

*Homogeneity as a Precondition for the Communitarian Ideal*

Communitarian thinkers exaggerate, then, the extent to which everyone in a particular collectivity has ever shared the same perspective on the world, the same values and interests, the same standards, loyalties, and so forth. They also exaggerate the extent to which different groups or societies each have their own *distinct* forms of social life, with their own unique concepts, interests, modes of social relationship, and the like. And they are wrong in their claims about the *actual* extent of uniformity in the three historical periods that they so often describe as exhibiting their community ideal: classical Athens, the High Middle Ages, and the founding period in America.

But they are correct in recognizing the importance of homogeneity as a precondition for realizing their conception of community and sustaining a collective identity. Durkheim, Tönnies, Tocqueville, and those communitarians writing today all emphasize the importance of homogeneity. All stress the many ways in which pluralism and diversity threaten the ideal social order to which they aspire.

People with the same national origin, ethnic or racial background, language, religion, and social or educational status are more likely than the members of a heterogeneous group to share a common history and to have similar values. There will be fewer divergent viewpoints and competing interests that can lead to conflict and threaten the group's well-being. In a culturally homogeneous group, then, the prevailing norms, customs, and standards will be more widely shared and accepted than in a highly heterogeneous group.

Central to the normative conception of community is the idea that the common good must take precedence over the good of individual group members. The realization of community requires individuals to accept and internalize a set of norms concerning the good of the collective. Consensus about values, meanings, and understandings helps assure community.

Individuals who grow up in a generally uniform group are likely to incorporate the same normative standards into their personalities, thereby themselves providing the restraining control necessary for peace and harmony. Once these social norms have been accepted and internalized, the community in a sense lives inside each of its members.

Communitarian writers recognize, of course, that individuals sometimes violate (or anticipate violating) the norms and values that they have internalized. But they argue that formal external controls are less often required in genuine communities than elsewhere. This is because a community's members monitor and control themselves. Implicit in the arguments of most communitarians (and sometimes explicit in those with a more sociological orientation) is the belief that the negative sanctions of guilt and shame work to minimize violations of the community's normative standards.

In brief, the realization and maintenance of community depends partly on the group members agreeing about what constitutes the com-

mon good and about the proper means to achieve it. Processes of socialization and education help assure such agreement. And the internaliza-
tion of the relevant norms and values then reduces any potential for
conflict between the interests of individual members and those of the
group. Anyone who violates the shared norms is expected to experience
the internal sanctions of guilt and shame. Thus, external sanctions are
generally unnecessary.[29]

As noted, people who have a common history and a similar cultural
background and spend their lives in one geographic locale are more
likely to share the same norms than are those whose backgrounds and
experiences are highly diverse. Furthermore, they are under the scrutiny
of others who also subscribe to those norms. When their behavior is known
by people with whom they have relatively enduring relationships and
with whom they have much in common, even anticipated violations of
the group's standards and expectations may give rise to feelings of guilt
and shame. Under such circumstances, there is likely to be a high degree
of conformity with the dominant standards and ideals of the community.

In a pluralistic culture, by contrast, individuals and groups will have
very different histories and experiences. With competing and sometimes
incompatible customs, values, and standards, normative consensus will
be lacking. Men and women will find it easier to gain new perspectives
and to accept other ways of thinking. People will be apt to have only a
weak attachment to the place where they live, and a developed con-
sciousness of kind will be missing.

Because of sharing little with others around them and having no
strong attachments to where they live, geographic mobility is likely to be
higher than in a less diverse group. Such mobility minimizes patterned
sequences of family relations, friendships, schooling, religious practice,
and work experiences, so that individuals often have only superficial relationships with those they meet. Without normative consensus about
the good and bad, right and wrong, and the common good for the
group, internal sanctions will be relatively weak and insignificant.

According to Sandel, homogeneity helps assure situated selves with
deep self-knowledge and clear identities. In fact, he relates this to a consideration of totalitarian movements, fragmentation, and social disorder. Sandel states boldly that "intolerance flourishes most where forms
of life are dislocated, unsettled, traditions undone. In our day, the totalitarian impulse has sprung less from the convictions of confidently situated selves than from the confusions of atomized, dislocated, frustrated
selves, at sea in a world where common meanings have lost their force."[30]

Sandel's empirical claim is, however, mistaken. This is shown by Ervin
Staub in his book *The Roots of Evil*, where he attempts to specify the con-

ditions underlying genocide and other group violence. One of the most important conditions, he finds, is a monolithic as opposed to a pluralistic culture or society. "In a monolithic culture there is limited variation in values and perspectives on life. In a monolithic society strong authority or totalitarian rule enforces uniformity."[31] Staub provides numerous instances of people being more susceptible to a narrow ideology in more homogeneous societies.

Contrasting homogeneous societies with those that are pluralistic, Staub writes: "In a pluralistic society with varied conceptions of reality and greater individual self-reliance, people will find it easier to change and gain new perspectives and accept new customs and mores. Reactions against initial harmful acts are more likely to occur and to inhibit the progression along the continuum of destruction."[32] Contrary to what Sandel asserts, Staub argues that it is pluralism, not homogeneity, that is associated with greater tolerance. "In a pluralistic society people are exposed to various values and beliefs and various ways of resolving conflicts; this makes it unlikely that a single cultural blueprint will be accepted and held with certainty."[33]

Cultural pluralism, then, is always a threat to community.[34] To show this more clearly, let me briefly consider two instances that reveal the significance of homogeneity and pluralism: Puritan America and the German hometowns of the seventeenth and eighteenth centuries.

### Puritan Boston

The Puritan settlement of Boston in 1630 represents a clear example of how community depends on social homogeneity and is threatened by heterogeneity. As I noted in chapter 2, John Winthrop's ideal community—his new Jerusalem, his city upon a hill—was very short-lived. This failure to build a lasting community had much to do with Boston's rapid change from a culturally uniform to a highly diverse composition.

The early Puritan settlers shared a similar cultural background. Most of them had been involved in agriculture and small household manufacturing in England. "As a result of the gathering together of first settlers through the personal solicitation of a small group, the rough screening and a natural screening inherent in the necessity of traveling across a dangerous ocean to an unsettled and forbidding land," writes Darrett Rutman in *Winthrop's Boston*, "there was a homogeneity about the first-comers to the town."[35]

This homogeneity was increased by the inclusiveness of the church. As Rutman emphasizes, "[I]t impressed a unity upon the population by demanding that all communicants undergo the common experience of formal admission: the confession of faith publicly given, the ceremonial offer and acceptance of the 'right hand of friendship,' and the acceptance of the covenant to walk in godly ways and give love and respect to all of the church."[36] Furthermore, of course, the fact that these original settlers had all chosen to leave sinful England to found a godly city was a crucial indication of the extent to which there was normative consensus about religious values.

One of the first disrupting factors of the ideal of a cohesive community was conflict about the distribution of land. But this was not the only conflict that created division in the early years of Puritan Boston. By itself, a division of opinion about the allotment of land might not have been decisive. In addition, the church—fundamental to Winthrop's ideal of community—soon proved unable to bind people together for the common good.

The original intention was that town and church government be one. And for a short period, they indeed were. This was largely a result of similarities among the settlers. Winthrop had screened them to assure that only those who supported the godliness of the venture and were diligent in their calling were accepted. He wanted no one who would be troublesome or disruptive. Winthrop and the other leaders continued to screen people in the New World. During the first few years, they refused permission for newcomers to settle unless there was testimony to their character and godliness.

As more and more settlers arrived, however, it became much too difficult to thoroughly screen all newcomers. Consequently, Boston's initially homogeneous population became increasingly heterogeneous. Instead of a population made up of people who came from a small number of English villages, with the men having been involved in the same sorts of work and with many people already knowing one another, there now arrived people from widely differing backgrounds. Many of the newcomers were devout and committed to the success of the community, but others were not. With the change to a much more varied population, the unity of congregation and town was broken only a few years after the founding of this city upon a hill.

As the result of differences between those with a local and those with a cosmopolitan orientation within the gentry; of competition between merchants, fishermen, and others within the "generality"; and of a division between town and church, and even within the church itself, fragmentation and dispute became widespread. More and more men sought material gain and opportunity elsewhere. By the end of the second decade, Winthrop's own sons were scattered from Rumney Marsh to Antigua in the West Indies, from New London in Connecticut to London.[37]

This example of early Boston illustrates the significance of cultural homogeneity for the sort of ideal community championed by communitarian writers today.[38] The importance of homogeneity as a precondition for community is also apparent from Mack Walker's research on German hometowns. Although Walker's *German Home Towns* is not concerned with precisely those sorts of genuine communities advocated by communitarians today, it is nevertheless highly relevant to my concerns here.[39]

## German Home Towns

What Walker calls the "home-towns" of seventeenth- and eighteenth-century Germany were distinct from both cities and villages. They were towns of maximally some ten thousand to fifteen thousand inhabitants, with between two thousand and three thousand *Bürger*, or communal citizens. These hometowns were self-sufficient units, free of outside commerce and distinct from the rural countryside. A general homogeneity in each town's population composition, its geographic separateness, and its historical stability were conditions of the existence of these German hometowns.

The hometownsman, Walker finds, was much more likely than either the peasant or the city dweller to live in the place where he had been born. Comparing the three places of residence, Walker writes:

> The hometownsman was far more intimately involved with the total life of his community than either the city dweller or the peasant because all of the spheres of his activities fell within the same boundary walls, and so did the activities of all his neighbors. The peasant lived close to his neighbors, but economically he was on his own and political power he had none; the city dweller lived by exchange, but among people who were not his neighbors and cousins and whose polity he did not actively share; the hometownsman lived by exchange among people he intimately knew and whose polity he fully shared.[40]

By the end of the eighteenth century, Walker estimates, there were some four thousand German hometowns—together making up about a quarter of the total German population.[41] Each of these isolated hometowns was regulated by a set of unwritten customs expressing the will and beliefs of the community. These customs—and the practices in which they were expressed—provided a source of integration and social cohesion.

A complex system of informal arrangements served to resolve internal disputes and "to smother conflicting emotions" without resort to formal procedures.[42] The smothering of friction, argues Walker, was "the internal key to the preservation of the community's individuality and autonomy."[43] Hometown standards and hometown means of coercion were diffuse and unspecialized, and they operated in all spheres of community life. The imposition of almost total conformity worked to suppress conflict and maintain social order.

The hometown weltanschauung shared a strong sense of hierarchy and status, although Walker says that this sense was far less important than the kind of moral equality that existed among men as citizens of the same hometown community. There was, in one sense, a real egalitarianism in hometown life: every hometownsman was equally subject "to limits placed both on opportunity to rise and upon liability to fall."[44]

It is interesting that Walker speaks only of the "hometownsman" and never of the "hometownswoman." But it is clear that no women, no poor men, no Jews, no radicals, and no other "outsiders" qualified for citizenship in these German hometowns. And to be without citizenship, as Walker notes, was not only to be without the vote but also to have no right to pursue a citizen's trade, to be eligible for office, to have an established home, to own community property, or to be able to marry.[45]

The community regarded every hometownsman personally as one citizen, workman, and neighbor. All three of these aspects were important for the grant of the *Bürgerrecht* by the community. Since a man's every transaction participated in all three areas, the hometown was constantly able to exercise both a monitoring and a sanctioning capacity. Walker points out that "the hometownsman did not leave his home and polity to do his productive work, returning at night to domestic and civic life in another life in another time of day; when he sold a suit of clothes his role as neighbor and citizen was involved."[46] A man's actions, in short, were known to everyone. There was no escaping the scrutiny of others.

And when a hometowner's conduct failed to meet community standards, sanctions came into play. "A bad craftsman," writes Walker, "found neither friends nor influence; the morally deviant found neither customers nor office; political contrariness tainted a man's workshop and the tavern he frequented. Community citizenship was what he had, and he had it all the time, his pride and his prison."[47]

Communal ties and communal membership rested on the rights of the German hometowns to choose their own members. "No shit-hens fly over the town wall" was the hometown refrain.[48] The hometown selected who its members should be through the imposition of indirect tests and long scrutiny so as to make sure of a candidate's suitability for membership. Both the rural peasantry and the nobility were regarded with resentment and contempt. And those whom Walker calls "movers and doers"—traveling merchants, court lawyers, and the academically trained, for instance—were also treated as aliens.[49] Community boundaries severely identified despised outsiders.

Membership in the German hometown was totally at the pleasure of an individual's fellow citizens. In order to marry, a man needed the approval of the community. He could lose his citizenship if he married an outsider whom the community would not accept or if he entered an "unsuitable" occupation. It was almost as difficult to leave a German hometown as to get in. Someone who renounced his citizenship was forced to pay an emigration tax, amounting to about 10 percent of his property.[50]

An emphasis on the primacy of communal membership, mistrust of floating individuals, and hostility toward the outside, argues Walker, were the hometown legacy to the Germany of the late nineteenth century and the first half of the twentieth.[51] While he is careful to avoid equating hometowns ideals with National Socialism, Walker points to obvious similarities between the hometown and the theory and practice of National Socialism. "The pogroms and political persecutions of the Third Reich are quite on the pattern of hometown drives after ground-rabbits and outsiders, now elevated into national state policy. The enemies National Socialism proclaimed to be German enemies were hometown enemies; it chose them for its guise as defender and restorer of the true Germany."[52] Whatever else may be said, the failure of the Third Reich ought to have effectively destroyed the idea of national community.

# III

## The Dangers of Pursuing the Communitarian Ideal

Although community in the full sense described by various nineteenth-century social theorists and by communitarian thinkers today has seldom been realized, the *quest* for a monolithic community has a long history. Whatever the impulse, desire, or romantic dream underlying the pursuit of community, history shows many attempts to achieve it. Such attempts continue to this day.

One lesson to be learned from this, I believe, is that the pursuit of community often has very negative consequences for those who are to be excluded from membership. This is true for those forms of social organization that do succeed as communities for at least a short period of time such as early Boston, for those highly restricted communities like classical Athens, and for those various attempts to achieve community during this century.

Any people aspiring to community must decide on the criteria of membership before they decide on anything else. It is in the nature of the communitarian ideal that membership is restricted to those having certain things in common: place of habitation, ancestors, language, tradition, religion, cultural patterns, and the like. The salience of these attributes rests not only on difference but also on an assumption of hierarchy. That is to say, evaluation of difference commonly has an explicitly normative basis. A genuine community is marked off from other groups and individuals by what its members see as *their* distinctive characteristics.

This is not to suggest, of course, that those aspiring to community consciously and as a group make an explicit decision about the criteria of membership. Instead, latent attitudes for and against certain racial, religious, or other groups often become fully manifest only when the move toward community is underway.

A frequent consequence of the salience of ancestry, tradition, religion, or other cultural characteristics, then, is that those who are different will be designated as *inferior* and excluded from political membership. In the case of Winthrop's communal experiment in early Boston, membership excluded as unworthy those who did not support the godliness of the venture or were not diligent enough in their calling. With the hometowns of seventeenth- and eighteenth-century Germany, the rural peasants, the nobility, and "movers and doers" were treated with suspicion and distrust, and excluded from membership. Community members were concerned that "no shit-hens fly over the town wall." To the extent that those property-owning men of the same racial background constituted a cultural community in classical Athens, women, slaves, and barbarians were defined as unworthy and deprived of the rights of citizenship.

The same mechanism seems to operate wherever a strong communitarian ideal is dominant. Common identification as a group with the same attributes always entails reference to those lacking such attributes and results in policies of exclusion. Certainly a collectivity that sees itself as a chosen people or its land as the promised land will attempt to exclude those who are different.[53]

The excluded may be defined as nonhuman barbarians, as heathens or heretics, as genetically deficient, or simply as strangers or outsiders. But they are always viewed as inferior. Concretely, those excluded from community membership have tended to be foreigners, women, racial and ethnic minorities, and the poor. One consequence of the homogeneity required for realizing the communitarian ideal, then, is oppositional differentiation from other, lesser individuals and groups.

Once a distinction is made between those inside and those outside the community, various mechanisms operate to keep the borders between them firmly drawn. Physical, social, psychic, and behavioral boundaries all help maintain the distinction between those who belong to the community and those who do not. These boundaries prevent or minimize the influence of people with different ideas or opposing values and ways of life.

Various rules about leaving the locale, about who is allowed to enter, and about the extent of permissible contact with visitors help maintain a community's physical separation from the surrounding environment. They function to create strong psychic boundaries concerning its membership. By preventing contaminating contact with outsiders—barbarians, Jews, blacks, gypsies, communists—the community avoids threats to its own status as unique and superior. The community itself is conceptualized positively and the outside negatively.[54]

Thus movement toward the realization of community is frequently accompanied by feelings of dislike, contempt, and even hatred toward individuals and groups with different traditions, languages, religions, racial origins, values, and real or mythical histories and experiences. The examples of the Puritan settlement in early Boston, the German hometowns of the seventeenth and eighteenth centuries, classical Athens, those intentional communities studied by sociologists and historians, such groups as the Mennonites and Amish, and—above all—the ominous emphasis on *das Volk* in Germany make it clear that hostility toward outsiders is often a consequence of differentiating one's own community from other groups.[55]

Such social differentiation may also, of course, have consequences for people who have heretofore considered themselves to be essentially like the dominant majority. In the same way that the logic of identity creates an insider/outsider distinction, it turns insiders into outsiders. In such instances, people may be excluded from membership or banned from the territory. This may occur because they are perceived as having a racial, religious, or social background different from what is valued in terms of the dominant ideal. This sometimes occurs in opposition to the excluded people's own self-definition. In other words, exclusion from the cultural community leads to exclusion from the wider political community.

The very *attempt* to achieve a monolithic community may create, then, a category of outsiders or enemies. This may be accompanied by the withdrawal or refusal of the rights of citizenship. The case of the Jews in Germany and Austria in the 1930s is a tragically clear example. In emphasizing the integrity of the organic *body* of the German *Volk* as the embodiment of racial-cultural superiority, Hitler and the Nazis made a sharp differentiation between "us" and "them." The achievement of genuine community, they believed, demanded the exclusion of those who were not racially pure. Gypsies, eastern Europeans, Jews, and many others were viewed as inferior and a threat to racial purity.[56]

Consider the situation in Vienna. Those Jews who migrated to Vienna at the turn of this century from their homes in Bohemia, Moravia, Galicia, and Hungary very quickly ceased to dress, talk, and behave like small-town "shtetl" Jews and became Viennese burghers. As Marsha Rozenblit points out, "they abandoned Yiddish for German, traditional Jewish names for proper German ones, Jewish costumes for the styles of . . . [modern] Europe."[57]

Viennese writers such as Arthur Schnitzler thought of themselves, says Steven Beller, as "Germans, members of German culture, people who spoke German and shared the literature." They showed a great love for things German, and "German became a synonym among Jews for all that was liberal, just, and progressive."[58]

This was for many non-Jews the problem. As Jews became more similar to their Christian countrymen in Germany, France, and elsewhere in Europe, they became culturally indistinguishable and socially invisible. Because of the disappearance of social and religious distinctions, Jews and Christians could not always be differentiated.

"Having become a citizen like any other and mixing with Christians through marriage," notes Patrick Girard, "the Jew was no longer recognizable."[59] For some anti-Semites, however, it was just this that was significant. Thus we find Edouard Drumont, the author of the pamphlet *Jewish France*, writing: "A Mr. Cohen, who goes to synagogue, who keeps kosher is a respectable person. I don't hold anything against him. I do have it in for the Jew who is not obvious."[60]

Differences had, therefore, to be created. As Hannah Arendt remarked, Judaism was replaced by Jewishness. "Jews had been able to escape from Judaism into conversion; from Jewishness there was no escape."[61] An earlier, cultural anti-Semitism came to be replaced by a much more vicious, racial anti-Semitism. With cultural anti-Semitism, Jewishness was defined as something based on certain cultural characteristics. But by becoming fully German, Jews felt that they would no longer be defined by those characteristics. With racial anti-Semitism, however, there was no possibility of Jews becoming Germans. In resting their own innate superiority on the basis of racial purity, Aryans defined their Germanness in a way that excluded those of Jewish ancestry.[62] Insiders had become outsiders and were now the enemy. A gemeinschaft of the blood had assured their exclusion.

The creation of differences and the devaluation of those who do not fit in appears to accompany every attempt to achieve a monolithic community. With Austria and Germany in the 1930s, with the Turkish genocide of the Armenians earlier in the century, and with the move toward independence and self-identity in eastern European countries in this last decade of the twentieth century, similar processes have been at work. Glorification of one's own group, its purity and greatness, leads to ostracism of those of another racial or national background.[63]

This can be seen with eastern Europe in recent years. The turmoil in the early 1990s brought a surge of anti-Gypsy feeling in Romania, Poland, and elsewhere. And thousands of Hungarians had to flee Romania because of ethnic hatred. In both Czechoslovakia and Yugoslavia, ill will and resentment against minorities was widespread. Those with minority status, as well as Gypsies, and the small surviving Jewish population in eastern Europe, have all experienced an increase in violence and prejudice since communism loosened its grip.

Ironically, the spread of democratic ideas and increased freedom of expression have been accompanied by an explosion of strong collective sentiments about community, tradition, identity, and the idea of one's people occupying a special place in history. This has led, in turn, to the smothering of democracy and the freedom of expression for those minorities who are perceived as outsiders. The Soviet Union and Yugoslavia have been the most obvious examples of this phenomenon.[64]

The moral thrust of the communitarian ideal, then, is simultaneously to unite and divide. This is the case with an intentional commune, a neighborhood, a village, a town, a city, or a nation. For the attempt to realize community not only requires a strong sense of solidarity and belonging but also seems to require the presence of enemies within and without.

Beyond this, one people's pursuit of community may be at odds with another people's vision of community. Conflict and even all-out war may result from the existence of multiple groups that are unalterably committed and obligated to the good of their particular group simply because it *is* theirs. History is rich in such examples.

## IV

### *The Failure of a Politics of the Common Good*

I noted earlier that the new communitarians advocate giving up the "politics of rights" for a "politics of the common good."[65] Imagine, then, that society is to be organized on the basis of a politics of the common good. What exactly *should* be the conception of the common good that people accept? MacIntyre repeatedly insists that we need "a conception of *the* good," Sandel says that we can know a good in common that we cannot know alone, and Bellah and his associates speak of the common good as "that which benefits society as a whole."[66] They go on to ask, "Is it possible that we could become citizens again and together seek the common good in the post-industrial, postmodern age?"[67]

If community in America or elsewhere were to be created by people coming to be united by a shared understanding of the common good, the question is *whose* conception of the common good this should be. The historical record certainly suggests that the conception would be one serving the interests of the rich and powerful. This has been so through the ages.

It is, in fact, a crucial weakness of the communitarians' celebration of the past that they almost totally ignore the extent to which the rhetoric of the common good has tended to benefit those with wealth, power, and privilege. As Susan Moller Okin observes, "Oppressors often claim that they, aristocrats or Brahmins or men, are fully human in ways that serfs or untouchables or women are not, and that while the rulers institutionalize equal justice among themselves, it is both just and in the common interest for them to require the other categories of people to perform functions supportive of the fully human existence of those capable of it."[68]

Aristotle's *Politics* is, of course, the originator of communitarian thinking and of the idea of a politics of the common good. For Aristotle, the Greek polis was the paradigmatic form of community required for assuring the common good. Society was viewed as an organism whose parts exercise the specific functions required by "our" way of life. In the *Politics*, the individual was perceived as an agent or extension of the state and was evaluated on the basis of his or her contribution to the good of society. A whole/part model was assumed, with the few and the many performing their respective functions.

As a blend or balance of the whole, the few and the many had their appropriate roles and special contributions toward achievement of the public good. The "few" or the "best" were the citizen elite, characterized by property and leisure, and by wisdom and experience. Their special virtue was to lead and to rule. The "many," or the remainder of the citizens, contributed to the common good through participating in the political process and being involved in decision making under the guidance and direction of the enlightened few.

As shown earlier, the politics of the common good favored by Aristotle and governing the institutional arrangements of ancient Athens required the subordination and exploitation of the vast majority of the population. For along with those parts of the organism which assured the good of the whole, there were those other "elements" whose functions were indispensable to society. Slaves, women, foreigners, craftsmen, and traders all fit into this category.

Aristotle considered the majority of human beings as intended by nature to be the instruments for assuring that the few—the rich and leisured—reach *their* highest good. This meant that 80 percent of the total population were excluded from membership in the Athenian community. Of course, the one-fifth of the population composed of Greek gentlemen were ruling with an eye to "the common good."[69] But pursuit of that common good rested on the exploitation and oppression of four-fifths of the population.

Athenian women had no political rights, few property rights, and were considered an inferior type of being. Marriage was a matter of paternal wishes and economic considerations, and females were treated as minors. Slaves were totally without rights, and males and females alike were unrestrictedly available for sexual relations with their masters. Flogging and other forms of physical punishment were common. Yet, communitarians barely mention slavery and patriarchy. From the liberal perspective, these social arrangements violated people's basic human rights. They were, therefore, morally unjustifiable.

Like communitarian thinkers today, nineteenth-century social theorists believed that something like a politics of the common good helped to provide community in the Middle Ages. As noted earlier, Christian society was seen as being composed of three orders: nobles, clergy, and peasants. Just as in ancient Athens, individuals were viewed as dependent on an organic social community and were subordinate in hierarchical relationships of political and religious authority. With this doctrine, the three orders formed one societal body or whole. Each, of course, had its own God-given function to perform.

The doctrine of the three orders was stressed by the church and the government as necessary for realization of the common good. The powerful controlled the lives of the weak, and those at the bottom of the natural hierarchy often suffered pain and humiliation. As I noted in chapter 4, the churchmen and warriors governed the economic and social life of the Middle Ages. The specialists in warfare, writes Georges Duby, "lived in idleness and looked upon productive tasks as unworthy of their rank and of that lofty freedom to which they claimed to reserve a preferential right for themselves."[70]

With regard to the workers, the bottom layer who made up the vast majority of the population, each "was persuaded that he or she had to supply the two elites of *oratores* and *bellatores*, those who prayed and those who fought, with the means to sustain their sloth and prodigality. Their specific function which, following the dictates of Providence, doomed them inescapably to a life of reputedly degrading manual labour, deprived them of full liberty."[71] But servility, oppression, exploitation, and feudal plunder are ignored by those communitarians who take medieval Europe as the model of communitarian harmony.

Medieval thought found its most complete expression of the common good in the writings of St. Thomas Aquinas, who provided a synthesis of Aristotelian and Christian conceptions of man and society. Aquinas accepted most of Aristotle's ideas about the origin, nature, and function of the state. He advanced a conception of law as "an ordinance for the common good." Aquinas argued that individuals can be judged only by their contributions to the good of the community; "since a man is part of the city, it is impossible for any man to be good, unless he is properly in conformity with the common good."[72]

The coordination of individual actions toward this common good is the function of "either the whole community or of some person acting in the place of the whole community."[73] Since the universe is governed by God, who is the embodiment of reason, and since all men are his creatures whom he loves, it follows that the ultimate source of all law is God. He has revealed a portion of that law in the form of the Ten Commandments. Monarchy, Aquinas argued, was most like God's method of ruling the universe. It was thus the best form of government. For Aquinas, the ultimate meaning of political society was in its conformity to God's will.

MacIntyre, in his recent *Whose Justice? Which Rationality?* declares his preference for the tradition of Catholic thought, as exemplified in Augustine and modified by Aquinas to include responses to the challenges presented by Aristotle's ethical views.[74] MacIntyre accepts that Catholic norms also derive their status from the political authority of the Catholic church, which, as Martha Nussbaum points out, "imposes agreement concerning basic principles, subduing the disobedient human will." She goes on to observe that "MacIntyre clearly approves of the inculcation of such agreements through a system of education controlled by religious authority."[75]

Like Aquinas, MacIntyre views the "common good" as that which is defined by the Catholic church and the pope, who is its legitimate head. Needless to say, the many millions who have suffered at the hands of the Catholic authorities in the name of the common good would not agree. The structure of the church and its various practices inspired by Aquinas have taken a heavy toll on humanity. Consider heresy trials, inquisitions, excommunications, and censorship, as well as the persecution of homosexuals and the legitimation of sexual repression and discrimination through restrictions on contraception and abortion.

The common good also occupies an important position for those American historians emphasizing the republican perspective. They argue that the revolutionary generation was schooled in the tradition of Aristotle and civic humanism, and that the subordination of the individual interests to the common good was an important part of this tradition. The authors of *Habits of the Heart* also observe that a concern with the common good was central to the founders of the republic.[76]

I pointed out in chapter 2 that the seventeenth-century English settlers in America viewed society as a living organism in which each of its component parts performed the functions necessary for the welfare of the whole. Each member of society was expected to fulfill the function that he or she was allotted, for each functioned for the sake of the common good and not for his or her own sake. All formed part of the great chain of being that ordered the entire universe.

Society was arranged hierarchically, with the king at the top, followed by the nobility and the wealthy gentry, on down to the servants and paupers at the very bottom. Rewards and privileges were distributed on the basis of the capacity of different groups and individuals to contribute to the common good of society.

We saw in earlier chapters that this doctrine of the common good was embraced by wealthy gentlemen in the American colonies to justify the dominant social arrangements. The rhetoric of the classical Aristotelian position was pronounced in America's founding period. Society was viewed as an organic whole, divided among the few and the many. They stood, of course, in a hierarchical relationship, and each had its own special functions and responsibilities.

In Massachusetts, Virginia, and the other colonies, the wealthy gentry saw themselves as the natural aristocracy. They made much of their special contribution to the functioning, health, and harmony of the social whole. Like Aristotle, they advocated a hierarchical political order resting on the natural right of the wise to rule the less wise.

From the perspective of their politics of the common good, it was for the good of the organic community that native Americans were totally excluded from the body politic in the Constitution. And the same held true for that 20 percent of the population who were black slaves. Women, poor men, and free blacks contributed to the welfare of the whole in ways appropriate to their positions in American society. Since women were judged to be incapable of self-control, they were excluded from citizenship in the name of the common good. It was similar with men without property, who, as I noted earlier, John Adams said "have no judgment of their own." Because free blacks were considered childlike, ignorant, and irresponsible, they could contribute most to the common good by being denied the franchise.

White men of wealth and influence were, of course, in a position to decide how the common good was to be defined and realized. And it was obvious to them that the good of society was best guaranteed when the power and authority were in the hands of men like themselves. The revolutionary generation, as shown earlier, was divided between a small group of independent gentlemen and everybody else.[77] The freedom of these rich men from manual labor, and from dependency on others, placed them in a position to exercise influence over the lives and destinies of ordinary men and women. They viewed themselves as a disinterested, enlightened elite. In their view, only they recognized fully what social arrangements were conducive to realizing the common good. The founders wanted to combine the principle of rule by a republican elite with the principle of consent by the people.

It was thus for the common good that gentlemen who were subject to the draft bought substitutes in the revolutionary war, that poor young men in their late teens and early twenties filled the enlisted ranks, and that the officer corps was made up of aristocratic gentlemen. By the 1780s, however, many ordinary Americans were not so certain that the privileged life of wealthy gentlemen was really conducive to realization of the common good. Their resentment gave rise to grave concern by aristocratic gentlemen about the democratic excesses of "the people." They feared the destruction of the natural elite by people who could not recognize their social superiors.[78] This was evident at the Constitutional Convention and thereafter with ratification of the Constitution.

The point here is, I hope, clear; one or another version of a politics of the "common good" has long served to mask the pursuit of special interests and a particular vision of how people ought to be together. And more often than not, it has been rich and powerful white men who have sought to pursue *their* vision of the common good. Whether intentionally or otherwise, various social arrangements benefiting the high-placed and wellborn have been viewed as necessary for the common good. More often than not, talk about the common good has tended to obscure questions about the abuse of power. Communitarian thinkers fail to recognize this.

They also fail to recognize the extent to which arguments for a politics of the common good have almost always taken the same *form* and involve the same *elements*. In classical Athens, medieval Europe, and the founding period of America alike, the same lines of argumentation were involved in doctrines about the common good. Beyond this, I believe, there exists today a version of a politics of the common good in many modern societies.

At least since the time of Aristotle's *Politics*, societies have been regarded as organisms whose parts exercise specific functions for the good of the whole. These parts are viewed as standing in a hierarchical relationship with one another, with each segment being expected to show deference to those above them and to pass on the duty of obedience to those below them. Broadly speaking, as we have seen, the division is between the "few" and the "many." Both groups are expected to stay in their assigned places and perform their proper functions.

The few are usually conceived of as a "natural" aristocracy or elite. They have sometimes been distinguished by birth, as with a hereditary nobility. In other instances, wealth and property have been the distinguishing characteristics. While in principle unusual wisdom, intelligence, or talent might place individuals among the natural aristocracy, it has most often been the material advantages associated with property, learning, and leisure that have assured inclusion among the few.

Along with the elite few, there has always been the vast multitude of the many. In one or another version of a politics of the common good, they may be perceived as an undifferentiated conglomerate or they may be viewed as distinguished on the basis of such characteristics as gender, race, and class position. Whatever the differences among them, the many are expected to accept the few as their natural leaders and to show them the proper deference and respect.

Whoever constitutes the natural aristocracy, it is understood that they may be called on to justify their privileged position in society. This is undoubtedly more true in recent centuries than in Aristotle's day. In any case, it is to be expected that the elite will justify their status as the "few" through reference to the valuable contributions they make to the society as a whole. Because of their presumably scarce and valuable talents, they claim right to a disproportionate share of societal rewards and privileges.

At the same time that the privileged few put forth the case for the social necessity and value of their contributions to the common good, they also usually provide a justification or defense of the very much less privileged position of the vast majority of the society's inhabitants. Aristotle, as we know, said that some men were slaves by nature and that it was thus "better" for them to be subjected to the rule of their masters. And in a book by a Virginia slaveholder, George Fitzhugh, published in 1854, it is asserted that "some men are born with saddles on their backs and others booted and spurred to ride them; *and the riding does them good.*"[79]

In other instances, as was seen earlier, individuals are described as being too dependent upon others to achieve much on their own behalf and thus need the guidance of the natural aristocrats in realizing their proper functions. Thus, the interests of women, blacks, and the poor were best looked after by white gentlemen in America's founding period. This required, so it was claimed, that they be kept in positions of legal and economic inferiority.

But as I noted in quoting Durkheim in an earlier chapter, in order for the majority of persons ("the many") to accept their lot, there must be some authority whose superiority they acknowledge and which tells them what is right. In medieval Europe and in seventeenth- and eighteenth-century America, the church generally gave its support to the unquestioning subordination that characterized the dominant relationships of patriarchy and hierarchy. Women, the poor, and people of color have been widely subjected to an ideological rhetoric in which the privileged elite justify the dominant social arrangements of their society. Not only organized religion but various universal patterns of socialization in the family, as well as formal educational practices, help assure the "naturalness" of relationships of dominance and inequality.

It is perhaps because they show so little awareness of the realities of power that communitarians advocate replacing the politics of rights with a politics of the common good. For in their many references to community in the past, they have almost nothing to say about the widespread physical and mental suffering connected with relationships of unequal power. But as the historian John Womack points out, it is often difficult to believe in other people's pain and suffering. " 'Niggers and Indians don't hurt like white people,' is what the rich believe. And what they believe counts most."[80] History, Womack emphasizes, can teach about pain and show that everybody hurts.

# Chapter 8

## A LIBERAL RESPONSE TO
## COMMUNITARIAN THOUGHT

COMMUNITARIAN thinkers use the historical thesis that community was sustained in earlier historical periods to support their moral and political theories. Much of the impact of their writings rests, in fact, on their depictions of the communal world of the past. Communitarians specify what is morally desirable, and the sorts of relations and social arrangements that ought to be dominant in contemporary societies, by appealing to the past as the source of their moral ideals. Tönnies and other nineteenth-century social theorists sometimes did the same. But in their writings, the moral dimension is much less explicit than with communitarian thinkers today. Nevertheless, both groups attempt to justify a particular way of life by appealing to patterns of social organization and behavior in the past.

The evidence I have presented in earlier chapters shows, of course, that communitarians have been mistaken in their claims about the prominence of community in times gone by. Given the general absence of community in the periods they celebrate, there can be no "renewal" or "restoration" of community. Even so, communitarians do strongly defend the moral urgency of achieving community today. And with or without the actual realization of community, MacIntyre, Sandel, Taylor, and Bellah and his collaborators insist on the superiority of their conceptions of morality and human society over those advanced by champions of individualism and the liberal perspective. Let me consider further, then, the communitarian and liberal standpoints.

## I

In their theories, both contemporary communitarian thinkers and their nineteenth-century counterparts emphasize the primacy of the collective life over that of the individual. That is, they ascribe supreme value to the community itself rather than to its individual members. Those of a communitarian persuasion judge the appropriateness of people's conduct in terms of the requirements of the collective. For them, what counts as good or bad, right or wrong, normal or abnormal on the part

175

of individuals' behavior is derivative from the needs of the community and its realization of the common good.

As I made clear in the previous chapter, however, there may be very serious costs or dangers associated with pursuit of the communitarian ideal. Racism, sexism, exclusion, forced emigration, deportation, and even eradication, I have suggested, are often involved in attempts to achieve community. It is just these sorts of things, of course, that concern liberal thinkers.

But communitarian theorists are writing in response to what they see as the failures of individualism and the liberal perspective. The hallmark of liberalism is, of course, devotion to the individual, especially his or her basic needs and interests. Contemporary communitarians direct their arguments at Kantian and utilitarian approaches in political and moral philosophy. They are especially critical of those sorts of rights-based theories that have been developed since the appearance of John Rawls's influential *A Theory of Justice* in 1971.[1] Liberal thinkers are not only seen as devaluing community, but they are accused of holding a defective conception of the self as well.

### Liberal and Communitarian Selves

"Rights-based liberalism," says Michael Sandel, "begins with the claim that we are separate, individual persons, each with our own aims, interests, and conceptions of the good, and seeks a framework of rights that will enable us to realize our capacity as free moral agents, consistent with a similar liberty for others."[2] With rights-based theories, he notes, a distinction is "drawn between the 'right' and the 'good'—between a framework of basic rights and liberties, and the conceptions of the good that people may choose to pursue within the framework." For liberals, claims Sandel, "it is precisely because we are essentially separate, independent selves that we need a neutral framework, a framework of rights that refuses to choose among competing purposes and ends. If the self is prior to its ends, then the right must be prior to the good."[3] Consequently, he says, liberals do not presuppose the superiority of one way of life over others.

Charles Taylor presents a similar view of the liberal tradition in his recent book, *Sources of the Self.* Along with providing a polemical account of liberal visions of the self, he provides a historical account of its intellectual genesis. While individuals were once firmly located in traditional communities, with a sustaining moral framework that was given in the general order of things, Taylor says that the liberal vision of the self as atomistic, autonomous, and disengaged has come to dominate modern thinking about the self and identity. Community is dissolved as we are divided from each other by the force of atomism, "a condition in which everyone defines his or her purpose in individual terms and only cleaves to society on instrumental grounds."[4]

A stress on freedom as self-determination, says Taylor, is characteristic of society today. Nowadays "morality is narrowly concerned with what we ought to *do* and not also with what is valuable in itself, or what we should admire or love."[5] According to contemporary liberal philosophers, Taylor writes, "the fully significant life is the one which is self-chosen."[6] Like Sandel, then, Taylor describes the liberal perspective in terms of words like atomistic, autonomous, and self-chosen.

But the accounts of Sandel and Taylor about how liberals conceive of individuals are highly misleading.[7] As does MacIntyre, they make it sound as if liberal psychology posits a world of independent and self-sufficient persons, each guided by his or her idiosyncratic aims, interests, and conceptions of the good and thus sharing little or nothing with one another. It is further suggested that liberals are unable to say anything at all about the value of one or another way of life.

This sort of communitarian account is a forgery of the liberal conception of the individual, and of the consequences of liberalism's neutrality. Liberal social and moral theorists recognize full well that no one has ever existed completely free of other persons. From the moment of birth, every individual is highly dependent on others. Everyone is interdependent, and no one is or ever was completely self-sufficient. No liberal thinker would claim otherwise. No liberal theorist believes that each individual has uniquely personal aims, interests, conceptions of the good, or anything else. Human beings live in society, and all societies have shared languages and various kinds of shared rules. This is a commonplace. And when communitarians claim that liberals posit separate individuals who are totally uninterested in the fate of others, this is again a caricature. Like everyone else, liberal thinkers recognize that a certain level of mutual interestedness arises for everyone as a result of his or her actual experiences in human society.

As to liberalism's neutrality about the value of various ways of life, Sandel and Taylor misrepresent the liberal position. So does MacIntyre when he says that liberalism is committed to "neutrality . . . between rival and competing sets of beliefs about the best way for human beings to live."[8]

But the liberal position concerns the neutrality of government toward conceptions of the good. "The idea," writes Will Kymlicka, "is that people are entitled to 'neutral concern' from the government—that is, equal concern regardless of their conception of the good (so long as it does not violate the rights of others), whether it is approved or disapproved of by the majority in society, or by state officials."[9] But liberalism is not, of course, neutral about matters of justice. It is, after all, a normative political philosophy.

Because liberalism is a theory of justice, it appeals to principles about people's basic human rights in judging the moral standing of various social arrangements. Liberal theorists insist that the individual is the benchmark of justice. This means that all judgments concerning the justice or injustice of people's conduct or of various social arrangements pertain ultimately to individuals. Even when liberals say that blacks, women, or one or another group have been treated unjustly, they mean that the individuals comprising that group have been so treated.

In any case, communitarians insist that they have a conception of the moral self which is very different from that assumed by the champions of individualism and liberal thinking. These conflicting visions of the self are described by Sandel as follows:

> Communitarian critics of rights-based liberalism say we cannot conceive ourselves as independent in this way, as bearers of selves wholly detached from our aims and attachments. They say that certain of our roles are partly constitutive of the persons we are—as citizens of a country, or members of a movement, or partisans of a cause. But if we are partly defined by the communities we inhabit, then we must also be implicated in the purposes and ends characteristic of those communities. As Alasdair MacIntyre writes: "what is good for me has to be the good for one who inhabits these roles." Open-ended though it be, the story of my life is always embedded in the story of those communities from which I derive my identity—whether family or city, tribe or nation, party or cause.[10]

Like Sandel and MacIntyre, Taylor discusses identity in terms of the horizons of community. He gives special importance to language and says that there is no individual sense of identity in the absence of other speakers. "I define who I am," writes Taylor, "by defining where I speak from, in the family tree, in social space, in the geography of social statuses and functions, in my intimate relations to the ones I love, and also crucially in the space of moral and spiritual orientations within which my most important defining relations are lived out."[11]

But what does it mean to say that certain roles are constitutive of the persons we are, "as citizens of a country, or members of a movement, or partisans of a cause"? What is intended in speaking of deriving one's identity from the communities we inhabit? How are we to understand defining our identities in terms of where we speak from, in the family tree, in social space, in the geography of social statuses and functions? Certainly no one would doubt that our aims and attachments are influenced by the positions we occupy, the roles we fulfill, the situations we find ourselves in. This is a sociological commonplace that everyone recognizes.

These communitarians seem to be suggesting something more than this, however. They claim not only that the *contents* of the individual's aims, preferences, interests, and the like are inescapably social but that the *self* is constituted by communal ends. In contrast to liberals, they argue that individual selves cannot be distinguished from those ends supplied by our roles as citizens, members of a family, and the like.

As Kymlicka points out, however, no matter how deeply implicated we find ourselves in the roles and practices of our society, we are capable of questioning the value and justification of those roles and practices. And while the specific roles and practices help constitute who we are, we all have the capacity to envision ourselves without our present relationships and preferences, and with *different* ones altogether.[12]

As I noted in the previous chapter, some communitarian writers relate their arguments about identity and self-understanding to the need for homogeneity in traditions, values, practices, and so forth. This sort of homogeneity, they say, provides more satisfactory conditions for the achievements of self-knowledge and an adequate sense of identity than does cultural pluralism. Like-mindedness in terms of shared understandings, meanings, perceptions, and interpretations helps assure deep self-understanding and a consistent sense of identity.

Both Sandel and Taylor refer to the importance of reflection in this regard. In order to "be capable of a deeper introspection than a 'direct self-knowledge' of our immediate wants and desires allows," writes Sandel, we must live in a community marked by common values, a spirit of benevolence, certain "shared final ends," and "a common vocabulary of discourse and a background of implicit practices and understandings within which the opacity of the participants is reduced if never finally dissolved."[13]

We must recognize, Sandel says, that "what at first glance appear as 'my' assets are more properly described as common assets in some sense; since others made me, and in various ways continue to make me, the person I am, it seems appropriate to regard them, in so far as I can identify them, as participants in 'my' achievements and common beneficiaries of the rewards they bring."[14] This means, he says, that our self-understanding is heightened by our seeing our identities in terms of our relational ties. And the more we share with others, the less opaque we are to one another and also to ourselves. Introspection or self-reflection, from this perspective, involves understanding who "we" are as a condition of understanding ourselves. One cannot speak of "I" without meaning "we."

Taylor seems to be saying very much the same thing in contrasting what he terms "radical reflexivity" with the classical notion of reflecting on a shared vision of order in the cosmos, on what is good or valuable for us, on our particular historic community, on what underlies our moral point of view, on what we have in common.

When the great classical moralists emphasized the importance of not living in unreflective habit and usage, says Taylor, they were emphasizing a third-person perspective. But the modern ideal of self-reflection, by contrast, "calls us to a separation from ourselves through self-objectification. This is an operation which can only be carried out in the first-person perspective."[15] It is a turn to the self as a self. "It calls on me to be aware of *my* activity of thinking or *my* process of habituation, so as to disengage from them and objectify them."[16] This sort of radical reflexivity, Taylor writes, is "intensely individual, a self-explanation, the aim of which is to reach self-knowledge by coming to see through the screens of self-delusion which passion or spiritual pride have erected."[17]

There are serious problems with the communitarians' view that we acquire our identity without our consent. MacIntyre, Sandel, and Taylor all emphasize that we are formed by others. Of course, liberals also agree that we are formed by others *to some extent.* They agree with communitarians that our identities are, to some extent, emergent, the products of our social relations, rather than self-creations. But communitarians go much further in this regard.

I quoted Sandel earlier as saying that "others made me, and in various ways continue to make me, the person I am."[18] And he says, "to have character is to know that I move in a history I neither summon nor command, which carries consequences none the less for my choices and conduct." He goes on to say that "it draws me closer to some and more distant from others; it makes some aims more appropriate, others less so. As a self-interpreting being, I am able to reflect on my history and in this sense to distance myself from it, but the distance is always precarious and provisional, the point of reflection never finally secured outside the history itself."[19] Reflection on one's identity may help one realize that there is "a certain ultimate contingency in my having wound up the person I am." Yet, "being the person I am, I affirm these ends rather than those, turn this way rather than that."[20]

Sandel is clear about rejecting the liberal perspective on autonomous individuals and self-understanding. So is Taylor in rejecting those views which emphasize the "primacy of self-fulfilment" and give absolutely central importance to the freedom to choose one's own mode of life.[21]

MacIntyre joins them in remarking that "I can only answer the question 'What am I to do?' if I can answer the prior question 'Of what story or stories do I find myself a part?' "[22]

All three of these communitarians believe that individual lives cannot be distinguished from their ends. By showing that our identities are constituted by communal ends, they believe they have shown that we nonarbitrarily choose our ends in the light of who and where we are. In their view, one's self and sense of identity is constituted entirely by one's physical and social locations: where one is born and grows up, the history in which one participates, one's relational ties and connections, one's roles, memberships, and the like.

But by arguing that the self cannot be distinguished from its place in the life and history of the community, communitarians run the risk of dissolving the self into a mere reflection of the various roles imposed by someone's social position or situation. For many persons, it is exactly the influence of this situated vision of the self that constitutes a problem for them. Certainly many women try to resist having their identity defined solely in terms of the roles and expectations connected with their gender.

Like communitarians, many feminist theorists today are critical of the "unencumbered self" ascribed to liberal thinkers. But they are also highly critical of the communitarians' notion of the "situated self." As Seyla Benhabib and Drucilla Cornell phrase their objection: "Precisely because to be a biological female has always been interpreted in gendered terms as dictating a certain psychosexual and cultural identity, the individual woman has always been situated in a world of roles, expectations, and social fantasies. Indeed, her individuality has been sacrificed to the 'constitutive definitions' of her identity as a member of a family, as someone's daughter, someone's wife, and someone's mother. The feminist subjects have disappeared behind their social and communal persona."[23] Exactly the same holds when someone's identity is dictated entirely by his or her race, ethnicity, or nationality.

Liberals reject, then, the idea that one's identity is determined by birth and upbringing, sex, race, or whatever. Such factors undoubtedly have their influence, but they are not all-decisive. Since liberals place a strong emphasis on leading our lives from the inside, they cannot accept the communitarian attempt to promote social confirmation by emphasizing the significance of inherited or ascribed status.

### Communitarian Obligations and Loyalties

Communitarians claim that the picture of the self as defined by its roles is far superior to the liberal picture of separate, autonomous individuals exercising choice, making promises, taking on voluntary obligations, and the like. Most especially, liberal thinkers are described as giving insufficient recognition and respect to those obligations that are imposed on someone by his or her situated self.

Sandel writes that "to some I owe more than justice requires or even permits, not by reason of agreements I have made but instead in virtue of those more or less enduring attachments and commitments which together partly define the person I am."[24] The individual, according to Sandel, is situated from the start, embedded in a history, among others to whom he or she has unavoidable obligations.

MacIntyre, Sandel, and Taylor all argue that we derive our identity from our community and that this in itself gives rise to valid obligations. MacIntyre speaks of both individuals and traditions as "socially embedded" in one or another particular mode of social and moral life.[25] Our allegiance to one or another tradition, he says, "requires the living out of some more specific modes of social relationship, each with its own canons of interpretation and explanation in respect of the behavior of others, each with its own evaluative practices."[26] Our embeddedness in specific forms of practice and types of community, according to MacIntyre, imposes obligations to that society and its culture.

Rejecting the argument of liberals that we can detach ourselves from our own particular society and evaluate its practices in the same way as we would those of any other society, MacIntyre identifies an individual's conception of morality with that of the society where he or she happens to be. He draws on this communitarian conception of morality in arguing that the individual always owes allegiance to that community in which he is embedded. He says that "once we recognize that typically moral agency and continuing moral capacity are engendered and sustained in essential ways by particular institutionalized social ties and particular social groups, it will be difficult to counterpoise allegiance to a particular society and allegiance to morality in the way in which the protagonists of liberal morality do."[27] MacIntyre goes on to say:

> *If* first . . . I can only apprehend the rules of morality in the version in which they are incarnated in some specific community; and *if* secondly . . . the justification of morality must be in terms of particular goods enjoyed within the life of particular communities; and *if* thirdly . . . I am characteristically brought into being and maintained as a moral agent only through the . . . moral sustenance afforded by my community, *then* it is clear . . . that my allegiance to the community and what it requires of me—even to the point of requiring me to die to sustain its life—could not meaningfully be contrasted with . . . what is morally required of me.[28]

Being so thoroughly embedded in the community, then, the individual is portrayed as lacking the intellectual independence to examine the community's morality and compare it either with morality elsewhere or with a set of independent standards. Detachment is viewed as impossible. For MacIntyre, moral reasoning cannot be understood except within its cultural and historical context. While liberals would argue that whether or not we ought to give allegiance to our society depends ultimately on the qualities of this particular nation and government, MacIntyre suggests that we owe allegiance to our community simply because it is *ours*.[29]

MacIntyre's position has much in common with that set forth by the sociologist Emile Durkheim and still accepted by many sociologists today. "History has established that except in abnormal cases, each society has in the main a morality suited to it," he writes, "and that any other would not only be impossible but also fatal to the society which attempted to follow it."[30] And elsewhere, Durkheim writes that "there is no one unique morality and we dare not condemn as immoral the moral systems that preceded ours, for the ideal that they represent was valid for the society in which they were established."[31]

We might expect the individual to experience conflicting loyalties in his or her commitments to family, nation, and "humanity." But Durkheim insists that these groups mutually complement each other. There is, however, a hierarchy among them. "The evidence suggests that familial goals are and should be subordinated to national objectives," writes Durkheim, "if for no other reason than that the nation is a social group at a higher level."[32] Humanity, too, ought to be subordinate to the nation. This is because "in contrast with the nation, mankind as source and object of morality suffers this deficiency: there is no constituted society."[33] Durkheim's morality is dominated by the idea of duties to various collectivities, especially to the state.

For Durkheim, as for MacIntyre and many other communitarian thinkers today, the only sources and measures of judgments about morality are those of a given society. There can be, then, no detached, independent standards by which the morality sanctioned by a particular society can be evaluated. Thus questions about the moral standing of a particular society, or about its political order and institutions, cannot even be raised.

The danger of communitarian thinking here is obvious. It obliterates individual autonomy entirely and dissolves the self into whatever roles are imposed by one's position in society. From the perspective of liberalism, someone who is totally absorbed in the community, whose conduct is guided entirely by the obligations and commitments that are imposed on him or her, and who lacks the ability to reflect critically on his or her

183

position, is no longer a moral agent. For liberals, there can be no moral agency without the freedom to examine any and all beliefs, traditions, practices, and social arrangements. Such freedom requires, of course, certain basic civil and political rights.

Despite the fact that being situated in a particular time and place does affect our perspective—just as communitarians say it does—this perspective is neither individually nor collectively so unique and idiosyncratic that we are totally unable to detach ourselves from where we are and question our local traditions, practices, and moral systems.

Whatever the actual extent of shared traditions, understandings, and perspectives in the past, most of us today are confronted continually by heterogeneous traditions, practices, and the like. These give rise to competing demands between individuals and groups, as well as within both. Because it is almost inevitable that our inheritances, obligations, and commitments will sometimes conflict with one another, we must find ways of choosing among them. In such instances, we often search for principles that transcend the particularities of our concrete situations. For liberals, these principles involve notions of basic rights and social justice.[34]

Thus liberals argue that the moral backgrounds and social practices of different societies *can* indeed be judged and evaluated. This means that the obligations stemming from membership in Nazi Germany or South Africa today, for example, far from being mandatory, ought to be vehemently rejected because of these societies' violations of basic human rights.[35]

## II

### The Necessity of Basic Human Rights

But the new communitarians object to the strong emphasis that liberals place on basic human rights. They are critical not only of the so-called unencumbered self endorsed by liberal philosophers but also of the liberal politics of rights. John Rawls, Robert Nozick, Ronald Dworkin, Alan Gewirth, and other liberal theorists are attacked for making human rights central to morality.[36] Bellah says that liberalism is to be avoided at all costs. "It is precisely the persistence of non-liberal practices," he writes, "that makes out society viable at all."[37]

Moral and political philosophy ought to be focused instead, the communitarians say, on virtue, the common good, and community. They argue that liberals are unable to defend their most basic principle: that "individual rights cannot be sacrificed for the sake of the general good."[38]

Much of what communitarian writers say about liberal philosophy and liberal politics is based on one-sided and mistaken interpretations of the liberal position. Recent appraisals of the communitarian attack on the liberal politics of rights make this clear. Since others have dealt at length with various aspects of the communitarians' criticism of liberalism, I will focus here on rights more generally.[39] Essentially, I am concerned with the question, What difference do rights make?

It is true, as communitarians point out, that there is no consensus among liberal philosophers about the proper conception of moral or human (as distinguished from legal) rights. It is also true that liberals disagree as to how the existence of rights can be established or justified. Nevertheless, liberal philosophers all share the view that rights express limits on what can be done to individuals for the sake of the general or common good. Whatever the language used to describe them, rights serve to *protect* the basics of our individual freedom and well-being.

Even though different justifications for moral rights have been set forth by liberal philosophers, they all emphasize the necessity of such rights. As to the question of why human beings can be said to have moral rights, perhaps the oldest answer is that people have rights because they are God's children or because they have intrinsic worth or dignity. A second sort of answer is provided by Nozick and others who say that people's possession of certain inalienable rights is self-evident: "Individuals have rights and there are things no person or group may do to them (without violating their rights)."[40] A third answer is that rights arise from formal or informal rules of institutions, such as promising.[41] A fourth is Rawls's argument that people choosing the constitutional structure of their society from behind a veil of ignorance would provide every person with certain basic rights.[42] And a fifth sort of answer—the one that I endorse—is that the primary criterion for all persons having moral rights is that all persons have certain needs or interests of human agency.[43] Whatever their different justifications, however, all advocates of moral rights agree that the morally independent individual is always the ultimate source of value.

Whereas communitarian thinkers are concerned with what is distinctive about a particular group or society, liberals focus on what is common to human beings everywhere. Communitarians see people as differing essentially according to culture and circumstances, while liberals argue that there are certain features of human beings and social life that are simply *there*, unchosen by us.

The capacities for love, logic, friendship, and humor, for example, are universal. We have no reason to expect that anthropologists, sociologists, or explorers in outer space or elsewhere are going to discover a people who are unfamiliar with love or friendship, who don't find some things funny, and who never smile or laugh. And it is difficult even to imagine human beings who reject logic and pay no attention to empirical evidence. They would not long survive. These capacities surely have the status of universals. They are not, that is, the product of local standards, conventions, traditions, or the like.[44]

Also universal is the need to control one's behavior by one's own unforced choice. Although there are a variety of defenses of liberal rights, most of them share an ideal of the person as having the autonomy to choose his or her own ends, projects, and commitments. Basic to the liberal position is the idea that people have certain fundamental moral rights that give rise to individual civil rights. To have civil rights, as Gewirth emphasizes, "requires not only the political and legal rights of expression, political participation, freedom from arbitrary arrest, and other traditional *civil* liberties; it requires also the economic and social goods without which the former rights lack an essential material and cultural basis."[45]

Related to this is the liberal view that, in Allen Buchanan's words, "the proper role of the state is to protect basic individual liberties, and not to make its citizens virtuous or to impose upon them any particular or substantive conception of the good life."[46]

Liberal rights are also necessary defenses against deliberate physical cruelty and psychological harm. William Galston observes that "liberalism was born in fear—of cruelty, of bloody conflict, of arbitrary and tyrannical authority."[47] At a very minimum, rights are protections against physical and mental suffering.

Of course, liberals see rights as pertaining to many more aspects of people's lives than their physical and psychological well-being. And they differ among themselves as to whether rights are absolute, may be overridden, or may be infringed.[48] But liberal philosophers agree that the fact that something would violate an individual's rights provides a strong moral reason for not doing it. Rights help assure a safe private and public life for everyone.[49] As Judith Thompson says, "assertions of rights have a kind of moral force that no other moral assertions do."[50]

As I see it, liberal political theory starts with the presumption that actual human needs—as experienced by people everywhere—must be an inescapable component in any theory. Linked to this is the presumption that these needs must be met under conditions of sociocultural and political pluralism. The aim of liberal political and moral theory is to specify the sorts of social, political, and economic arrangements required to satisfy people's basic needs. It follows, then, that the justificatory test for any such institutional arrangements is how well they actually meet these needs.[51]

Although it is communitarians who have appropriated the language of "the common good," a concern with the common good is central to the liberal position. The common good for communitarians, Kymlicka notes, is the pursuit of "shared ends which define the community's way of life."[52] He contrasts this with the liberal conception of the common good, in which the aim is for the state to promote "the interests of the members of the community."[53] Liberals see rights as putting constraints on the pursuit of the shared ends that constitute the common good for communitarians. From the liberal perspective, individuals are free to pursue any end they choose so long as they do not violate the rights of others.

Another way of distinguishing between a communitarian and liberal conception of the common good is to point out that communitarians interpret the common good collectively, while liberals interpret it individually. With a collective interpretation, the common good means the good either of all the individuals in a community summed together or the good of the community taken as a collective distinct from its individual members. Not only communitarians but also utilitarians generally hold this collective conception of the common good. They either ignore individual rights altogether or assign a subordinate role to the rights of individuals, making them derivative from duties toward the social whole.

When the common good is conceived of distributively or individualistically, on the other hand, it refers to goods that are common to—that is, held equally by—each of the individual members of the group or community. In the case of rights, this means that realization of the common good cannot involve violations of the rights of some individuals for the good of the community.

In fact, a concern for the common good requires that society be regulated by recognition of and respect for everyone's basic rights and for the institutional arrangements to which they give rise. Recognition of each individual's basic rights imposes obligations on everyone else to act in ways that are of benefit to all. Along with the negative obligation not to interfere with people's basic rights (which I have defended elsewhere as the rights to freedom and to well-being), there is the positive obligation to help provide and support those policies and programs necessary for every person to exercise his or her basic rights.[54] Justice requires that everyone be treated with equal concern, and each individual thus has a strong personal interest in assuring justice not only for himself but for everyone else as well. This means that a concern with the common good is unavoidable in a liberal conception of the just society. From the perspective of the politics of rights, then, an emphasis on individual rights requires a conscientious concern for the common good.[55]

In my view, a liberal politics of the common good is much more likely than the communitarian version to assure solidarity (since people in a just society must show concern for one another), to encourage participation (since liberalism respects people who are different), to assure shared values (since everyone believes in the moral equality of all persons), and perhaps to promote territorial ties as well (since institutional arrangements satisfy people's needs in a just society). In other words, a liberal politics of the common good will help realize and sustain the normative conception of community set forth by communitarian theorists.[56]

## III

### *Individuals, Communities, and the Myth of Isolation*

Most thinking about community assumes a rather simple and direct relationship between past and present. At one or another time and place there was community, and then it collapsed. Where there once was community, we now find only isolated individuals. The communitarian critique of liberal society today often takes the form of an individual/community dichotomy: separate, unconnected individuals on the one hand, and the larger community on the other.

Remarking on this, the sociologist Amitai Etzioni emphasizes the importance of what he terms the "human arch." He observes that an "arch is composed of bricks and cannot exist without them, but the bricks without the arch are merely a pile of rubble." Etzioni goes on to say that the *human* arch is composed "partly of community and partly of individuals situated within the arch."[57] Although he never specifies exactly what he intends by "community," Etzioni's point is clear: we cannot conceive of community without individuals, or of individuals outside one or another community.

Like communitarians, Etzioni accuses liberal theorists of neglecting the community "both as a sociological reality and as a moral claim"; and like liberals, he criticizes communitarians for "neglecting individual actors, rights, and a critical stance against the community." In common with many others today, however, Etzioni contrasts isolated individuals with the community as a collectivity.

But clearly much social space is to be found between the two extremes of the atomic "unencumbered self" and the all-embracing community. Yet communitarian critics seem content to accept the either/or formulation that has long been employed by social theorists. Whether they conceive of community at the level of the nation-state or on a more restricted scale, communitarian writers consistently speak in terms of the individual/community dichotomy. If the individual is not deeply embedded in the community, he is viewed as standing completely alone.

This tendency is apparent in Michael Walzer's recent examination of the communitarian critique of liberalism, where he argues that the central issue between liberals and their communitarian critics is the pattern of social relations in modern society. "Liberalism," writes Walzer, "is best understood as a theory of relationship, which has voluntary associations at its center and which understands voluntariness as the right of rupture or withdrawal."[58] But this right to withdraw, Walzer argues, places groups continually at risk. Insofar as liberalism tends toward instability and dissociation, he says, it requires periodic communitarian correction.

Walzer recognizes that the nation-state is not the most important social union for most people today, and notes that "all sorts of other groups continue to exist and to give shape and purpose to the lives of their members."[59] These groups, too, are continually at risk because of people's freedom to leave them if they so desire. In the United States today, people "live in a society where individuals are relatively dissociated and separated from one another, or better, where they are continually separating from one another."[60] Such separation, according to Walzer, gives rise to intermittent feelings of sadness and discontent. He agrees with communitarians that liberal society is fragmentation in practice. People are far less often involved in communal activities than in earlier historical periods, says Walzer, and this adversely affects social relations in American society. Walzer and the communitarians share the view that there has been an enormous decline in those sorts of personal relationships that provide the experience of community.

In emphasizing the consequences of community decline for American society today, Walzer has much in common with Tönnies, Durkheim, and many other sociologists who argue that the lack of communal forms of association intermediate between the individual and the state leaves the individual isolated and vulnerable, and threatens the social order of society.

In the gesellschaft, says Tönnies, "everybody is by himself and isolated, and there exists a condition of tension against all others."[61] Durkheim writes that "where the state is the only environment in which men can live communal lives, they inevitably lose contact, become detached, and thus society disintegrates. A nation can be maintained only if, between the state and the individual, there is intercalated a whole series of secondary groups near enough to the individuals to attract them strongly in their sphere of action and drag them in this way, into the general torrent of social life."[62] Nineteenth-century theorists and communitarians today agree that individuals are no longer enclosed in such groups. The absence of community, in short, results in an atomized existence for most people.

But if some sort of mediating social relations between the individual and the state are required, there is no reason why such relations must be defined in terms of membership in discrete "groups." There are obviously social ties other than those based on membership in densely knit, tightly bounded, mutually supportive collectivities. If social relationships are an important source of concern and belonging, of cohesion and solidarity in society, why must they rest on membership in one or another communal group? If attachments among individuals provide the supports and constraints necessary for human functioning and social order, why must these attachments exist within the context of community?

Communitarians today follow Durkheim in seeing the community or group as the most meaningful source of social attachment or connection. "There is pleasure in saying 'we,' rather than 'I,' " writes Durkheim, "because anyone in a position to say 'we' feels behind him a support, a force on which he can count, a force that is much more intense than that upon which isolated individuals can rely."[63] But there are other "we" relations than those involving community membership.

This has been shown clearly by American and European social scientists over the past twenty-five years or so. Instead of conceiving of community as a space within which social contacts occur, they consider the perspective of the individual and the network of social relations in which he or she is involved. The focus is on interpersonal ties rather than on bounded groups.[64]

Claude Fischer, for example, says that "the lowering of social and spatial barriers and the consequent increase in the freedom to choose social relations have not led to less communal social ties." Instead, he suggests that ascribed membership in various collectivities may, over time, have been replaced by voluntary involvement in personal communities. These "personal communities" are not locality-based groups with a shared history and common values, but rather involve relatives, friends, neighbors, co-workers, and others with whom individuals have regular social contacts.

In Fischer's words: "The disintegration of the monolithic community has perhaps led to the proliferation of many personal communities, each more compatible and more supportive to the individual than ascribed corporate groups."[65] Like most sociologists today, Fischer assumes that these "monolithic" communities once existed and have now disappeared. My discussion in earlier chapters calls that assumption into question.[66]

Although I know of no comparable evidence about personal communities in earlier historical periods, I suspect that personal communities in classical Athens, medieval Europe, and early America were also (in Fischer's words) "more compatible and more supportive to the individual than ascribed corporate groups."

I indicated earlier that Tönnies and Durkheim were mistaken in thinking that medieval guilds were genuine communities whose members shared the same norms and values, as well as feelings of attachment and solidarity with one another. These social theorists clearly exaggerated in claiming that a guild embraced the whole man or attached its members more thoroughly than the family. I suggested that craft guilds probably involved the same sorts of friendly feelings shared by members of trade unions today, and the more convivial guilds (fraternities) were in many ways like private clubs or fraternal organizations in modern society. For those guild members with no friends or family in the medieval town, the guild was undoubtedly very important. It is unlikely, however, that the loyalty of most guild members ever outweighed their ties to family and friends.

In fact, throughout history relationships with family, friends, neighbors, and co-workers have undoubtedly been far more significant for most people than their membership in a guild or some other form of communal life.[67] Just as today, it is likely that people in the past were involved in networks of overlapping relationships that served as sources of both social constraint and support. Individuals must have oriented themselves to specific persons—and, of course, sometimes to specific groups—who had special significance for them. These special persons and groups would have served as points of reference for the individual, and their norms and values would have helped provide a basis for his or her sense of what was good, right, important, desirable, and the like.[68]

Fischer is correct in what he says about the consequences of an increase in people's "freedom to choose" the social relationships in which they become involved. People today have not only more freedom to decide whom to spend their time with than did people in the past, but also more freedom to decide about the frequency and duration of such contacts. Compared with the situation in classical Greece, medieval Europe, and America's founding period, men and women today have many more options as to whom they will marry, where they will work, how they will worship, and the like. Individual liberal rights allow for the free exercise of choice as to one's involvements and protect against unreflective, herd solidarity.

Contrary to the view of communitarian writers that social relationships arising from people's ascribed position in the community were more significant than social relationships today, it seems to me that relationships based on voluntary choices have a far deeper significance than those based on blind obedience or unthinking acquiescence. Relationships of intimacy between friends or lovers, characterized by the sharing of thoughts and feelings, are more likely to arise from free choice than from social imposition. From a Kantian perspective, those commitments that we actively arrive at ourselves are more truly our own than those that are simply imposed on us.[69] And the less dependent individuals are on social collectivities, the better able they are to make such commitments.

This is not to claim that voluntary choices about personal relationships are peculiar to modern society. People have almost always had some choice about their personal involvements. But various structural changes over the centuries have strongly altered the meanings of the concepts voluntary and personal. To see this, let us examine briefly the three periods that have concerned me in this book.

We saw earlier that in classical Greece individuals from different families and villages came together out of their mutual need for common defense. Without this unity, everyone was vulnerable to the threats of other city-states. Although the Athenian polis was an arena for conflicting interests and conflicting classes, citizens there voluntarily entered into personal relationships to help assure their safety and well-being. At least as compared with kinship and marriage, such relationships were certainly voluntary.

Voluntary personal relationships were also widespread in the Middle Ages. Men bound themselves together in the feudal relationship of vassalage. That is, some men voluntarily subordinated themselves to more powerful men for reasons of security and economic survival. And they voluntarily participated in various sorts of associations that provided mutual insurance and protection, economic benefits, a decent burial, and warmth and sociability for people who were away from their homes and families.

Many important personal relationships in the Middle Ages were modeled on the idea of a blood relationship. Yet the ties thus created were usually characterized in terms of the word "friend." In Marc Bloch's words: "The general assumption seems to have been that there was no real friendship save between persons united by blood."[70] He notes that a "common synonym for vassal was 'friend,' and it was widely held that 'Thy friends will be my friends, thy enemies my enemies.' "[71] From the end of the Middle Ages, says Bloch, noblemen who attached themselves to a great man for protection agreed in writing to the "promise of friendship."[72] This was often the case, he observes, throughout seventeenth-century Europe.

This was true in eighteenth-century America as well. We saw in an earlier chapter that relationships between rich Virginia planters and their poorer neighbors and between the planters and their British creditors were described as relationships between friends. At that time, Rhys Issac notes, a "friend was a person, whether of higher, lower, or equal status, related by the expectation of a mutual exchange of services."[73]

Just as with many relationships in classical Athens and medieval Europe, these relationships in Virginia were voluntary in nature. And just as was the case in those earlier periods, these personal relationships were characterized by instrumentality and exchange. When men spoke of friendship in such instances, they recognized it as being shaped by calculations of interest. These "friendships" were protections against numerous vulnerabilities in a highly dangerous and uncertain world.

Allan Silver, who has written widely on the historical vicissitudes of the notion of friendship, quotes Adam Smith's remarks about friendship in precommercial society:

> The necessity or conveniency of mutual accommodation very frequently produces a friendship not unlike that which takes place among those who are born to live in the same family. Colleagues in office, partners in trade, call one another brothers; and frequently feel towards one another as if they really were so. . . . The Romans expressed this sort of attachment by the word *necessitude*, which . . . seems to denote that it was imposed by the necessity of the situation.[74]

Necessitous relationships are not, of course, the sorts of close personal relationships that one would today describe as involving warm and intimate friendships.

Smith argues that it was the replacement of *necessitude* by commercial society that made possible relationships based on sympathy and personal attraction, unconstrained by necessity. More recent societal changes have gone still further in that direction. "In modern society and states, with their unprecedented depersonalization of economy, polity, and administration," writes Silver, "concern for personal safety and the advancement of competitive interests are addressed—to an extent not earlier imaginable—by impersonal means."[75]

As institutionalized arrangements have come to provide more and more for people's safety, employment, education, medical care, and other basic needs, personal relationships dominated by exchange, instrumentality, and calculation have decreased. The greater availability of various impersonal arrangements has allowed for the development of a conception of friendship different from that found in earlier historical periods. Instead of friendships being viewed as relationships of mutual convenience, as they often were in the past, friendships today are more likely to be informal, intimate, private, and unspecialized.

Thus while contemporary communitarian writers often insist that traditional conceptions of friendship and close personal relationships were superior to what we find in modern society, Silver's recent work suggests just the opposite.[76] Such factors as the advent of commercial society, the establishment of a pervasive division of labor, and the creation of institutionalized means for securing various individual and collective goals provide the conditions for close personal friendships today. At least as far as friendships are concerned, the individual's freedom of choice is far more extensive than in past centuries.

Some relationships are, of course, based on calculations of interest and exchange. And people do often lack close and intimate involvements with others. It is in these cases especially, I believe, that groups are important sources of emotional satisfaction. The less able the individual is to satisfy the need for connection through various close, personal relationships, the greater will be the likelihood that he or she will find communal membership attractive.

In any case, communitarians are correct in recognizing people's need for relatedness to others.[77] Social ties, attachments, and fellow feeling are indeed important to our well-being. But communitarian writers go wrong in defining this relatedness in terms of the group or collective. The satisfactions inherent in connection with others, the feelings of security and support, need not find their source in the community. Communitarians exaggerate the benefits of communal membership and minimize its destructive potential.


# IV

I have now considered the communitarian project in terms of its historical, moral, and practical dimensions. For the most part, my conclusions have been very negative. Although communitarian thinkers are concerned with opening our eyes to the weaknesses of individualism and the liberal perspective, the danger is that they will blind us to those failures of communitarian thinking that liberal theory has helped us to escape.

The communitarian theorists whose work I have examined in these pages give an idealized and misleading account of community in the past. Contrary to their many claims, community was not prominent in the three places most often chosen as their points of comparison: classical Athens, medieval Europe, and the founding period of America. Like many others who misread history, these communitarians encourage a feeling of loss and emptiness. This, in turn, helps make people vulnerable to the manipulation of the symbols of community.

In their celebration of the ecstasy of belonging, communitarian writers exhibit a frightening forgetfulness about the past. They fail to acknowledge that the quest for community often involves domination for some and subordination for others. In attacking post-Enlightenment liberalism and the politics of rights, communitarian theorists threaten to rob individuals of their most basic protections against abuses of power. In emphasizing the importance of community for people's everyday lives, communitarians fail to see that it is attachment rather than membership that is a general human value.

Anyone who takes seriously the fate of ordinary people in the sorts of communities advocated by MacIntyre, Sandel, Taylor, Bellah and his associates, and those who have reacted to their writings with praise and enthusiasm cannot ignore the historical experiences of our world. With that I agree. But I disagree about *what* is to be learned by looking backward. Communitarians emphasize the peace and harmony of earlier times and places, while I see even more domination, subordination, exploitation, and human suffering than surrounds us today. So while I share much of their disenchantment with life in the modern age, I reject their idealized portrayal of the past. If those were the good times, Lord protect us against the bad.

# NOTES

## Introduction

1. Tönnies, *Community and Society*; Durkheim, *Division of Labor*; and Weber, *From Max Weber.*

2. Nor should contemporary communitarianism be confused with that of the 1960s, which was inspired by Marxist ideas of equal political power and collective ownership of property. Instead, communitarians today find their inspiration in Aristotle and Hegel.

3. As far as communitarianism is concerned, MacIntyre is best known for two books: *After Virtue* and *Whose Justice? Which Rationality?* Sandel is most important for his critical study of the liberal perspective: *Liberalism and the Limits of Justice.*

4. See Taylor, *Philosophy* and *Sources.*

5. By Robert Bellah, Richard Madsen, William M. Sullivan, Ann Swidler, and Steven M. Tipton.

6. It has already stimulated a companion volume: Reynolds and Norman, *Community in America.* Wolfe also takes a turn toward the communitarianism of Bellah and his associates: see *Whose Keeper?*

7. Lasch, "Communitarian Critique," 61.

8. Michael Walzer is sometimes included among the ranks of the major communitarian thinkers today. But I exclude him from consideration here since he is in most respects closer to liberalism. He makes this clear in Walzer, "Communitarian Critique."

9. Some other important works with a communitarian thrust are Barber, *Strong Democracy*; Ketcham, *Individualism and Public Life*; Auerbach, *Justice*; Bay, *Strategies of Political Emancipation*; Abramson, *Liberalism and Its Limits*; and Sullivan, *Reconstructing Public Philosophy.* Sullivan, a philosopher, is one of the authors of *Habits of the Heart.*

10. MacIntyre, *After Virtue*, 147. I shall focus mainly on *After Virtue* rather than on the more recent *Whose Justice? Which Rationality?* It is the former book where MacIntyre's critique of liberalism is most developed and where he is most explicit about the need for community. As MacIntyre himself emphasizes, any changes in his views do not affect any of the "main contentions" in *After Virtue.* See MacIntyre, *Whose Justice?* x.

11. Ibid.

12. Bellah et al., *Habits.*

13. Taylor, *Sources,* 510.

14. Durkheim, Weber, and Tönnies made the same kinds of charges a century ago.

15. This is less true of Charles Taylor than of the other communitarians considered here. That is to say, he is generally less specific than the others about

197

exactly when community reigned. But that it *did* once reign is, for him, not in question. He says that while post-seventeenth-century writers ask about how the community gets started, "previously that people were members of a community went without saying." Taylor, *Sources*, 193.

16. MacIntyre, *After Virtue*, 181.
17. Ibid., 146.
18. Ibid., 52.
19. Sandel, *Liberalism*, 179.
20. Sandel, "Procedural Republic," 93.
21. Bellah et al., *Habits*, 253.
22. Ibid.
23. Ibid., 255.
24. This lack of clarity has been clearly recognized by various political theorists. See, for example, Wallach, "Liberals, Communitarians, and Political Theory," and Plant, "Community."
25. A recent consideration of "the resurfacing of communitarianism" is Anderson et al., "Roundtable on Communitarianism."
26. Plant, "Community," 49. The same holds among historians. Appleby says that *community* is a word with a connotative significance that is seldom ever spelled out by historians as to its intended meaning. See Appleby, "Value and Society," 307. Nor are sociologists always explicit about the meaning of community.
27. Bellamy, *Looking Backward, 2000–1887*. First published in 1888.
28. Sandel, *Liberalism*, and Bellah et al., *Habits*, see the goal as rediscovering or reclaiming certain communal tendencies that are still within our cultural tradition, while MacIntyre and Taylor see the necessary changes as involving deep transformations of contemporary society.
29. For important discussions of the communitarian perspective, Gutmann, "Communitarian Critics"; Hirsch, "Threnody of Liberalism"; Wallach, "Liberals, Communitarians, and Political Theory"; Buchanan, "Assessing"; Etzioni, "I & We Paradigm"; Herzog, "Questions for Republicans"; Kymlicka, *Liberalism, Community and Culture*; Larmore, *Patterns of Moral Complexity*; Galston, *Liberal Purposes*; and Tomasi, "Individual Rights and Community Virtues."
30. Durkheim, *Moral Education*, 240.
31. Sandel, "Introduction," in Sandel, *Critics*, 6.

## CHAPTER 1
### UNCOVERING THE COMMUNITARIAN IDEAL

1. MacIntyre, *After Virtue*, 146.
2. Ibid., 158.
3. Ibid., 162.
4. Ibid., 233.
5. MacIntyre, *Whose Justice?* 67.
6. Sandel, *Liberalism*, 172–73.

7. Ibid., 148–50.
8. Ibid., 150.
9. Ibid.
10. Charles Taylor, *Hegel* (Cambridge: Cambridge University Press, 1975). Reprinted in Sandel, *Critics*, 177–78.
11. Ibid., 179.
12. Ibid., 197.
13. Taylor, *Sources*, 36.
14. Bellah et al., *Habits*, 333. Italics in original.
15. This is a widely held position among sociologists in the communitarian tradition. See, for example, Nisbet, *Community and Power*.
16. MacIntyre, *After Virtue*, 124, 234, 245.
17. Sandel, *Liberalism*.
18. It is not always clear, however, that they are not attributing too specific a view of the "political" to Aristotle. Since the basic meaning of "political" in Greek is "of the polis," all activity in classical Greece was political because it took place within the polis. Aristotle certainly emphasized the extent to which the good of the polis ought to be a concern for all members of the community. Thus, each individual was expected to be widely involved in the activities of the polis rather than to live a solitary life. Matters that are common to the polis ought to concern everyone. But this does not mean that men were expected always to be politically active in the modern specific sense of political involvement. For an excellent discussion of the distinction between narrow political participation and participation in the wider social life of the polis, see Mulgan, "Aristotle and Political Participation."
19. Bellah et al., *Habits*, 335.
20. Ibid., 154.
21. Ibid., 251.
22. Sandel, *Liberalism*; MacIntyre, *After Virtue*.
23. Bellah et al., *Habits*, 153.
24. Sandel, *Liberalism*, 152.
25. Barber, *Strong Democracy*, 152.
26. Aristotle, *Nicomachean Ethics* IX.1171a10.
27. Ibid. IX.1171a11–12.
28. Ibid. VIII.1160a.
29. Bellah et al., *Habits*, 333.
30. Sandel, *Liberalism*, 150.
31. Bellah et al., *Habits*, 154.
32. Sandel, *Liberalism*, 179. The obligation to help someone in distress when an individual can do so at little or no cost to himself is an example of such a natural duty or obligation.
33. For discussions of universal needs, see Braybrooke, *Meeting Needs*; Moore, *Injustice*; an earlier book of my own, Phillips, *Equality, Justice and Rectification*; and Nussbaum, "Human Flourishing."
34. Toulmin, *Human Understanding* 1:491.
35. Sandel, "Introduction," in Sandel, *Critics*, 7.

36. Surprisingly, communitarians themselves seldom provide a detailed theoretical consideration of the notion of the common good. Two very useful discussions by theorists of a much more liberal persuasion are provided by Connolly, *Appearance and Reality*, 90–119, and Kymlicka, *Liberalism, Community and Culture*, 76–99.
37. Novick, *That Noble Dream*, 8.
38. Kammen, *Selvages*, 107.
39. Ibid.
40. For an excellent discussion of recent changes in the topics and methods of historical inquiry, see Stone, *Past and Present Revisited*, especially chap. 1, "History and the Social Sciences in the Twentieth Century."
41. Kammen, *Selvages*, 166.

CHAPTER 2
ONCE UPON A TIME IN AMERICA

1. These historians write in opposition to the long-influential view of Louis Hartz that America was from the beginning preoccupied with Locke and with individual private rights. See Hartz, *The Liberal Tradition in America*. Hartz's position has been vigorously attacked in several historical studies, the most important of which are Bailyn, *The Pamphlets of the American Revolution* and *The Ideological Origins of the American Revolution*; Wood, *The Creation of the American Republic*; and Pocock, *The Machiavellian Moment*. Interesting discussions of different versions of republicanism are found in Shalhope, "Republicanism and Early American Historiography," and Kramnick, "The 'Great National Discussion.' "
2. "Neo-Lockeian" attacks on the republican claims have severely criticized their position. The best known is Diggins, *The Lost Soul of American Politics*. Also relevant here is Appleby, *Capitalism and a New Social Order*. For an excellent discussion of the liberal-republican debate and an interesting review of several recent books on that subject, see Matthews, "Liberalism, Civic Humanism, and the American Political Tradition."
3. MacIntyre, *After Virtue*, 220.
4. Bellah et al., *Habits*, 285.
5. Ibid., 30.
6. Ibid., 256, 303.
7. Sullivan, *Reconstructing Public Philosophy*.
8. Ibid., 21.
9. Ibid., 12.
10. Ibid., 18.
11. Although Sullivan discusses republicanism at greater length in his own book than in the collective project, it is clear that both books assume the existence of the republican tradition in early America. In their discussion of the "division of labor," the five authors indicate that Sullivan had major responsibility for the drafting of chapters 2, 6, and 10, the three chapters which most often refer to republicanism in America's founding period. See Bellah et al., *Habits*, 331.

12. Sandel, "State and Soul."
13. For good introductions to the historiography of the founding period, see, in addition to the works cited in notes 1 and 2, Morgan, *Birth of the Republic*; Greene, *Reinterpretation of the American Revolution*; Kelley, *Cultural Pattern*; Young, *American Revolution*; Jensen, *Founding of a Nation*; Main, *Social Structure*; McDonald, *Novus Ordo Seclorum*; and Beeman et al., *Beyond Confederation*.
14. Kammen, *Selvages*, 168.
15. At the time of the birth of the American republic, native Americans found themselves on lands claimed by the United States. While the North American continent was their homeland and while they dominated nearly half the territory of the United States, these indigenous people had no wish to be part of the American republic. Nor did America's founders wish to have them. The Constitution simply excluded them from the body politic and placed them in the category of *resident* "foreign" nations. As Meinig remarks, "it was clear that in general Americans regarded Indians as enemies and encumbrances." Meinig, *Shaping of America* 1:393. These native Americans are not included, then, in the following account of America's early history and founding.
16. Jones, *Colonial Wealth*.
17. Ibid.
18. Pesson, *Riches, Class, and Power*. See also Sheridan, "Domestic Economy."
19. Jones, *Colonial Wealth*.
20. Main, *Social Structure*, 217.
21. Morgan, *Inventing the People*, 248–49.
22. See the very excellent discussions by Murrin, "Roof Without Walls," and by Davis, *Sectionalism*.
23. The following were useful to my understanding of early Massachusetts: Demos, *A Little Commonwealth*; Greene and Pole, *Colonial British America*; Greven, *Four Generations*; Kelley, *Cultural Pattern*; Lockridge, *New England Town* and *Settlement and Unsettlement*; Miller, *New England Mind*; Morgan, *Puritan Family*; Smith, *City upon a Hill*; Ulrich, *Good Wives*; Wood, *Creation*; and Zuckerman, *Peaceable Kingdom*.
24. See, for example, McWilliams, *Idea of Fraternity*, chap. 5, and Diggins, *Lost Soul*. This is to some degree the case with Bellah et al., *Habits*, as well.
25. Murrin, "Roof without Walls," 347. Simpson's recent book, *Mind and the American Civil War*, gives heavy emphasis to the opposition between Massachusetts and Virginia.
26. Bender, *Community*, 45–119.
27. Ibid., 108. Bellah et al., *Habits*, cite Bender in support of their claim that locality-based community was widespread well into the nineteenth century, 38–39, 160.
28. As noted by the historians Greene and Pole, *Colonial British America*, the "gemeinschaft-gesellschaft" model was used more widely by colonial historians than any other model over the past thirty years or so. But, as they also note, this model has come to be seen as unsatisfactory in more recent research by colonial historians, 11.

29. See, for important work, Glass and Eversley, *Population in History*; Vinovskis, *American Historical Geography*; and Nugent, *Structures of American Social History*.
30. Wrigley and Schofield, *Population History*, 175. This book is the definitive summary of the many early publications of the Cambridge Group for the History of Population and Social Structure in England. More than anyone else, Peter Laslett's work has opened up research concerning various facets of local life in early modern England. See Laslett, *World We Have Lost*.
31. Ibid., 471.
32. McManis, *Colonial New England*, 14.
33. Ibid.
34. Dunn, "Servants and Slaves," 160.
35. McManis, *Colonial New England*, 39.
36. Allen, *In English Ways*, 234–35.
37. Ibid.
38. Macfarlane, *Origins*, 163.
39. Lemon, "Spatial Order," 100. See also Breen, *Puritans and Adventurers*, and, for the economic background in England at the time, Thirsk, *Economic Policy and Prospects*.
40. For an excellent discussion of the restriction of voting and officeholding to church members in early Massachusetts, see Haskins, *Law and Authority*, chap. 6, "Communities of Visible Saints."
41. Ibid., 29.
42. Laslett, *World We Have Lost*, 27.
43. Ibid., 23–47, and Haskins, *Law and Authority*, 97.
44. Durkheim, *Socialism and Saint-Simon*, 200.
45. Laslett, *World We Have Lost*, 74.
46. See Wrigley and Schofield, *Population History*, 565.
47. Laslett, *World We Have Lost*, 186.
48. While it is seldom remarked upon, *all* initial learning about the role differentiation associated with age, sex, and status, as well as about hierarchy, solidarity, and the allocation of resources and rewards, takes place in a family setting. As various feminist theorists have argued in recent years, the mother has a lopsidedly asymmetric influence in terms of what the child learns in the first years of its life. For a systematic and thorough consideration of the significance of family structure throughout history, see Levy, *Our Mother-Tempers*. In the case of seventeenth-century England and early America, the family and the church together assured that everyone learned the appropriate behavior for people in different positions.
49. Allen, *In English Ways*, 25, 79, 89–90, 111, 134, 202.
50. Lemon, "Spatial Order," 98.
51. Lockridge, *New England Town*, 11–12.
52. Haskins, *Law and Authority*, 44–45.
53. See, for example, Koehler, *Search for Power*, and Cott, *Bonds of Womanhood*.
54. Ulrich, *Good Wives*, 7.
55. Salmon, *Women and Property*, 123.

56. See Potter, "Demographic Development," 123–56.
57. Ibid.
58. Lemon, "Spatial Order," 91.
59. Ibid., 92.
60. See the excellent discussion in McManis, *Colonial New England*, 53.
61. Ibid., 55.
62. Ibid., 56–57.
63. Lemon, "Spatial Order," 87.
64. McManis, *Colonial New England*, 62.
65. Haskins, *Law and Authority*, 73.
66. Lockridge, *New England Town*, 15.
67. Allen, *In English Ways*, 23.
68. Ibid., 91–92.
69. Quoted in Carroll and Noble, *Free and Unfree*, 55.
70. In the following discussion, I draw on Rutman's excellent study of early Boston. He uses documentary evidence concerning the government, the church, the land, and commercial activities, as well as letters, pamphlets, and other sources, to draw a portrait of Boston during its first decades. His concern, he writes, "is to assess the nature of the difference between the ideal which lay behind Winthrop's migration of 1630 and the reality of the settled community as revealed in institutional development." See Rutman, *Winthrop's Boston*, vii. The figures on population are from 57, 80.
71. Ibid., 44, 282.
72. Ibid., 87.
73. Ibid., 246.
74. Ibid., 249.
75. Ibid., 164.
76. Ibid., 256.
77. I draw here on the research of Boyer and Nissenbaum. It is based on the analysis of a variety of documentary materials, with what they describe as "probably as large a body of firsthand documentation as existed for any seventeenth-century community in British America." Boyer and Nissenbaum, *Salem Possessed*, x.
78. Ibid., 39.
79. Ibid., 88.
80. McManis, *Colonial New England*, 69.
81. Hall, "Family Structure and Economic Organization," 38–61.
82. Degler, *At Odds*, 7–8, 178–80.
83. Bender, *Community*, and Flaherty, *Privacy*.
84. Cook, *Fathers of the Towns*, xiv.
85. Lockridge, *New England Town*; Greven, *Four Generations*; and Henretta, "Families and Farms."
86. See, for example, Allen, *In English Ways*, 233–34.
87. Potter, "Demographic Development," 135.
88. Billington, *Westward Expansion*, 104.
89. Potter, "Demographic Development," 135.

90. See, for example, Zuckerman, *Peaceable Kingdom.*
91. Nelson, *Americanization of Common Law,* 37–38.
92. Conflict between neighbors had also been very common in seventeenth-century Massachusetts, and there was an incredible amount of litigation. For an excellent study of this, see Konig, *Law and Society in Puritan Massachusetts.*
93. Allen, *In English Ways,* 241.
94. Cook, *Fathers of the Towns.*
95. McManis, *Colonial New England,* 74.
96. This was true even for some women, since Boston offered a range of new occupations open to at least a few women. Some worked as silversmiths, in paper mills, as distillers, woodworkers, leather workers, and barbers. See Degler, *At Odds,* 365. There were also so-called she-merchants, shopkeepers and tavern owners who were taking over from their dead husbands. See Dexter, *Colonial Women of Affairs.* See also Norton, *Liberty's Daughters.*
97. Kelley, *Cultural Pattern,* 50–58.
98. Lockridge, *Settlement and Unsettlement,* 39.
99. Wright, *Cultural Life,* 39–40.
100. Lockridge, *Settlement and Unsettlement,* 27.
101. Meinig, *Shaping of America,* 148.
102. Carroll and Noble, *Free and Unfree,* 52.
103. Lemon, "Spatial Order," 103.
104. Dunn, "Servants and Slaves," 160. By 1650, when the population was about 20,000, more than half were probably in servitude. See Meinig, *Shaping of America,* 147.
105. Meinig, *Shaping of America,* 149. See also Morgan, *American Slavery–American Freedom.*
106. Potter, "Demographic Development," 142.
107. Ibid., 143.
108. Morgan, *American Slavery–American Freedom.*
109. See the discussion in Dunn, "Servants and Slaves."
110. Sidney W. Mintz and Richard Price, *An Anthropological Approach to the Afro-American Past: A Caribbean Perspective,* ISHI Occasional Papers on Social Change, no. 2 (Philadelphia, 1976), 1:4–11. Quoted in T. H. Breen, "Creative Adaptations: Peoples and Cultures," in Greene and Pole, *Colonial British America,* 200.
111. Dunn, "Servants and Slaves," 168.
112. Mintz and Price, *Anthropological Approach,* 10 (see note 110, above).
113. Potter, "Demographic Development," 135.
114. Morgan, *American Slavery–American Freedom.*
115. The following are especially useful for an understanding of Virginia in the founding period: Breen, *Tobacco Culture*; Brown and Brown, *Virginia 1705–1786*; Isaac, *Transformation*; Jones, *Present State of Virginia*; Kelley, *Cultural Pattern;* Lewis, *Pursuit of Happiness*; Lockridge, *Settlement and Unsettlement*; McDonald, *Novus Ordo Seclorum*; Morgan, *American Slavery–American Freedom*; Sydnor, *Gentlemen Freeholders*; Tapolar, *Sociology of Colonial Virginia*; Bertelson, *Lazy South*; and Wood, *Creation.*

NOTES TO CHAPTER 2

116. Isaac, *Transformation*, 229.
117. Sheridan, "Domestic Economy," 63.
118. Lewis, *Pursuit of Happiness*, 147–48.
119. Ibid.; Wyatt-Brown, *Southern Honor*; Taylor, *Cavalier and Yankee*.
120. Wyatt-Brown, *Southern Honor*, 293–97, 300–308.
121. Waterman, *Mansions of Virginia*.
122. No one knows exactly how many slaves there were in Virginia at the time. For estimates of the percentage, see Michael Mullin, *Flight and Rebellion*; Sydnor, *Revolutionaries in the Making*; and Jones, *Colonial Wealth*.
123. Isaac, *Transformation*, 31, 306.
124. Ibid., 30.
125. Meinig, *Shaping of America*, 248.
126. Lewis, *Pursuit of Happiness*, 19.
127. Ibid., 44–45. As in Massachusetts, the church helped assure the maintenance of the privileged position of the wealthy gentry. Beyond this, Christian indoctrination was apparently intended to keep slaves docile and contented.
128. Bushman, "High-Style and Vernacular," 88.
129. Ibid., 92.
130. Lewis, *Pursuit of Happiness*, 18.
131. See Roeber, *Faithful Magistrates*.
132. See the discussion in Fliegelman, *Prodigals and Pilgrims*, 27–28, and Lewis, *Pursuit of Happiness*.
133. For an interesting consideration of the leisure ethic in the South, see Burnaby, *Travels*.
134. Wood provides a good discussion. See Wood, "Interests and Disinterestedness," 85.
135. Pesson, *Riches, Class, and Power*.
136. Lewis, *Pursuit of Happiness*, 108.
137. Quoted in Lockridge, *Settlement and Unsettlement*, 92.
138. Isaac, *Transformation*; Lockridge, *Settlement and Unsettlement*.
139. Kelley, *Cultural Pattern*, 60–61.
140. Lockridge, *Settlement and Unsettlement*, 100.
141. Lemon argues that the intensity of the religious uprising is at least partly accounted for by their opposition to a very much "property-minded" society at the time. Lemon, "Spatial Order," 116.
142. Pole, *American Constitution*, 4.
143. Speck, "Context," 401.
144. Galvin, *Three Men*, 59.
145. Morris and Morris, *Encyclopedia*, 85–86.
146. Ibid., 86–87. See also Jensen, *Founding of a Nation*, 65.
147. Galvin, *Three Men*, 90.
148. Morris and Morris, *Encyclopedia*, 91.
149. Maier, *Old Revolutionaries*, 22.
150. Rogers, *Empire and Liberty*.
151. Galvin, *Three Men*, 222.

152. Ibid., 229.
153. Ibid., 230.
154. Morgan, *American Slavery–American Freedom*, 381.
155. Sydnor, *Gentlemen Freeholders*.
156. Breen, *Tobacco Culture*; Lewis, *Pursuit of Happiness*, 134–35.
157. Isaac, *Transformation*, 113.
158. Breen, *Tobacco Culture*, 142. See also Lewis, *Pursuit of Happiness*, 110–11.
159. Breen, *Tobacco Culture*.
160. See Hutson, "Country, Court, and Constitution"; Murrin, "Great Inversion," 368–453; and Stone, *Past and Present Revisited*, chap. 11, "Court and Country."
161. Aristotle, *Politics* VII.ix.1328–29.
162. Jefferson, *Notes*, 164–65.
163. Breen, *Tobacco Culture*, 127–28.
164. Morgan, *American Slavery-American Freedom*, 383–84.
165. Breen, *Tobacco Culture*, 127–28.
166. Ibid., 207.
167. Morris and Morris, *Encyclopedia*, 87.
168. Ibid., 92.
169. Breen, *Tobacco Culture*, 188–91.
170. Ibid., 202.
171. Morris and Morris, *Encylopedia*, 98.
172. Ibid., 102.
173. Ibid., 107.
174. Ibid.
175. All quoted in McDonald, *Novus Ordo Seclorum*, 78.
176. Murrin, "Roof without Walls."

CHAPTER 3
THE COMMUNITARIAN IDEAL AND THE
AMERICAN REALITY

1. Tocqueville, *Democracy* 1:319.
2. Ibid., 26–45.
3. Ibid., 112.
4. Ibid., 321.
5. Ibid., 51–54.
6. Ibid., 199.
7. Bellah et al., Habits, 306.
8. Ibid., 175.
9. Ibid., 38.
10. Ibid., 39.
11. Wood, "Interests and Disinterestedness," 85.
12. See Pocock, *Machiavellian Moment*, chaps. 12 and 14. For an interesting consideration of the continuing importance of property in America, see Scott, *In Pursuit of Happiness*.

13. The right to vote and participate politically also depended on property ownership. For only such men could be relatively free of the influence of those
on whom they were dependent. "Such is the frailty of the human heart, that
very few men who have no property have any judgment of their own," declared John Adams just a few weeks before Independence. "Generally speaking," he said, "even white women, whom nature had made . . . fittest for
domestic cares," and children, who had "no judgment or will of their own,"
had "as good judgments, and as independent minds, as those men who are
wholly destitute of property." Quoted in Greene, *All Men*, 26–27.

14. Quoted in ibid., 6.

15. Quoted in ibid., 5, 7–8. For discussions of philosophical influence on the
founding fathers, see Howe, "European Sources," and White, *Philosophy*.

16. Even disagreements between Federalists and Anti-Federalists concerning the
ratification of the Constitution were defined mainly in terms of the views
and opinions of "the men who mattered." As Wiebe points out: "Appropri-
ately the gentry addressed their speeches and pamphlets, rich with learned
allusions and first principles, to one another, not to the people, who would
have to receive their instructions from others closer to them in the hierarchy." Wiebe, *Opening*, 40. "For the Founding Fathers," write Carroll and
Noble, "the American was a white Anglo-Saxon Protestant male." *Free and
Unfree*, 134.

17. This hierarchy of natural distinctions was reinforced in each and every
American family as well as in the preaching and practices of the church. In
the church as elsewhere in American society at the time, gatherings always
began with people arranging themselves in a rough order of leaders and
followers.

18. Fowler makes clear in his recent book that there is more interest in commu-
nity during the time of the American Revolution than for any other period.
See Fowler, *Dance with Community*, especially chap. 4, "Rummaging through
American History."

19. Sandel, *Liberalism*, 152.

20. Meinig, *Shaping of America*, 218.

21. Main, *Social Structure*, 193. A century later, Thernstrom shows, around 50%
of the residents at any date would not be found living there ten years later.
"This was not a frontier phenomenon, or a big-city phenomenon," he
writes, "but a national phenomenon." Thernstrom, *The Other Bostonians*,
225. Today, of course, the rate of geographical mobility in the United States
is even greater. Annually, some 20% of the population changes residence.
See Brown, *Migration and Politics*. Yet it is not necessarily the case—as communitarians seem to assume—that relationships and attachments are today
*more* often disrupted by "moving on" than was the case two centuries ago.
After all, the telephone and various improvements in transportation make
it much easier for people nowadays to keep in touch with friends and family
from the places they have left.

22. Bellah et al., *Habits*, 153.

23. MacIntyre, *Whose Justice?* 24–25.

24. Quoted in Carroll and Noble, *Free and Unfree*, 133.
25. Ward, "Immigration," 502–3.
26. Ibid.; Kelley, *Cultural Pattern*; and Feingold, *Zion in America*.
27. Pole, *Pursuit of Equality*, 42.
28. These figures are based on analyses of probate inventories and estate records from the time. See Jones, *Colonial Wealth*.
29. Main, *Social Structure*, 276.
30. Morgan writes that "the social hierarchy in the colonies nowhere reached the exalted heights that it did in England, but a hierarchy nevertheless existed and persisted in every colony." See Morgan, *Inventing the People*, 248–49.
31. Greene, "Uneasy Connection," 35.
32. Cook, *Fathers of the Towns*, 179.
33. Ibid., 178.
34. Ibid., 174.
35. Ibid., 172.
36. Pole, *Pursuit of Equality*, 28.
37. Main, *Social Structure*, 41–42.
38. Morgan, *American Slavery–American Freedom*, 388.
39. Pole, *Pursuit of Eqality*, 33.
40. Breen, *Tobacco Culture*, 32. See also Lockridge, *Settlement and Unsettlement*, 83.
41. I draw here on Pesson, *The Log Cabin Myth*.
42. Although Washington and Jefferson have long been celebrated in American history textbooks, recent scholarship corrects the one-sided picture of these two men. One aspect of this concerns their position on slavery. For excellent studies of their attitudes and behavior in regard to the ownership of slaves, see Davis, *Problem of Slavery*; Matthews, *Radical Politics*; and Miller, *Wolf by the Ears*.
43. For excellent studies, see Lemon, "Spatial Order," and, especially, James A. Henretta, "Wealth and Social Structure," in ibid., 262–89.
44. The quotation is from Greene, *All Men*, 7.
45. In what follows, I draw heavily on Royster, *A Revolutionary People*.
46. Ibid., 132.
47. Ibid., 71. See also Shy, *A People Numerous and Armed*.
48. Hoerder, "Boston Leaders and Crowds," 266.
49. Royster, *A Revolutionary People*, 129, 268. Only some 20% were married, 268. Morgan notes that the men of the Continental army "were generally drawn from the lowest ranks of society, from the poor and landless." Morgan, *Inventing the People*, 162.
50. Royster, *A Revolutionary People*, 268.
51. Ibid., 211.
52. Ibid., 72–73.
53. Ibid., 312.
54. Ibid., 312.
55. Ibid., 274–75.
56. Nor was there a common vocabulary of discourse. Kramnick finds that along with republicanism there were also the idioms of power and the state, of

Lockean liberalism, and of work-ethic Protestantism. See Kramnick, "Great National Discussion." It seems clear to me that these different idioms very often reinforced one another and generally supported the privileged position of the gentry.

57. Barber, *Strong Democracy*, 261.
58. See the excellent discussion in Greene, *All Men*.
59. Williamson, *American Suffrage*, 12–15.
60. Zilversmit, *First Emancipation*, 113.
61. Greene, *All Men*, 19.
62. Williamson, *American Suffrage*, 19.
63. Ibid., 365.
64. Greene, *All Men*, 22. Jefferson, however, favored universal white-manhood suffrage. In different versions of his proposed model constitution for the state of Virginia, Jefferson suggested that all white men be given sufficient land to assure that they would have suffrage. See Matthews, *Radical Politics*, 35, 79–81. Matthews also notes, however, that Jefferson "was unwilling to make suffrage genuinely universal by extending it beyond white males. On at least two occasions, Jefferson explicitly argued for the disfranchisement of women, in order to 'protect' them from the world of public affairs. And the possibility of giving the vote to black Americans appears never to have surfaced in his mind." *Radical Politics*, 80–81.
65. Mansbridge, *Beyond Adversary Democracy*.
66. Tocqueville, *Democracy* 1:61.
67. Ibid., 67.
68. Bellah et al., *Habits*, 200.
69. Mansbridge, *Beyond Adversary Democracy*, 131.
70. Writing about Dedham in the seventeenth century, Mansbridge notes the following. "Even though no more than fifty-eight men were eligible to come to the Dedham town meeting and to make the decisions for the town, even though the decisions to which they addressed themselves were vital to their existence, even though each absence from the meeting brought a fine, and even though a crier personally visited the house of every later-comer half an hour after the meeting had begun, only 74 percent of those eligible actually showed up at a typical meeting between 1636 and 1644. This must come close to the highest attendance one can expect, on the average, in a geographically based direct democracy." Mansbridge, *Beyond*, 130–31. For her own study of Selby, Vermont, Mansbridge reports average attendance figures of between 30% and 35% in the nineteenth century, and about 25% in the early 1970s.
71. Brown, *Middle-Class Democracy*, 389.
72. Furthermore, Morgan points out, the same people rarely voted in every election. Morgan, *Inventing the People*, 305.
73. It seems likely that a slightly higher percentage of the eligible voters may have cast a vote in Virginia than in Massachusetts. This may be partly accounted for by the "public" nature of voting in Virginia. Every voter had to ascend a platform on which the candidates were seated. He was called by name by the sheriff, announced his vote, and was then personally

thanked by the candidate to whom he gave it. See the description in ibid., 185.

74. Lockridge, *Settlement and Unsettlement.*

75. John M. Murrin, "Political Development," in Greene and Pole, *Colonial British America,* 444.

76. Williamson, *American Suffrage.* See also Pole, *Foundations of American Independence,* 200.

77. Cook, *Fathers of the Towns,* 37–38.

78. Ibid., 93.

79. Ibid., 159.

80. See Maier, *From Resistance to Revolution,* 85–91.

81. As with geographical mobility and shared values, it is not clear to what extent people today differ from those 200 years ago in regard to participation. Certainly many more people today have the franchise, and at least as high a percentage vote. On the other hand, I do have the impression that people today feel more "distanced" from the political process (and from their representatives and leaders) than was the case in the founding period. Whatever the differences, the communitarians' picture of participation in the past is an idealization. For an interesting recent approach to democratic participation, see Beitz, *Political Equality.*

82. Carroll and Noble, *Free and Unfree,* 116.

83. Quoted in Murrin, "Roof without Walls," 343.

84. Ibid., 344.

85. Ibid.

86. Ibid.

87. Royster, *A Revolutionary People,* 109.

88. Quoted in McCoy, "James Madison," 238.

89. Kelley, *Cultural Patterns,* 89.

90. See McCoy, "James Madison."

91. An analysis of the geographical references made by delegates to the Continental and Confederation congresses revealed that about 47% of the geographical references were made to New England, 17% to the North, 28% to the South, and only 8% to the middle states. Cited in ibid., 235.

92. Ibid., 229.

93. Farrand, *Records* 1:486; 2:100.

94. Ibid. 1:476. Italics in original.

95. Finkelman speaks of this as the "dirty compromise" between delegates from New England and the Deep South. The former supported the right of the Carolinas and Georgia to continue to import slaves. In turn, South Carolina supported New England's demands for giving Congress power to regulate all commerce—a matter much more important to New England than to the southern states. See Finkelman, "Slavery and the Constitutional Convention," 214.

96. Ibid., 224.

97. See the discussion in Lynd, *Class Conflict.* Nevertheless, some Anti-Federalists were clearly embarrassed by the support for slavery in the Constitution. For an excellent discussion, see Finkelman, "Antifederalists," 182–207.

98. See Kelley, *Cultural Pattern.*
99. Greene and Pole, *Colonial British America,* 13.


CHAPTER 4
LIFE IN THE MIDDLE AGES: AN OVERVIEW

1. MacIntyre, *After Virtue,* 160.
2. Comte, *Positive Polity*; Weber, *Economy and Society*; Simmel, *Selected Writings*; and Durkheim, *Division of Labor.* See also the interesting discussion of German and French thinkers in Liebersohn, *Fate and Utopia.*
3. Nisbet, *Sociological Tradition,* 14.
4. Liebersohn, *Fate and Utopia,* 2.
5. Tönnies, *Fundamental Concepts.*
6. Liebersohn, *Fate and Utopia,* 13.
7. Tönnies, *Fundamental Concepts,* 17–23. For definitions of the two terms used by Tönnies—*Wesenwille* (essential will) and *Kürwille* (arbitrary will)—I utilize Tönnies, *On Social Ideas,* 174.
8. Tönnies, *Fundamental Concepts,* 53–73.
9. Ibid., 88.
10. Ibid., 273.
11. Ibid., 270.
12. Ibid., 28.
13. This seems to me obvious despite Tönnies' denials that he has "taken sides" for gemeinschaft and against gesellschaft. See Tönnies, *On Social Ideas,* 208.
14. Nisbet, *Sociological Tradition,* 16.
15. Tönnies, *Fundamental Concepts,* 60.
16. Ibid., 267.
17. Ibid., 61.
18. Ibid., 213.
19. Ibid., 45–46.
20. Ibid., 174.
21. Ibid., 189.
22. Ibid., 62.
23. Ibid., 26, 267.
24. Ibid., 68.
25. Ibid., 26.
26. Here Tönnies relies on Gierke for his claims.
27. Tönnies, *Fundamental Concepts,* 49.
28. Ibid., 261.
29. Ibid., 265.
30. Ibid., 70.
31. Ibid., 57.
32. Ibid., 73.
33. Ibid., 57.
34. Ibid., 242.
35. Ibid., 245.

36. Ibid., 247.
37. Ibid., 266.
38. Ibid., 268.
39. Ibid.
40. MacIntyre, *After Virtue*, 245.
41. Tönnies, *Fundamental Concepts*, 270.
42. Nisbet, *Community and Power*, 80–82. See also the extended discussion of the gemeinschaft-gesellschaft typology in Bender, *Community*, 17–24, 29–43, 143–47.
43. These authors are all mentioned by Tönnies himself as relevant to his studies in writing *Gemeinschaft and Gesellschaft*. See Tönnies, *On Social Ideas*, chap. 6, "Development of Sociology in Germany in the Nineteenth Century." Many of these same scholars also had a considerable influence on Marx and Engels. See, for example, Hobsbawm's introduction in Marx, *Pre-Capitalist Economic Formation*.
44. Tönnies, *On Social Ideas*, 26.
45. For an excellent discussion, see Murray, *Germanic Kinship*.
46. Tönnies, *Fundamental Concepts*, 48, 272.
47. Ibid., 48.
48. Ibid., 268.
49. Murray, *Germanic Kinship*, 178.
50. See Walker, *German Home Towns*, 418.
51. Cited in ibid., 148.
52. Ibid., 2.
53. Ibid., 424.
54. Ibid., 424–25.
55. For a detailed discussion of the various influences on Tönnies, see Mitzman, *Sociology and Estrangement*.
56. Among those publications that I have found particularly useful for understanding the Middle Ages are Black, *Guilds and Civil Society*; Bloch, *Feudal Society*; Duby, *Early Growth, Chivalrous Society*, and *Age of Cathedrals*; Goody et al., *Family and Inheritance*; Goff, *Medieval Civilization*; Kamenka and Neale, *Feudalism, Capitalism, and Beyond*; Kirshner and Morrison, *Medieval Europe*; LeRoy Ladurie, *Montaillou*; Macfarlane et al., *Reconstructing Historical Communities*; Macfarlane, *Origins*; Mitterauer and Sieder, *European Family*; Mundy, *Europe in the High Middle Ages*; Postan, *Cambridge Economic History, Essays on Medieval Agriculture*, and *Medieval Economy*; and, most especially, Reynolds, *Kingdoms and Communities*.
57. For a good discussion of the methods available to a scholar nowadays, see Duby, *Chivalrous Society*. See also Stone, *Past and Present Revisited*.
58. See, for example, MacPherson, *Possessive Individualism*; Marx, *Critique of Political Economy*; and Weber, *Protestant Ethic*.
59. See, for example, Reynolds, *Kingdoms and Communities*; and Shahar, *Fourth Estate*.
60. Duby, *Early Growth*, 165. See also Duby, *Chivalrous Society* and *Age of Cathedrals*.
61. See Murray, *Reason and Society*, 96–97. Murray argues that the doctrine of the

three orders was partly a propaganda device utilized by those who fought and those who prayed in an attempt to assure the continuation of the existing hierarchical division.

62. For discussions of the Middle Ages in terms of feudalism, see Bloch, *Feudal Society*, and Postan, *Medieval Economy*.

63. Reynolds, *Kingdoms and Communities*, 223.

64. Murray, *Reason and Society*.

65. Reynolds, *Kingdoms and Communities*, 223.

66. Duby, *Chivalrous Society*. For a detailed examination of the nobility and France and Germany from 500 to 1100, see Reuter, *Medieval Nobility*.

67. Murray, *Reason and Society*, 343–46.

68. Ibid., 348.

69. See, for example, Postan, *Medieval Economy*.

70. See the description in LeRoy Ladurie, *Montaillou*, 19.

71. Duby, *Chivalrous Society*.

72. Ibid., 9.

73. See Herlihy, *Medieval Households*, 157. "The study of medieval households requires the use of scattered, diverse, and usually difficult sources," he notes, "but even out of them a coherent picture emerges."

74. Goody, "Evolution of the Family," 124. See also Mitterauer and Sieder, *European Family*, and Herlihy, *Medieval Households*.

75. Duby, *Chivalrous Society*.

76. Herlihy, *Medieval Households*, 111.

77. Ibid., 144.

78. See, for example, Razi, *Life, Marriage and Death*, 86.

79. M. M. Postan and J. Z. Titow, "Heriots and Prices in Winchester Manors," in Postan, *Cambridge Economic History*, 159–60, 180–83; and Razi, *Life, Marriage and Death*, 43–44.

80. LeRoy Ladurie, *Montaillou*, 41–47.

81. Postan, *Medieval Economy*; Mitterauer and Sieder, *European Family*; Razi, *Life, Marriage and Death*; and Herlihy, *Medieval Households*.

82. Shahar, *Fourth Estate*, 181.

83. Mitterauer and Sieder, *European Family*; Herlihy, *Medieval Household*, 135, reports that in 1427 the average size of Florentine households was only 3.8 persons, and 4.4 in all of Tuscany. Only 3.6% had 10 or more persons, i.e., were truly large households.

84. Murray, *Germanic Kinship*, 222.

85. Ibid.

86. Shahar, *Fourth Estate*, 240.

87. See, for example, LeRoy Ladurie, *Montaillou*.

88. Shahar, *Fourth Estate*, 196–97.

89. Ibid., 191.

90. McNamara and Wemple, "Sanctity and Power," 114.

91. Shahar, *Fourth Estate*, 191.

92. Ibid., 194.

93. Ibid., 150.

94. Ibid.; McNamara and Wemple, "Sanctity and Power"; and Casey, "Cheshire Cat," 224–49.
95. Postan, *Medieval Economy*, 223.
96. Ibid.
97. Murray, *Germanic Kinship*, 177. Also see Bloch, *Marxism and Anthropology*.
98. See, for example, Duby, *Chivalrous Society*, and Macfarlane, *Origins*.
99. See Macfarlane, *Origins*, and Mitterauer and Sieder, *European Family*.
100. Pounds, *Historical Geography of England*.
101. Reynolds, *Kingdoms and Communities*, 101. Because she seems to have considered more sources and secondary authorities concerning collective organization in medieval Europe—more than 800 in total—than any other historian of the Middle Ages, Reynolds's book is especially relevant to the following discussion.
102. Black, *Guilds and Civil Society*, 50.
103. Reynolds, *Kingdoms and Communities*, 112–13. Also Duby, *Chivalrous Society*.
104. Reynolds, *Kingdoms and Communities*, 124–25.
105. Ibid., 102.
106. Ibid., 144–45.
107. Ibid., 139.
108. Ibid.; Homans, *English Villagers*; and Razi, *Life, Marriage and Death*.
109. See, for example, LeRoy Ladurie, *Montaillou*.
110. Postan, *Agrarian Life* and *Medieval Economy*.
111. Reynolds, *Kingdoms and Communities*, 124–25.
112. Ibid., 138.
113. Tönnies, *Fundamental Concepts*, 57.
114. Ridley, *Living in Cities*.
115. Girouard, *Cities and People*.
116. Little, *Religious Poverty*, 223. In addition to those involved in the primary (i.e., food-producing) sector of the economy, then, the medieval town consisted of artisans and industrial workers constituting the secondary sector, and the totally new tertiary sector made up of the merchants, the bankers, the industrial entrepreneurs, and the professionals. This sector came to be dominant in terms of power and influence in the medieval town.
117. Kirshner and Morrison, *Medieval Europe*, 86.
118. Postan, *Medieval Economy*.
119. Reynolds, *Kingdoms and Communities*, 168.
120. Ibid., 198–202.
121. Hook, *Siena*, 13.
122. Reynolds, *Kingdoms and Communities*, 188.
123. Cited in ibid., 190.
124. See, for example, Mumford, *City in History*.
125. Ridley, *Living in Cities*, 94–95.
126. Ibid.
127. Reynolds, *Kingdoms and Communities*, 250–331.

128. Ibid., 25.
129. Ibid., 258–59, 272–74.
130. Ibid., 33.

## CHAPTER 5
### THE COMMUNITARIAN IDEAL AND
### MEDIEVAL REALITY

1. See Pounds, *Historical Geography of England*, 339–40. Most of them came from no greater distance than about 15 miles (the length of a day's journey).
2. Duby, *Early Growth*, 80.
3. Razi, *Life, Marriage and Death*. See also Hilton, *English Peasantry*.
4. Duby, *Early Growth*, 117.
5. Ibid., 240–41.
6. Quoted in Tönnies, *Fundamental Concepts*, 67.
7. Ibid., 53, 267.
8. LeRoy Ladurie, *Montaillou*, 53.
9. Ibid., 130–31.
10. Ibid., 131.
11. Ibid., 266.
12. Reynolds, *Kingdoms and Communities*, 139.
13. Ibid., 148.
14. LeRoy Ladurie, *Montaillou*, 354.
15. Ibid., 354.
16. Shahar, *Fourth Estate*, and Power, *Medieval Women*.
17. Shahar, *Fourth Estate*, 12.
18. Ibid., 92.
19. Gurr, "Violent Crime."
20. Ibid., 307.
21. Hook, *Siena*, 33.
22. Girouard, *Cities and People*, 74–75.
23. See Bartlett, *Trial by Fire and Water*.
24. Ibid., 33.
25. Shahar, *Fourth Estate*, 19–21.
26. Ibid., 218.
27. Ibid., 16.
28. Ibid., 17.
29. Ibid., 90. See also LeRoy Ladurie, *Montaillou*.
30. Saltman, "Feudal Relationships," 522.
31. Reynolds, *Kingdoms and Communities*, 146.
32. Ibid., 102.
33. Razi, *Life, Marriage and Death*, 77–79.
34. Ibid., 122.
35. LeRoy Ladurie, *Montaillou*.
36. Kirshner and Morrison, *Medieval Europe*, 85.
37. Ibid., 184.

38. Ibid.
39. Ibid., 185.
40. These are discussed in Bowsky, "Medieval Citizenship."
41. Reynolds, *Kingdoms and Communities*, 186.
42. Ibid., 191.
43. Ibid., 192.
44. Ibid.; Duby, *Chivalrous Society*.
45. See, for example, Reynolds, *Kingdoms and Communities*, 224.
46. See Duby, *Early Growth*, for an explicit argument in this connection.
47. Ibid., 164.
48. MacIntyre, *After Virtue*, 160.
49. Hook, *Siena*.
50. Duby, *Chivalrous Society*.
51. Mollat, *The Poor*, 175.
52. Ibid., 129.
53. Ibid., 21–23.
54. See Tribe, *American Constitutional Law*, and Auerbach, *Justice*.
55. Auerbach, *Justice*.
56. Razi, *Life, Marriage and Death*, 1. Italics added.
57. Further, of course, the recoverable statistics of criminal prosecutions are less a measure of the total incidence of misconduct than an index of the willingness of villagers to take one another to court. Thus, the actual amount of miscount was undoubtedly higher.
58. See, for example, Reynolds, *Kingdoms and Communities*; Hook, *Siena*; and Girouard, *Cities and People*.
59. Cited in Black, *Guilds and Civil Society*, 12–13.
60. Reynolds, *Kingdoms and Communities*, 70.
61. Ibid., 72.
62. Ibid.
63. Ibid., 73.
64. Of course, craft organizations never involved close emotional ties of brotherhood and solidarity. At most, they probably involved the same sorts of friendly feelings shared by members of a trade union today.

CHAPTER 6

COMMUNITY AND THE GOOD LIFE IN
CLASSICAL ATHENS

1. MacIntyre, *After Virtue*, 112.
2. Ibid., 111.
3. Ibid., 137.
4. Ibid., 139.
5. Aristotle, *Politics* I.i.1252a1–2.
6. Ibid. III.ix.1280a26–1280b31.
7. MacIntyre, *Whose Justice?* 105.
8. Aristotle, *Politics* I.v.1254a1–8.

9. Aristotle, *Nicomachean Ethics* I.1097b.
10. Aristotle, *Politics* I.ii.1252a25–27.
11. Ibid. I.xiii.1259b40.
12. Ibid. I.xiii.1259b32ff.
13. Ibid. I.xii.1259b42.
14. Ibid. I.xiii.1259b19–29.
15. Ibid. I.xiii.1259b43.
16. Aristotle, *Eudemian Ethics* II,1218b-1219a.
17. Aristotle, *Politics* I.ii.1252a27; I.vii.1255b7.
18. Aristotle, *Nicomachean Ethics* VIII.1162a22.
19. Aristotle, *Eudemian Ethics* VII.1238b.
20. Aristotle, *Politics* I.v.1254a28.
21. Ibid. I.iv.1253b26.
22. Ibid. I.xi.1259a39.
23. Aristotle, *Generation of Animals* IV.766a.
24. Aristotle, *Politics* I.xiii.1260a24ff.
25. Ibid. III.iv.1277b19.
26. Ibid. III.iv.1277b21–22.
27. Ibid. VII.viii.1328a34.
28. Ibid. VII.viii.1328a35–36.
29. Ibid. VII.viii.1328b14.
30. Ibid. VII.viii.1328b18.
31. Ibid. VII.ix.1329a19.
32. Ibid. VII.ix.1328b33ff; 1329aff.
33. Ibid. VII.ix.1329a27–36.
34. Ibid. VII.ix.1329a2ff.
35. Ibid. VII.x.1330a25–27.
36. Ibid. IV.xi.1295b1–3.
37. Ibid. IV.xi.1295a3–16.
38. Ibid. IV.xi.1295b28–30.
39. Ibid. IV.xi.1296a8.
40. Ibid. III.xi.1281a39.
41. Ibid. III.xi.1282a24ff.
42. Ibid. III.xi.1282a15.
43. Ibid. VI.iii.1318a11ff.
44. Ibid. IV.iv:1291a43.
45. Ibid. IV.ix.1294a37–39.
46. Ibid. IV.xiii.1297b1–2.
47. In what follows, I make use of Adkins, *Merit and Responsibility*; de Ste. Croix, *Class Struggle*; Davies, *Propertied Families*; Ehrenberg, *Greek State*; Finley, *Ancient Economy* and *Politics*; Forrest, *Emergence of Greek Democracy*; Hignett, *Athenian Constitution*; Jones, *Athenian Democracy*; MacDowell, *The Law*; Ostwald, *Nomos*; Rhodes, *Athenian Boule*; and Stanton *Athenian Politics*.
48. de Ste. Croix, *Class Struggle*, 42.
49. Ibid., especially chap. 2, "Class, Exploitation, and Class Struggle."

50. Ibid., and Finley, *Politics*.
51. Finley, *Politics*, 31.
52. For the lower estimate, see Ehrenberg, *Greek State*, 33; for the higher, Finley, *Politics*, 80.
53. de Ste. Croix, *Class Struggle*, 95. Another group of noncitizens was made up of "metics" or "resident foreigners"; these men were citizens elsewhere. They were liable to paying taxes and performing military service while living as resident aliens. See MacDowell, *The Law*, 76–78.
54. de Ste. Croix, *Class Struggle*.
55. Ibid.
56. Ibid., 114–15.
57. Aristotle, *Politics* VII.iv.1326b28.
58. Quoted in de Ste. Croix, *Class Struggle*, 115. Also see Mosse, *Ancient World at Work*.
59. The resemblance with the position of the wealthy in medieval Europe and early America is striking.
60. Finley, *Politics*, 2.
61. de Ste. Croix, *Class Struggle*, 140.
62. Aristotle, *Politics* I.iii.1253b28.
63. de Ste. Croix, *Class Struggle*, 141.
64. Rhodes, *Athenian Boule*.
65. Finley, *Politics*; Jones, *Athenian Democracy*.
66. Finley, *Politics*, 140. See also de Ste. Croix, *Class Struggle*, 290.
67. MacDowell, *The Law*, 35.
68. Ibid., 172.
69. Jones, *Athenian Democracy*, 168.
70. Aristotle, *Politics* VI.vii.1321a31–32.
71. See, for example, Adkins, *Merit and Responsibility*, 202, and Davies, *Propertied Families*, 95.
72. Finley, *Politics*, 35.
73. Ibid., 45.
74. Jones, *Athenian Democracy*, 167.
75. Finley, *Politics*, 139.
76. Ibid.
77. Aristotle, *Politics* IV.xiii.1297b4.
78. Ibid. III.viii.1279a25–26.
79. Ibid. III.vii.1279b26ff.
80. Ibid. III.vii.1279a9–10.
81. de Ste. Croix, *Class Struggle*, 290.
82. Aristotle, *Politics.* IV.iv.1292a8–9.
83. Ibid. IV.iv.1292a32.
84. Ibid. VI.iii.1318a20.
85. de Ste. Croix, *Class Struggle*, 284.
86. Finley, *Ancient Slavery*, 72.
87. de Ste. Croix, *Class Struggle*, 65, 146. Also see Jameson, "Agriculture and Slavery."

88. Finley, *Ancient Slavery*, 80.
89. Ibid., 96.
90. de Ste. Croix, *Class Struggle*, 142.
91. Aristotle, *Politics* I.iv.1255b26.
92. Ibid. I.v.1254b19.
93. Ibid. VII.x.1330a25.
94. Ibid. VII.mxi.1330a26.
95. Adkins makes the same point. See Adkins, "Connection between *Ethics* and *Politics*," 42.
96. Pomeroy, *Goddesses, Whores, Wives, and Slaves*, 64.
97. Ibid., 85.
98. Ibid., 68.
99. In what follows, I draw on de Ste. Croix, *Class Struggle*, and on Schaps, *Economic Rights*,
100. Schaps, *Economic Rights*.
101. Ibid., 53.
102. de Ste. Croix, *Class Struggle*, 101.
103. Aristotle, *Politics* I.v.1254b16. For excellent critiques of Aristotle's sexism, see Elshtain, *Public Man, Private Woman*; Okin, *Women in Western Political Thought*; and Lloyd, *Men of Reason*.
104. MacIntyre, *After Virtue*, 127.
105. Ibid.
106. Ibid., 129.
107. Ibid., 129–30.
108. Finley, *Ancient Slavery*, 80.
109. Finley, *Politics*, 59. As noted earlier, Ehrenberg, *Greek State*, provides a much lower estimate of the number of citizens.
110. Okin, *Justice, Gender, and Family*, 55.
111. Finley, *Politics*, 125–26.
112. Hansen, "How Many Athenians?"
113. Finley, *Politics*, 74.
114. See, for example, Ehrenberg, "Polypragmosyme."
115. Rhodes, *Athenian Boule*, 39.
116. Ibid., 79.
117. Ibid., 5–6.
118. Finley, *Politics*, 25.
119. Moore, *Injustice*, 40.
120. Ibid.
121. Finley, *Politics*, 34.
122. de Ste. Croix, *Class Struggle*, 191, 200.
123. Walzer, *Spheres of Justice*, 71.
124. MacIntyre, *After Virtue*, 146.
125. Ibid.
126. Ibid.
127. Okin, *Justice, Gender, and Family*, 54.
128. Ibid., 245.

CHAPTER 7
LEARNING FROM HISTORY

1. Bender, *Community*, 4.
2. Quoted in Liebersohn, *Fate and Utopia*, 1.
3. Kymlicka speaks of communitarians as having "a romanticized view of earlier communities." Kymlicka, *Liberalism, Community and Culture*, 85.
4. At the same time, some of them emphasize the need to avoid a narrow sectarian view and to give serious attention to historical work. Bellah and his associates point to the absence of a sense of history among contemporary Americans, including social scientists. They advocate a "synoptic view, at once philosophical, historical, and sociological" in scholarly research, and stress the importance of "getting the story right for scholarship" in describing America's founding period. See Bellah et al., *Habits*, 298, 302. Sullivan also remarks on the lack of historical awareness, especially among liberals, in the United States today, and contrasts this with those writers in the republican tradition whose work is much more historically informed. Sullivan, *Reconstructing Public Philosophy*, 18.
5. Durkheim, *Elementary Forms*, 30.
6. See, for example, Bloch, *Royal Touch*; LeRoy Ladurie, *Peasants of Languedoc*; Stoianovich, *French Historical Method*; and Burke, "History of Mentalities."
7. The enormous influence of Durkheim on Bloch especially is discussed by Rhodes, "Durkheim and Bloch." See also Fink, *Marc Bloch*.
8. Reynolds, "Social Mentalities and Medieval Scepticism."
9. Ibid., 27.
10. Ibid.
11. Ginzburg similarly criticizes the methodology of the history of mentalities for its "decidedly classless character." Against this assumption, he makes clear that there were enormous differences between the culture of the dominant classes and the culture of the subordinate classes in sixteenth-century Europe. Ginzburg, *Cheese and Worms*, xxiii.
12. Becker, *Political Parties in New York*; Beard, *Economic Interpretation of the Constitution*.
13. Brown, *Middle-Class Democracy*; McDonald, *We the People*.
14. Lerner, "Constitution of the Thinking Revolutionary," 39.
15. Bailyn, *Ideological Origins*, 43.
16. Even if Americans had all perceived the world through the same republican lens, Rakove points out that they did not all *act* accordingly. "For however much lip service Americans paid to the concept of the virtuous republican who knew how to subordinate private interest to the common good," he observes, "remarkably few of them learned to prefer the duties of public office to the contentments of private life. The exaltation of civic life that was so central to the classical republican tradition never became dominant in America even during the Revolution, when patriot constraints were most effective." Rakove, "Structure of Politics," 265.
17. Appleby, "Republicanism and Ideology," 468. See also Appleby, *Capitalism and a New Social Order*.

18. For an excellent discussion of these matters, see Onuf, "Reflections on the Founding."
19. For a detailed consideration of sociological approaches to culture, see Wuthnow, *Meaning and Moral Order.*
20. Bellah et al., *Habits,* 335.
21. Ibid., 37.
22. Ibid., 38.
23. I noted earlier that his mistaken views about America's founding period were due partly to his having borrowed liberally from *The Federalist Papers.* He apparently accepted Jay's description of the homogeneity of the American people as the literal truth. See Schleifer, *Tocqueville's "Democracy."* For some of the Federalist writers, the term *people* referred to men of wealth, standing, and importance in the colonies, and not to the rank and file. For an interesting discussion of this tendency, see White, *Philosophy of the American Revolution.*
24. Tocqueville, *Democracy* 1:434.
25. Ibid. 2:212.
26. Schneck, "Habits of the Head," 644.
27. Galston, *Liberal Purposes,* 25–26.
28. Ibid., 27.
29. However, the evidence shows otherwise. Even in a very homogeneous group, some persons are simply not motivated to always observe the prevailing norms and values. Hechter makes it clear that social controls are necessary even for those communities that are supposedly exemplary instances of gemeinschaft. See Hechter, *Group Solidarity.*
30. Sandel, "Introduction," in Sandel, *Critics,* 7.
31. Staub, *Roots of Evil,* 19.
32. Ibid., 235.
33. Ibid.
34. This is made clear in Staub, *Roots of Evil.*
35. Rutman, *Winthrop's Boston,* 138.
36. Ibid., 98–99.
37. Ibid., 256.
38. Kanter's study of "intentional" communities—groups who choose to live permanently together away from the larger society of which they form a part—finds that homogeneity in terms of religious, social, or education background is the most important factor contributing to the success of a communal group. Kanter, *Commitment and Community.* See also Veysey, *Communal Experience.*
39. Walker, *German Home Towns.*
40. Ibid., 33.
41. Ibid., 32.
42. Ibid., 53.
43. Ibid., 55.
44. Ibid., 133.
45. Ibid., 140.
46. Ibid., 137–38.

47. Ibid., 138.
48. Ibid., 31.
49. Ibid., 121.
50. Ibid., 140.
51. Ibid., 417.
52. Ibid., 427–28.
53. Communitarians often fail to see the dangers associated with a people emphasizing their own special territory, history, traditions, language, values, and the like. Taylor, however, makes a point of acknowledging these dangers in his most recent book. Speaking of communal identity at the level of the nation, he says that "in one way or another, a nation in order to have an identity requires and develops a certain picture of its history, genesis, development—its sufferings and its achievements." But, he also observes, this need for identity "frequently combines a chauvinistic appeal to the national personality or will with a drive to power which justifies recourse to the most effective industrial and military means. The extreme case of this repulsive phenomenon was Nazi Germany." Taylor, *Sources*, 415–16.
54. Kanter, *Commitment and Community*, 84–92, gives a good description with regard to the intentional communities that she studied.
55. In addition to Kanter, *Commitment and Community*; Veysey, *Communal Experience*; and Hechter, *Group Solidarity*, other important discussions are Taylor's excellent *Community, Anarchy and Liberty*; Hostetler, *Amish Society*; Lemon, "Weakness of Place"; and Fitzgerald, *Cities on a Hill*.
56. For an excellent discussion of the processes by which insiders are turned into outsiders, see Staub, *Roots of Evil*.
57. Rozenblit, *Jews of Vienna*, 6.
58. Beller, *Vienna and the Jews*, 151.
59. Girard, "Antisemitism," 70.
60. Quoted in ibid. Sometimes it seems that things have not changed very much. In his recent novel *Deception*, Philip Roth reports the following episode. Three Jewish men were taking a Sunday walk in Chelsea (London). They passed two men who, judging by their clothes, were some sort of professionals. As they did, they heard them mumbling out loud. The narrator asked one of the men what was bothering them, what they were mumbling about. "At first he glared back at me. Then he gestured at his own clothes and he shouted, 'You don't even dress right.' " The narrator says that he kept puzzling over the man's behavior, "and then it dawned on me: the reason my clothes just like his were wrong was *because* they were just like his. What with my beard and my looks and my gesticulations, I should have been wearing a caftan and a black felt hat. I should have been wrapped in a prayer shawl. I shouldn't have been in clothes like his *at all*." Roth, *Deception*, 106.
61. Arendt, *Origins of Totalitarianism*, 87.
62. Beller, *Vienna and the Jews*, 162. See also Rozenblit, *Jews of Vienna*.
63. See Staub, *Roots of Evil*. See also Horowitz, *Taking Lives*.
64. Although his concern is specifically with genocide rather than group violence more generally, Melson's analysis of the factors preceding geno-

cide has a broader application. Melson, "Provocation or Nationalism," 79–80.

65. Sandel, "Introduction," in Sandel, *Critics*, 6.
66. MacIntyre, *After Virtue*, 204, his italics; Sandel, *Liberalism*, 183; and Bellah et al., *Habits*, 335.
67. Bellah et al., *Habits*. The "common good" is also given much attention by other communitarian writers. See, for example, Taylor, *Sources*; Sullivan, *Reconstructing Public Philosophy*; Ketcham, *Individualism and Public Life*; and Jackson, *Matters of Justice*.
68. Okin, *Justice, Gender, and Family*, 67.
69. Aristotle, *Politics* III.vii.1279a26.
70. Duby, *Early Growth*, 167.
71. Ibid., 168.
72. Quoted in Morrall, *Political Thought in Medieval Times*, 76.
73. Ibid.
74. MacIntyre, *Whose Justice?*
75. Nussbaum, "Recoiling from Reason," 36.
76. Bellah et al., *Habits*, 252.
77. Wood provides an excellent extended discussion of the distinction between "patricians and plebians" in his recent book. See Wood, *Radicalism*, 24–42. Because his book appeared just as I was completing my own, I have not been able to incorporate his arguments and conclusions into the earlier chapters.
78. Wood, *Radicalism*, provides a good discussion of the assault on aristocracy and the reactions of gentlemen to the actions of the common folk.
79. George Fitzhugh, *Sociology for the South, or the Failure of Free Society* (Richmond, Va., 1854). Quoted in de Ste. Croix, *Class Struggle*, 417.
80. Interview with John Womack in Abelove et al., *Visions of History*, 261.

## CHAPTER 8
### A LIBERAL RESPONSE TO COMMUNITARIAN THOUGHT

1. Rawls, *Theory of Justice*. Others being criticized are Dworkin, *Taking Rights Seriously*, and Gewirth, *Reason and Morality*. My own recent work also stresses rights and justice. See Phillips, *Just Social Order*.
2. Sandel, "Introduction," in Sandel, *Critics*, 4.
3. Ibid., 3, 5.
4. Taylor, *Sources*, 413.
5. Ibid., 84.
6. Ibid.
7. Kymlicka offers an especially systematic and detailed exploration of these communitarian claims. See Kymlicka, *Liberalism, Community and Culture*, chap. 4, "Communitarianism and the Self."
8. MacIntyre, "Patriotism," 7.
9. Kymlicka, *Liberalism, Community and Culture*, 76.

10. Sandel, "Introduction," in Sandel, *Critics*, 5–6.
11. Taylor, *Sources*, 35.
12. Kymlicka, *Liberalism, Community and Culture*, 54. Galston objects to this view because he sees this conception of individuality as tending "to exclude individuals and groups that do not place a high value on personal autonomy and reasonable plans of life." See Galston, *Liberal Purposes*, 153. But contrary to what he suggests, development toward autonomy is something experienced by every normal human being. This has its origin in early childhood, as the individual acquires a sense of separation and differentiation. Beyond this, the process of growing up necessarily involves some revisions in the life plans of everyone. Unfortunately, most moral and political theorists forget the fact that we have not always been adults. Even Okin's recent book on justice and the family gives surprisingly little attention to how children begin to acquire a sense of morality as they learn that their own pursuit of autonomy will often come into conflict with others who are doing the same. See Okin, *Justice, Gender, and Family*.
13. Sandel, *Liberalism*, 172–73.
14. Ibid., 143.
15. Taylor, *Sources*, 175.
16. Ibid.
17. Ibid., 181.
18. Sandel, *Liberalism*, 143.
19. Ibid., 179.
20. Ibid., 180.
21. Taylor, *Sources*, 507.
22. MacIntyre, *After Virtue*, 216.
23. Benhabib and Cornell, "Introduction: Beyond the Politics of Gender," in Benhabib and Cornell, *Feminism as Critique*, 12.
24. Sandel, *Liberalism*, 179.
25. MacIntyre, *Whose Justice?* 349.
26. Ibid., 391.
27. MacIntyre, "Patriotism," 10.
28. Ibid., 10–11.
29. Ibid.
30. Durkheim, *Sociology and Philosophy*, 56.
31. Durkheim, "Pragmatism and Sociology," 433.
32. Durkheim, *Moral Education*, 74.
33. Ibid., 76.
34. It is important to note here that liberals do not object to patriotism or loyalty per se. Within the limits set by violations of individuals' basic rights, there is no objection to people having a special concern for the well-being and flourishing of their own country or any other community.
35. See Gewirth, "Human Rights."
36. Rawls, *Theory of Justice*; Nozick, *Anarchy, State, and Utopia*; Dworkin, *Taking Rights Seriously*; and Gewirth, *Reason and Morality*. While communitarians sometimes speak of "the primacy of rights" in liberal thought, this is a mis-

taken characterization. It is, rather, needs and interests inescapably connected with being a human agent that have primacy.

37. Bellah, "A Response," 182.

38. Sandel, "Introduction," in Sandel, *Critics*, 4.

39. See, for example, Gutmann, "Communitarian Critics"; Wallach, "Liberals, Communitarians, and Political Theory"; Buchanan, "Assessing"; Gewirth, "Ethical Universalism and Particularism" and "Rights and Virtues"; Kymlicka, *Liberalism, Community and Culture*; and Galston, *Liberal Purposes*.

40. Nozick, *Anarchy, State, and Utopia*, ix.

41. See, for example, Hart, "Are There Any Natural Rights?" and Melden, *Rights and Duties*.

42. Rawls, *Theory of Justice*.

43. Gewirth, *Reason and Morality*. See also Phillips, *Just Social Order*.

44. See my discussions in Phillips, *Equality, Justice and Rectification*, and in "Fundamental Rights and the Supportive State."

45. Gewirth, "Moral Foundations," 128.

46. Buchanan, "Assessing," 854.

47. Galston, *Liberal Purposes*, 12. This emphasis on pain and humiliation has been a central theme in the writings of Judith Shklar. See, for example, Shklar, *Ordinary Vices* and "Injustice, Injury, and Inequality."

48. See, for example, Martin and Nickel, "Recent Work."

49. This is at least ideally the case. But most liberal political theorists—and the actual social and legal arrangements in society—ignore the private realm of familial, domestic, and sexual relations. See, for example, Pateman, *Disorder of Women*; Okin, *Justice, Gender, and Family*; and Young, *Justice and the Politics of Difference*.

50. Thompson, *Rights, Restitution, and Risk*, 254. But, of course, rights and justice do not exhaust the content of morality. Although my focus in this volume has been on communitarian and liberal conceptions of morality, I recognize the need for a far broader conception of morality. I am in basic agreement with Taylor's comments about morality being concerned with questions about our life as a whole, both with what we are and with what we do. He writes: "We want our lives to have meaning, or weight, or substance, or to grow towards some fulness, or however the concern is formulated." This means, he says, "our *whole* lives." Taylor, *Sources*, 50, 58. Becker, Hampshire, and Louden also advance broad conceptions of morality. See Becker, *Reciprocity*; Hampshire, *Innocence and Experience*; and Louden, *Morality and Moral Theory*. Personal character, individual actions, and institutional arrangements all ought to be of concern to any full-fledged moral theory. In a book concerned with what might be termed "the sociology of morality," I intend to deal with morality in terms of these various components.

51. For a similar view of liberal political theory, see Becker, *Reciprocity*, 499–500.

52. Kymlicka, *Liberalism, Community and Culture*, 77.

53. Ibid., 76.

54. See my extended discussion in Phillips, *Just Social Order*.

55. I draw here on Gewirth's discussion of the two main meanings of the "common good." Gewirth, *Human Rights*, 236–37.
56. I discuss and defend many features of such a just society elsewhere. See Phillips, *Just Social Order*.
57. Etzioni, "I & We Paradigm," 173.
58. Walzer, "Communitarian Critique," 21.
59. Ibid., 17.
60. Ibid., 11.
61. Tönnies, *Community and Society*, 74.
62. Durkheim, *Division of Labor*, 28.
63. Durkheim, *Moral Education*, 240.
64. See, for example, Fischer, *Networks and Places* and *To Dwell Among Friends*; Hunter, "Private, Parochial and Public Social Orders; and Wellman et al., "Networks as Personal Communities."
65. Fischer, *Networks and Places*, 202.
66. See also Tilly, "Misreading, then Rereading."
67. As Levy reminds us, throughout history most people have spent more time in family contexts than in any other social context, and family interests, priorities, and loyalties generally have cut deeper than any other attachments. See Levy, *Our Mother-Tempers*, 48, 61.
68. Determining the structure and quality of different individuals' social relationships in the past would involve the study of diaries, correspondence, autobiographies, and other such materials. For many periods, of course, such materials are nonexistent. But only those sorts of materials would allow answers to questions about people's networks of social relations in the past.
69. For an excellent argument in this regard, see Christine M. Korsgaard, "Personal Identity." See also Piper, "Two Conceptions."
70. Bloch, *Feudal Society* 1:124.
71. Ibid., 231–32.
72. Ibid. 2:450.
73. Issac, *Transformation*, 113. Perkin similarly speaks of eighteenth-century "friends" as "all those who expected or, reciprocally, from whom one could expect the benefits of patronage." See Perkin, *Origins*, 46–51.
74. Quoted in Silver, "Friendship in Commercial Society," 1481. The quotation is from Smith, *Theory of Moral Sentiments*.
75. Silver, "Friendship and Trust," 283.
76. See also Silver, " 'Trust' in Theory," and "Curious Importance of Small Groups." For an excellent discussion of the importance of friendship and the dangers of community, see Friedman, "Feminism and Modern Friendship." See also Baron, "Impartiality and Friendship."
77. Surprisingly, however, not even the most recent communitarian writing mentions the important research of Gilligan and the ideas of other feminists who emphasize connection and care. See Gilligan, *In a Different Voice*; Noddings, *Caring*; and the various essays in Kittay and Meyers, *Women and Moral Theory*.

# BIBLIOGRAPHY

Abelove, Henry, Betsy Blackmar, Peter Dimock, and Jonathan Schneer, eds. *Visions of History*. New York: Pantheon Books, 1983.

Abramson, Jeffrey B. *Liberalism and Its Limits*. Boston: Beacon Press, 1986.

Adkins, Arthur W. H. "The Connection between Aristotle's *Ethics* and *Politics*." *Political Theory* 12 (February 1984): 29–50.

———. *Merit and Responsibility: A Study in Greek Values*. Oxford: Oxford University Press, 1960.

Allen, David Grayson. *In English Ways: The Movements of Societies and the Transferal of English Local Law and Custom to Massachusetts Bay in the Seventeenth Century*. New York: Norton, 1982.

Anderson, Ken, Paul Piccone, Fred Siegel, and Michael Taves. "Roundtable on Communitarianism." *Telos* 76 (Summer 1988): 2–32.

Appleby, Joyce. *Capitalism and a New Social Order: The Republican Vision of the 1790s*. New York: New York University Press, 1984.

———. "Republicanism and Ideology." *American Quarterly* 37 (1985): 450–68.

———. "Value and Society." In *Colonial British America: Essays in the New History of the Early Modern Era*, edited by Jack P. Greene and J. R. Pole. Baltimore: Johns Hopkins University Press, 1984.

Arendt, Hannah. *The Origins of Totalitarianism*. London: Allen & Unwin, 1962.

Aristotle. *Eudemian Ethics*. Translated by H. Rackham. Loeb Classical Library, 1935.

———. *The Generation of Animals*. Translated by A. L. Peck. Loeb Classical Library, 1943.

———. *Nicomachean Ethics*. Translated by Martin Ostwald. Indianapolis: Bobbs-Merrill, 1962.

———. *The Politics*. Translated by T. A. Sinclair. New York: Penguin Books, 1982.

Auerbach, Jerold. *Justice without Law*. New York: Oxford University Press, 1975.

Bailyn, Bernard. *The Ideological Origins of the American Revolution*. Cambridge, Mass.: Harvard University Press, 1967.

———. *The Pamphlets of the American Revolution*. Cambridge, Mass.: Harvard University Press, 1965.

Barber, Bernard. *Strong Democracy: Participatory Politics for a New Age*. Berkeley: University of California Press, 1984.

Baron, Marcia. "Impartiality and Friendship." *Ethics* 101 (July 1991): 836–57.

Bartlett, Robert. *Trial by Fire and Water: The Medieval Judicial Ordeal*. Oxford: Clarendon Press, 1988.

Bay, Christian. *Strategies of Political Emancipation*. South Bend, Ind.: Notre Dame Press, 1981.

Beard, Charles A. *An Economic Interpretation of the Constitution of the United States*. New York: Macmillan, 1913.

Becker, Carl L. *The History of Political Parties in the Province of New York, 1760–1776.* Madison: University of Wisconsin Press, 1909.

Becker, Lawrence C. *Reciprocity.* Boston: Routledge & Kegan Paul, 1986.

Beeman, Richard, Stephen Botein, and Edward C. Carter, II, eds. *Beyond Confederation: Origins of the Constitution and American National Identity.* Chapel Hill: University of North Carolina Press, 1987.

Beitz, Charles. *Political Equality.* Princeton: Princeton University Press, 1989.

Bellah, Robert N. "A Response: The Idea of Practices in *Habits.*" *Soundings* 49 (Spring/Summer 1986): 181–87.

Bellah, Robert N., Richard Madsen, William M. Sullivan, Ann Swidler, and Steven M. Tipton. *Habits of the Heart: Individualism and Commitment in American Life.* Berkeley: University of California Press, 1985.

Bellamy, Edward. *Looking Backward, 2000–1887.* 1888. Reprint. New York: Penguin Books, 1982.

Beller, Steven. *Vienna and the Jews, 1867–1938: A Cultural History.* Cambridge: Cambridge University Press, 1989.

Bender, Thomas. *Community and Social Change in America.* New Brunswick, N.J.: Rutgers University Press, 1978.

Benhabib, Seyla, and Drucilla Cornell, eds. *Feminism as Critique.* Minneapolis: University of Minnesota Press, 1987.

Bertelson, David. *The Lazy South.* New York: Oxford University Press, 1967.

Billington, Ray Allen. *Westward Expansion: A History of the American Frontier.* New York: Macmillan, 1960.

Black, Antony. *Guilds and Civil Society in European Political Thought from the Twelfth Century to the Present.* London: Methuen, 1984.

Bloch, Marc. *Feudal Society.* Translated by L. A. Manyon. 2 vols. Chicago: University of Chicago Press, 1961.

―――. *The Royal Touch.* Translated by J. E. Anderson. London: Routledge & Kegan Paul, 1973.

Bloch, Maurice. *Marxism and Anthropology: The History of a Relationship.* Oxford: Clarendon Press, 1983.

Bowsky, W. M. "Medieval Citizenship: The Individual and the State in the Commune of Siena, 1287–1355." *Studies in Medieval and Renaissance History* 4 (1967): 193–243.

Boyer, Paul, and Stephen Nissenbaum. *Salem Possessed: The Social Origins of Witchcraft.* Cambridge, Mass.: Harvard University Press, 1974.

Braybrooke, David. *Meeting Needs.* Princeton: Princeton University Press, 1987.

Breen, T. H. *Puritans and Adventurers: Change and Persistence in Early America.* New York: Oxford University Press, 1980.

―――. *Tobacco Culture: The Mentality of the Great Tidewater Planters on the Eve of Revolution.* Princeton: Princeton University Press, 1985.

Brown, Robert E. *Middle-Class Democracy and the Revolution in Massachusetts, 1691–1788.* Ithaca: Cornell University Press, 1955.

Brown, Robert E., and Katherine B. Brown. *Virginia 1705–1786: Democracy or Aristocracy?* East Lansing: Michigan State University Press, 1964.

Brown, Thad. A. *Migration and Politics.* Chapel Hill: University of North Carolina Press, 1973.

Buchanan, Allen E. "Assessing the Communitarian Critique of Liberalism." *Ethics* 99 (July 1989): 852–82.

Burke, Peter. "The History of Mentalities in Great Britain." *Tijdschrift voor Geschiedenis* 93 (1980): 529–40.

Burnaby, Andrew. *Travels through the Middle Settlements of North-America in the Years 1759 and 1760.* Ithaca: Cornell University Press, 1960.

Bushman, Richard L. "American High-Style and Vernacular Cultures." In *Colonial British America: Essays in the New History of the Early Modern Era*, edited by Jack P. Greene and J. R. Pole. Baltimore: Johns Hopkins University Press, 1984.

Carroll, Peter N., and David W. Noble. *The Free and the Unfree: A New History of the United States.* New York: Penguin Books, 1977.

Casey, Kathleen. "The Cheshire Cat: Reconstructing the Experience of Medieval Women." In *Liberating Women's History*, edited by Bernice A. Carroll. Urbana: University of Illinois Press, 1976.

Comte, Auguste. *The Positive Polity.* Translated by Harriet Martineau. 3 vols. New York: Calvin Blanchard, 1955.

Connolly, W. E. *Appearance and Reality in Politics.* Cambridge: Cambridge University Press, 1981.

Cook, Edward M., Jr. *The Fathers of the Towns: Leadership and Community in Eighteenth-Century New England.* Baltimore: Johns Hopkins University Press, 1976.

Cott, Nancy F. *The Bonds of Womanhood: Women's Sphere in New England, 1780–1835.* New Haven: Yale University Press, 1977.

Davies, J. K. *Athenian Propertied Families, 600–300 B.C.* Oxford: Oxford University Press, 1971.

Davis, David Brian. *The Problem of Slavery in the Age of Revolution, 1770–1823.* Ithaca: Cornell University Press, 1975.

Davis, Joseph L. *Sectionalism in American Politics: 1774–1787.* Madison: University of Wisconsin Press, 1977.

Degler, Carl. *At Odds: Women and Family in America from the Revolution to the Present.* New York: Oxford University Press, 1980.

Demos, John. *A Little Commonwealth: Family Life in Plymouth Colony.* New York: Oxford University Press, 1970.

de Ste. Croix, G.E.M. *The Class Struggle in the Ancient Greek World.* London: Duckworth, 1984.

Dexter, Elisabeth Anthony. *Colonial Women of Affairs: Women in Business and the Professions in America before 1776.* Rev. ed. Boston: Houghton Mifflin, 1931.

Diggins, John Patrick. *The Lost Soul of American Politics: Virtue, Self-Interest, and the Foundations of Liberalism.* New York: Basic Books, 1984.

Duby, Georges. *The Age of the Cathedrals.* Translated by Eleanor Levieux and Barbara Thompson. London: Croon, Helm, 1981.

———. *The Chivalrous Society.* Translated by Cynthia Postan. Berkeley: University of California Press, 1980.

———. *The Early Growth of the European Economy.* Translated by Howard B. Clarke. Ithaca: Cornell University Press, 1974.

Dunn, Richard S. "Servants and Slaves: The Recruitment and Employment of Labor." In *Colonial British America: Essays in the New History of the Early Modern*

*Era*, edited by Jack P. Greene and J. R. Pole. Baltimore: Johns Hopkins University Press, 1984.

Durkheim, Emile. *The Division of Labor in Society*. Translated by George Simpson. New York: Free Press, 1949.

———. *The Elementary Forms of the Religious Life*. Translated by Joseph W. Swain. New York: Free Press, 1965.

———. *Moral Education*. Translated by Everett K. Wilson and Herman Schnurer. New York: Free Press, 1973.

———. "Pragmatism and Sociology." In *Essays on Sociology and Philosophy*, edited by Kurt H. Wolff. New York: Harper Torchbooks, 1964.

———. *Socialism and Saint-Simon*. Edited by Alvin W. Gouldner. Yellow Springs, Ohio: Antioch Press, 1958.

———. *Sociology and Philosophy*. Translated by D. F. Pocock. Glencoe, Ill.: Free Press, 1953.

Dworkin, Ronald. *Taking Rights Seriously*. London: Duckworth, 1979.

Ehrenberg, V. L. *The Greek State*. London: Methuen, 1969.

———. "Polypragmosyme: A Study in Greek Politics." *Journal of Hellenic Studies* 67 (1947): 46–47.

Elstain, Jean Bethke. *Public Man, Private Woman: Women in Social and Political Thought*. Princeton: Princeton University Press, 1981.

Etzioni, Amitai. "Toward an I & We Paradigm." *Contemporary Sociology* 18 (March 1989): 171–75.

Farrand, Max, ed. *The Records of the Federal Conventions of 1787*. Rev. ed. New Haven: Yale University Press, 1966.

Feingold, Henry L. *Zion in America: The Jewish Experience from Colonial Times to the Present*. New York: Twayne Publishers, 1974.

Fink, Carole. *Marc Bloch: A Life in History*. Cambridge: Cambridge University Press, 1989.

Finkelman, Paul. "Antifederalists: The Loyal Opposition and the American Constitution." *Cornell Law Review* 70 (November 1984): 182–207.

———. "Slavery and the Constitutional Convention: Making a Covenant with Death." In *Beyond Confederation: Origins of the Constitution and American National Identity*, edited by Richard Beeman, Stephen Botein, and Edward C. Carter, II. Chapel Hill: University of North Carolina Press, 1987.

Finley, M. I. *The Ancient Economy*. Berkeley: University of California Press, 1973.

———. *Ancient Slavery and Modern Ideology*. London: Chatto & Windus, 1980.

———. *Politics in the Ancient World*. Cambridge: Cambridge University Press, 1983.

Fischer, Claude S. *Networks and Places: Social Networks in an Urban Society*. New York: Free Press, 1977.

———. *To Dwell among Friends: Personal Networks in Town and City*. Berkeley: University of California Press, 1982.

Fitzgerald, Frances. *Cities on a Hill*. New York: Simon and Schuster, 1986.

Flaherty, David H. *Privacy in Colonial New England*. Charlottesville: University of Virginia Press, 1972.

Fliegelman, Jay. *Prodigals and Pilgrims: The American Revolution against Patriarchal Authority, 1780–1800*. Cambridge: Cambridge University Press, 1982.

Forrest, W. G. *The Emergence of Greek Democracy*. London: Weidenfeld and Nic-
olsen, 1978.

Fowler, Robert Booth. *The Dance with Community: The Contemporary Debate in American Political Thought*. Lawrence: University Press of Kansas, 1991.

Friedman, Marilyn. "Feminism and Modern Friendship: Dislocating the Community." *Ethics* 99 (January 1989): 275–90.

Galston, William A. *Liberal Purposes: Goods, Virtues, and Diversity in the Liberal State*.
New York: Cambridge University Press, 1991.

Galvin, John R. *Three Men of Boston*. New York: Thomas Y. Crowell, 1976.

Gewirth, Alan. "Ethical Universalism and Particularism." *The Journal of Philosophy*
65 (June 1988): 283–302.

———. "Human Rights and Conceptions of the Self." *Philosophica* 18 (1988):
129–49.

———. *Human Rights: Essays on Justification and Application*. Chicago: University
of Chicago Press, 1982.

———. "Moral Foundations of Civil Rights Law." *The Journal of Law and Religion*
5 (1987): 125–47.

———. *Reason and Morality*. Chicago: University of Chicago Press, 1978.

———. "Rights and Virtues." *Review of Metaphysics* 38 (June 1985): 739–62.

Gilligan, Carol. *In a Different Voice*. Cambridge, Mass.: Harvard University Press,
1982.

Ginzburg, Carlo. *The Cheese and the Worms: The Cosmos of a Sixteenth-Century Miller*.
Translated by John and Anne Tedeschi. New York: Penguin Books, 1984.

Girard, Patrick. "Historical Foundations of Antisemitism." In *Survivors, Victims,
and Perpetrators: Essays on the Nazi Holocaust*, edited by Joel E. Dinsdale. Washington: Hemisphere Publishing Company, 1980.

Girouard, Mark. *Cities and People*. New Haven: Yale University Press, 1985.

Glass, David V., and D. E. C. Eversley, eds. *Population in History*. London: Edward
Arnold, 1974.

Goff, Jacques le. *Medieval Civilization: 400–1500*. Translated by Julia Barrow. Oxford: Basil Blackwell, 1989.

Goody, Jack. "The Evolution of the Family." In *Household and Family in Past Time*,
edited by Peter Laslett and Richard Walls. Cambridge: Cambridge University Press, 1972.

Goody, Jack, Joan Thirsk, and E. P. Thompson, eds. *Family and Inheritance*. Cambridge: Cambridge University Press, 1976.

Greene, Jack P. *All Men Are Created Equal*. Oxford: Clarendon Press, 1976.

———. "An Uneasy Connection: An Analysis of the Preconditions of the American Revolution." In *Essays on the American Revolution*, edited by James H. Hutson. Chapel Hill: University of North Carolina Press, 1972.

———, ed. *The Reinterpretation of the American Revolution, 1763–1789*. New York:
Harper & Row, 1968.

Greene, Jack P., and J. R. Pole, eds. *Colonial British America: Essays in the New
History of the Early Modern Era*. Baltimore: Johns Hopkins University Press,
1984.

Greven, Philip J., Jr. *Four Generations: Population, Land, and Family in Colonial America*. Ithaca: Cornell University Press, 1970.

Gurr, T. R. "Historical Trends in Violent Crime: A Critical Review of the Evidence." *Crime and Justice: An Annual Review of Research* 3 (1981): 295–343.

Gutmann, Amy. "Communitarian Critics of Liberalism." *Philosophy and Public Affairs* 14 (Summer 1985): 308–22.

Hall, Peter Dobkin. "Family Structure and Economic Organization: Massachusetts Merchants, 1700–1850." In *Family and Kin in Urban Communities, 1700–1930*, edited by Tamara K. Hareven. New York: New Viewpoints, 1977.

Hampshire, Stuart. *Innocence and Experience.* London: Penguin Books, 1989.

Hansen, M. H. "How Many Athenians Attended the Ecclesia?" *Greek, Roman and Byzantine Studies* 17 (1976): 115–34.

Hart, H. L. A. "Are There Any Natural Rights?" *The Philosophical Review* 44 (April 1955): 175–91.

Hartz, Louis. *The Liberal Tradition in America: An Interpretation of American Political Thought since the Revolution.* New York: Harcourt, Brace, 1955.

Haskins, George Lee. *Law and Authority in Early Massachusetts.* New York: Macmillan, 1960.

Hechter, Michael. *Principles of Group Solidarity.* Berkeley: University of California Press, 1987.

Henretta, James A. "Families and Farms: *Mentalité* in Pre-Industrial America." *William and Mary Quarterly* 30 (January 1978): 3–32.

Herlihy, David. *Medieval Households.* Cambridge, Mass.: Harvard University Press, 1985.

Herzog, Don. "Some Questions for Republicans." *Political Theory* 14 (August 1986): 473–93.

Hignett, C. *A History of the Athenian Constitution.* Oxford: Oxford University Press, 1952.

Hilton, R. H. *The English Peasantry in the Late Middle Ages.* Oxford: Oxford University Press, 1975.

Hirsch, H. N. "The Threnody of Liberalism: Constitutional Liberty and the Renewal of Community." *Political Theory* 14 (August 1986): 423–49.

Hoeder, Dick. "Boston Leaders and Boston Crowds." In *The American Revolution: Explorations in the History of American Radicalism*, edited by Alfred F. Young. DeKalb: Northern Illinois University Press, 1976.

Homans, George. *English Villagers of the Thirteenth Century.* Cambridge, Mass.: Harvard University Press, 1942.

Hook, Judith. *Siena: A City and Its History.* London: Hamish Hamilton, 1979.

Horowitz, Irving Louis. *Taking Lives: Genocide and State Power.* New Brunswick, N.J.: Transaction Books, 1980.

Hostetler, John A. *Amish Society.* Rev. ed. Baltimore: Johns Hopkins University Press, 1969.

Howe, Daniel Walker. "European Sources of Political Ideas in Jeffersonian America." *Reviews in American History* 10 (December 1982): 28–44.

Hunter, Albert. "Private, Parochial and Public Social Orders: The Problem of Crime and Incivility in Urban Communities." In *The Challenge of Social Con-*

*trol.* edited by Gerald B. Suttles and Mayer N. Zald, 230–42. Norwood, N.J.: Ablex, 1985.

Hutson, James. "Country, Court, and Constitution." *William and Mary Quarterly* 38 (1981): 337–68.

Isaac, Rhys. *The Transformation of Virginia, 1740–1790.* Chapel Hill: University of North Carolina Press, 1982.

Jackson, Michael. *Matters of Justice.* London: Croon Helm, 1986.

Jameson, Michael H. "Agriculture and Slavery in Classical Athens." *Classical Journal* 73 (1977–78): 122–45.

Jefferson, Thomas. *Notes on the State of Virginia.* Edited by William Peden. Chapel Hill: University of North Carolina Press, 1955.

Jensen, Merrill. *The Founding of a Nation: A History of the American Revolution, 1763–1776.* New York: Oxford University Press, 1968.

Jones, A. H. M. *Athenian Democracy.* New York: Praeger, 1957.

Jones, Alice Hanson. *American Colonial Wealth: Documents and Methods.* Vol. 3. New York: Arno Books, 1977.

Jones, Hugh. *The Present State of Virginia, from Whence Is Inferred a Sort View of Maryland and North Carolina.* Edited by Richard L. Morton. Chapel Hill: University of North Carolina Press, 1956.

Kamenka, Eugene, and R. S. Neal, eds. *Feudalism, Capitalism, and Beyond.* London: Edward Arnold, 1975.

Kammen, Michael. *Selvages & Biases: The Fabric of History in American Culture.* Ithaca: Cornell University Press, 1987.

Kanter, Rosabeth Moss. *Commitment and Community: Communes and Utopias in Sociological Perspective.* Cambridge, Mass.: Harvard University Press, 1972.

Kelley, Robert. *The Cultural Pattern in American Politics: The First Generation.* New York: Knopf, 1979.

Ketcham, Ralph. *Individualism and Public Life.* Oxford: Blackwell, 1987.

Kirshner, Julius, and Karl F. Morrison, eds. *Western Civilization.* Vol. 4. *Medieval Europe.* Chicago: University of Chicago Press, 1986.

Kittay, Eva, and Diana T. Meyers, eds. *Women and Moral Theory.* Savage, Md.: Rowman and Littlefield, 1987.

Koehler, Lyle. *A Search for Power: The "Weaker Sex" in Seventeenth-Century New England.* Urbana: University of Illinois Press, 1980.

Konig, David T. *Law and Society in Puritan Massachusetts: Essex County, 1629–1692.* Chapel Hill: University of North Carolina Press, 1979.

Korsgaard, Christine M. "Personal Identity and the Unity of Agency: A Kantian Response to Parfit." *Philosophy and Public Affairs* 18 (Spring 1989): 101–32.

Kramnick, Isaac. "The 'Great National Discussion': The Discourse of Politics in 1787." *William and Mary Quarterly* 35 (January 1988): 3–32.

Kymlicka, Will. *Liberalism, Community and Culture.* Oxford: Clarendon Press, 1989.

Larmore, Charles. *Patterns of Moral Complexity.* New York: Cambridge University Press, 1987.

Lasch, Christopher. "The Communitarian Critique of Liberalism." *Soundings* 49 (Spring/Summer 1986): 60–76.

Laslett, Peter. *The World We Have Lost: England before the Industrial Age.* 2d ed. New York: Charles Scribner's Sons, 1973.

Lemon, James T. "Spatial Order: Households in Local Communities and Regions." In *Colonial British America: Essays in the New History of the Early Modern Era,* edited by Jack P. Greene and J. R. Pole, 86–122. Baltimore: Johns Hopkins University Press, 1984.

———. "The Weakness of Place and Community in Early Pennsylvania." In *European Settlement and Development in North America,* edited by James R. Gibson, 190–207. Toronto: University of Toronto Press, 1978.

Lerner, Ralph. "The Constitution of the Thinking Revolutionary." In *Beyond Confederation: Origins of the Constitution and National Identity,* edited by Richard Beeman, Stephen Botein, and Edward C. Carter, II. Chapel Hill: University of North Carolina Press, 1987.

LeRoy Ladurie, Emmanuel. *Montaillou.* Translated by Barbara Bray. New York: Vintage Books, 1979.

———. *The Peasants of Lanquedoc.* Translated by John Day. Urbana: University of Illinois Press, 1974.

Levy, Marion J. *Our Mother-Tempers.* Berkeley: University of California Press, 1989.

Lewis, Jan. *The Pursuit of Happiness: Family and Values in Jefferson's Virginia.* New York: Cambridge University Press, 1983.

Liebersohn, Harry. *Fate and Utopia in German Sociology, 1870–1923.* Cambridge, Mass.: MIT Press, 1989.

Little, Lester K. *Religious Poverty and the Profit Economy in Medieval Europe.* London: Paul Elek, 1978.

Lloyd, Genevieve. *The Men of Reason: 'Male' and 'Female' in Western Philosophy.* London: Methuen, 1984.

Lockridge, Kenneth A. *A New England Town: The First Hundred Years, Dedham, Massachusetts, 1636–1736.* New York: Norton, 1970.

———. *Settlement and Unsettlement in Early America: The Crisis of Political Legitimacy before the Revolution.* New York: Cambridge University Press, 1981.

Louden, Robert B. *Morality and Moral Theory: A Reappraisal and Reaffirmation.* New York: Oxford University Press, 1992.

Lynd, Staughton. *Class Conflict, Slavery, and the United States Constitution.* Indianapolis: Bobbs-Merrill, 1967.

McCoy, Drew. "James Madison and Visions of American Nationality in the Confederate Period: A Regional Perspective." In *Beyond Confederation: Origins of the Constitution and American National Identity,* edited by Richard Beeman, Stephen Botein, and Edward C. Carter, II. Chapel Hill: University of North Carolina Press, 1987.

McDonald, Forrest. *Novus Ordo Seclorum: The Intellectual Origins of the Constitution and American National Identity.* Chapel Hill: University of North Carolina Press, 1987.

———. *We the People: The Economic Origins of the Constitution.* Chicago: University of Chicago Press, 1958.

MacDowell, Douglas M. *The Law in Classical Athens.* London: Thames and Hudson, 1978.

Macfarlane, Alan. *The Origins of English Individualism.* Oxford: Basil Blackwell, 1978.

Macfarlane, Alan, Sarah Harrison, and Charles Jardine. *Reconstructing Historical Communities.* Cambridge: Cambridge University Press, 1977.

MacIntyre, Alasdair. *After Virtue: A Study in Moral Theory.* London: Duckworth, 1981.

———. "Is Patriotism a Virtue?" Lindley Lecture, University of Kansas Philosophy Department, 1984.

———. *Whose Justice? Which Rationality?* London: Duckworth, 1988.

McManis, Douglas R. *Colonial New England: A Historical Geography.* New York: Oxford University Press, 1975.

McNamara, Jo Ann, and Suzanne F. Wemple. "Sanctity and Power: The Dual Pursuit of Medieval Women." In *Becoming Visible: Women in European History,* edited by Renate Bridenthal and Claudia Koonz. Boston: Houghton Mifflin, 1977.

MacPherson, C. B. *The Political Theory of Possessive Individualism.* New York: Oxford University Press, 1964.

McWilliams, Wilson Carey. *The Idea of Fraternity in America.* Berkeley: University of California Press, 1974.

Maier, Pauline. *From Resistance to Revolution: Colonial Radicals and the Development of American Opposition to Britain, 1765–1776.* New York: Vintage Books, 1974.

———. *The Old Revolutionaries: Political Lives in the Age of Samuel Adams.* New York: Vintage Books, 1982.

Main, Jackson Turner. *The Social Structure of Revolutionary America.* Princeton: Princeton University Press, 1965.

Mansbridge, Jane J. *Beyond Adversary Democracy.* Chicago: University of Chicago Press, 1980.

Martin, Rex, and James W. Nickel. "Recent Work on the Concept of Rights." *American Philosophical Quarterly* 17 (1980): 165–80.

Marx, Karl. *A Contribution to the Critique of Political Economy.* In Karl Marx and Friedrich Engels, *Selected Writings.* London: Lawrence & Wishart, 1968.

———. *Pre-Capitalism Economic Formation.* Translated by Jack Cohen. Edited by Eric Hobsbawn. London: Lawrence & Wishart, 1964.

Matthews, Richard K. "Liberalism, Civic Humanism, and the American Political Tradition: Understanding Genesis." *The Journal of Politics* 49 (November 1987): 1127–53.

———. *The Radical Politics of Thomas Jefferson: A Revisionist View.* Lawrence: University Press of Kansas, 1986.

Meinig, D. W. *The Shaping of America: A Geographical Perspective on 500 Years of History.* Vol. 1. New Haven: Yale University Press, 1986.

Melden, A. I. *Rights and Duties.* Oxford: Basil Blackwell, 1977.

Melson, Robert. "Provocation or Nationalism: A Critical Inquiry into the Armenian Genocide of 1915." In *The Armenian Genocide in Perspective,* edited by Richard G. Hovannisian. New Brunswick, N.J.: Transaction Books, 1986.

Miller, John Chester. *The Wolf by the Ears.* New York: Free Press, 1977.

Miller, Perry. *The New England Mind: From Colony to Province.* Cambridge, Mass.: Harvard University Press, 1953.

Mitterauer, Michael, and Reinhard Sieder. *The European Family.* Oxford: Basil Blackwell, 1982.

Mitzman, Arthur. *Sociology and Estrangement.* New York: Knopf, 1973.

Mollat, Michael. *The Poor in the Middle Ages: An Essay in Social History.* Translated by Arthur Goldhammer. New Haven: Yale University Press, 1986.

Moore, Barrington, Jr. *Injustice: The Social Bases of Obedience and Revolt.* New York: M. E. Sharpe, 1978.

Morgan, Edmund S. *American Slavery–American Freedom: The Ordeal of Colonial America.* New York: Norton, 1975.

———. *The Birth of the Republic, 1763–1789.* Chicago: University of Chicago Press, 1956.

———. *Inventing the People: The Rise of Popular Sovereignty in England and America.* New York: Norton, 1988.

———. *The Puritan Family.* New York: Knopf, 1966.

Morrall, John B. *Political Thought in Medieval Times.* Toronto: University of Toronto Press, 1980.

Morris, Richard B., and Jeffrey B. Morris, eds. *Encyclopedia of American History.* New York: Harper and Row, 1976.

Mosse, Claude. *The Ancient World at Work.* New York: Norton, 1969.

Mulgan, Richard. "Aristotle and the Value of Political Participation." *Political Theory* 18 (May 1990): 195–215.

Mullin, Michael. *Flight and Rebellion: Slave Resistance in Eighteenth-Century Virginia.* New York: Oxford University Press, 1972.

Mumford, Lewis. *The City in History: Its Origins, Its Transformations, and Its Prospects.* Harmondsworth: Penguin Books, 1966.

Mundy, John H. *Europe in the High Middle Ages, 1150–1309.* London: Longman, 1973.

Murray, Alexander C. *Germanic Kinship Structure: Studies in Law and Society in Antiquity and the Early Middle Ages.* Toronto: Pontifical Institute of Medieval Studies, 1983.

———. *Reason and Society in the Middle Ages.* Oxford: Clarendon Press, 1978.

Murrin, John M. "The Great Inversion, or Court versus Country: A Comparison of the Revolutionary Settlements in England (1688–1721) and America (1776–1866)." In *Three British Revolutions: 1641, 1688, 1776,* edited by J. G. A. Pocock. Princeton: Princeton University Press, 1980.

———. "A Roof without Walls: The Dilemma of American National Identity." In *Beyond Confederation: Origins of the Constitution and American National Identity,* edited by Richard Beeman, Steven Botein, and Edward C. Carter, II. Chapel Hill: University of North Carolina Press, 1987.

Nash, Gary B. "Social Development." In *Colonial British America: Essays in the New History of the Early Modern Era,* edited by Jack P. Greene and J. R. Pole. Baltimore: Johns Hopkins University Press, 1984.

Nelson, William E. *Americanization of the Common Law: The Impact of Legal Change on Massachusetts, 1760–1830.* Cambridge, Mass.: Harvard University Press, 1973.

Nisbet, Robert. *Community and Power.* New York: Oxford University Press, 1967.

———. *The Sociological Tradition.* New York: Basic Books, 1961.

Noddings, Nel. *Caring.* Berkeley: University of California Press, 1984.

Norton, Mary Beth. *Liberty's Daughters: The Revolutionary Experience of American Women, 1750–1800.* Boston: Little, Brown, 1980.

Novick, Peter. *That Noble Dream: The "Objectivity Question" and the American Historical Profession.* New York: Cambridge University Press, 1988.

Nozick, Robert. *Anarchy, State, and Utopia.* New York: Basic Books, 1974.

Nugent, Walter. *Structures of American Social History.* Bloomington: Indiana University Press, 1981.

Nussbaum, Martha C. "Human Flourishing and Social Justice: In Defense of Aristotelian Essentialism." *Political Theory* 20 (May 1992): 202–46.

———. "Recoiling from Reason." *The New York Review* 36 (December 7, 1989): 35–36.

Okin, Susan Moller. *Justice, Gender, and the Family.* New York: Basic Books, 1989.

———. *Women in Western Political Thought.* Princeton: Princeton University Press, 1979.

Onuf, Peter S. "Reflections on the Founding: Constitutional Historiography in Bicentennial Perspective." *William and Mary Quarterly* 46 (April 1989): 341–75.

Ostwald, M. *Nomos and the Beginnings of the Athenian Democracy.* Oxford: Oxford University Press, 1969.

Pateman, Carole. *The Disorder of Women.* London: Polity Press, 1989.

Perkin, Harold. *The Origins of Modern English Society, 1780–1880.* Toronto: University of Toronto Press, 1972.

Pesson, Edward. *The Log Cabin Myth: The Social Background of the Presidents.* New Haven: Yale University Press, 1984.

———. *Riches, Class, and Power before the Civil War.* Lexington, Mass.: Heath, 1973.

Phillips, Derek L. *Equality, Justice and Rectification.* London: Academic Press, 1979.

———. "Fundamental Rights and the Supportive State." *Theory and Society* 17 (July 1988): 571–88.

———. *Toward a Just Social Order.* Princeton: Princeton University Press, 1986.

Piper, Adrian M. S. "Two Conceptions of the Self." *Philosophical Studies* 48 (1985): 173–97.

Plant, Raymond. "Community: Concept, Conception, and Ideology." *Politics and Society* 8 (1978):49–78.

Pocock, J. G. A. *The Machiavellian Moment: Florentine Political Thought and the Atlantic Republican Tradition.* Princeton: Princeton University Press, 1975.

Pole, J. R. *The American Constitution: For and against.* New York: Hill and Wang, 1987.

———. *Foundations of American Independence, 1763–1815.* New York: Bobbs-Merrill, 1972.

———. *The Pursuit of Equality in American History.* Berkeley: University of California Press, 1978.

Pomeroy, Sarah B. *Goddesses, Whores, Wives, and Slaves: Women in Classical Antiquity.* New York: Schocken Books, 1975.

Postan, M. M. *Essays on Medieval Agriculture and General Problems of the Medieval Economy.* Cambridge: Cambridge University Press, 1973.

————. *The Medieval Economy and Society.* London: Penguin Books, 1975.

Postan, M. M., ed. *The Cambridge Economic History of Europe.* Vol. 1. *The Agrarian Life of the Middle Ages.* Cambridge: Cambridge University Press, 1973.

Potter, Jim. "Demographic Development and Family Structure." In *Colonial British America: Essays in the New History of the Early Modern Era.* edited by Jack P. Greene and J. R. Pole. Baltimore: Johns Hopkins University Press, 1984.

Pounds, N. J. G. *An Historical Geography of England, 450 B.C.–A.D. 1330.* Cambridge: Cambridge University Press, 1976.

Power, Eileen. *Medieval Women.* Cambridge: Cambridge University Press, 1975.

Rakove, Jack N. "The Structure of Politics at the Accession of George Washington." In *Beyond Confederation: Origins of the Constitution and National Identity,* edited by Richard Beeman, Stephen Botein, and Edward C. Carter, II. Chapel Hill: University of North Carolina Press, 1987.

Rawls, John. *A Theory of Justice.* Cambridge, Mass.: Harvard University Press, 1971.

Razi, Zvi. *Life, Marriage and Death in a Medieval Parish.* Cambridge: Cambridge University Press, 1980.

Reuter, Timothy. *The Medieval Nobility.* Amsterdam: North-Holland Publishing Company, 1978.

Reynolds, Charles H., and Ralph V. Norman, eds. *Community in America: The Challenge of Habits of the Heart.* Berkeley: University of California Press, 1988.

Reynolds, Susan. *Kingdoms and Communities in Western Europe, 900–1300.* Oxford: Clarendon Press, 1984.

————. "Social Mentalities and the Case of Medieval Scepticism." *Transactions of the Royal Historical Society,* 6th ser. 1 (1991): 21–41.

Rhodes, P. J. *The Athenian Boule.* Oxford: Oxford University Press, 1972.

Rhodes, R. Colbert. "Emile Durkheim and the Historical Thought of Marc Bloch." *Theory and Society* 5 (January 1978): 45–73.

Ridley, Anthony. *Living in Cities.* London: Heinemann, 1971.

Roeber, A. G. *Faithful Magistrates and Republican Lawyers: Creators of Virginia Legal Culture, 1680–1810.* Chapel Hill: University of North Carolina Press, 1981.

Rogers, Alan. *Empire and Liberty: American Resistance to British Authority, 1755–1763.* Berkeley: University of California Press, 1974.

Roth, Philip. *Deception.* New York: Simon and Schuster, 1990.

Royster, Charles. *A Revolutionary People at War: The Continental Army and American Character, 1775–1783.* Chapel Hill: University of North Carolina Press, 1979.

Rozenblit, Marsha L. *The Jews of Vienna, 1867–1914: Assimilation and Identity.* Albany: State University of New York, 1984.

Rutman, Darrett T. *Winthrop's Boston.* Chapel Hill: University of North Carolina Press, 1965.

Salmon, Marylynn. *Women and the Law of Property in Early America.* Chapel Hill: University of North Carolina Press, 1986.

Saltman, Michael. "Feudal Relationships and the Law: A Comparative Enquiry." *Comparative Studies in Society and History* 29 (July 1987): 520–27.

Sandel, Michael. *Liberalism and the Limits of Justice*. Cambridge: Cambridge University Press, 1982.

———. "The Procedural Republic and the Unencumbered Self." *Political Theory* 12 (February 1984): 81–96.

———. "The State and the Soul." *New Republic* (June 10, 1985): 39–40.

———, ed. *Liberalism and Its Critics*. Oxford: Basil Blackwell, 1984.

Schaps, David M. *Economic Rights of Women in Ancient Greece*. Edinburgh: Edinburgh University Press, 1979.

Schleifer, J. T. *The Making of Tocqueville's "Democracy in America."* Chapel Hill: University of North Carolina Press, 1982.

Schneck, Stephen Frederick. "Habits of the Head: Tocqueville's America and Jazz." *Political Theory* 17 (November 1989): 638–62.

Scott, William B. *In Pursuit of Happiness: American Conceptions of Property from the Seventeenth to the Twentieth Century*. Bloomington: Indiana University Press, 1977.

Shahar, Shulamith. *The Fourth Estate: A History of Women in the Middle Ages*. Translated by Chaya Galai. London: Methuen, 1983.

Shalhope, Robert E. "Republicanism and Early American Historiography." *William and Mary Quarterly* 30 (April 1982): 334–56.

Sheridan, Richard B. "The Domestic Economy." In *Colonial British America: Essays in the New History of the Early Modern Era*, edited by Jack P. Greene and J. R. Pole, 49–85. Baltimore: Johns Hopkins University Press, 1984.

Shklar, Judith. "Injustice, Injury, and Inequality." In *Justice and Equality: Here and Now*, edited by Frank Lucash, 13–33. Ithaca: Cornell University Press, 1986.

———. *Ordinary Vices*. Cambridge, Mass.: Harvard University Press, 1984.

Shy, John. *A People Numerous and Armed: Reflections on the Military Struggle for American Independence*. New York: Oxford University Press, 1976.

Silver, Allan. "The Curious Importance of Small Groups in American Sociology." In *Sociology in America*, edited by Herbert J. Gans, 61–72. London: Sage, 1990.

———. "Friendship and Trust as Moral Ideals: An Historical Inquiry." *European Journal of Sociology* 30 (1989): 274–97.

———. "Friendship in Commercial Society: Eighteenth-Century Social Theory and Modern Sociology." *American Journal of Sociology* 95 (May 1990): 1474–1504.

———. " 'Trust' In Social and Political Theory." In *The Challenge of Social Control*, edited by Gerald D. Suttles and Mayer N. Zald, 52–67. Norwood, N.J.: Ablex, 1985.

Simmel, Georg. *Selected Writings in Sociology and Social Philosophy*. Translated by T. M. Bottomore. New York: McGraw-Hill, 1956.

Simpson, Lewis P. *Mind and the American Civil War: A Meditation on Lost Causes*. Baton Rouge: Louisiana State University Press, 1990.

Smith, Adam. *The Theory of Moral Sentiments*. Edited by D. D. Raphael and A. L. Macfie. Oxford: Clarendon Press, 1976. Originally published in 1759 and 1791.

Smith, Page. *As a City upon a Hill*. New York: Knopf, 1966.

Smith, Roger M. "The 'American Creed' and American Identity: The Limits of Liberal Citizenship in the United States." *Western Political Quarterly* 41 (June 1988): 225–51.

Speck, W. A. "The Internationalist and Imperial Context." In *Colonial British America: Essays in the New History of the Early Modern Era*, edited by Jack P. Greene and J. R. Pole. Baltimore: Johns Hopkins University Press, 1984.

Stanton, G. R. *Athenian Politics, c 800–500 B.C.: A Sourcebook*. London: Routledge & Kegan Paul, 1990.

Staub, Ervin. *The Roots of Evil: The Origins of Genocide and Other Group Violence*. New York: Cambridge University Press, 1989.

Stoianovich, Traian. *French Historical Method: The* Annales *Paradigm*. Ithaca: Cornell University Press, 1976.

Stone, Lawrence. *The Past and the Present Revisited*. London: Routledge & Kegan Paul, 1987.

Sullivan, William M. *Reconstructing Public Philosophy*. Berkeley: Univerity of California Press, 1982.

Sydnor, Charles S. *American Revolutionaries in the Making*. New York: Free Press, 1965.

———. *Gentlemen Freeholders: Political Practices in Washington's Virginia*. Chapel Hill: University of North Carolina Press, 1952.

Tapolar, Morris. *The Sociology of Colonial Virginia*. New York: Philosophical Library, 1960.

Taylor, Charles. *Philosophy and the Human Sciences: Philosophical Papers*. 2 vols. Cambridge: Cambridge University Press, 1985.

———. *Sources of the Self: The Making of the Modern Identity*. Cambridge, Mass.: Harvard University Press, 1989.

Taylor, Michael. *Community, Anarchy and Liberty*. Cambridge: Cambridge University Press, 1982.

Taylor, William R. *Cavalier and Yankee: The Old South and American National Character*. Garden City, N.Y.: Doubleday Anchor Books, 1963.

Thernstrom, Stephan. *The Other Bostonians: Property and Progress in the American Metropolis, 1880–1970*. Cambridge, Mass.: Harvard University Press, 1973.

Thirsk, Joan. *Economic Policy and Prospects: The Development of a Consumer Society in Early Modern England*. Oxford: Clarendon Press, 1978.

Thompson, Judith Javis. *Rights, Restitution, and Risk: Essays in Moral Theory*. Edited by William Parent. Cambridge, Mass.: Harvard University Press, 1986.

Tilly, Charles. "Misreading, then Rereading, Nineteenth-Century Social Change." In *Social Structures: A Network Approach*, edited by Barry Wellman and S. D. Berkowitz, 332–58. New York: Cambridge University Press, 1988.

Tocqueville, Alexis de. *Democracy in America*. The Henry Reeve Text as revised by Francis Bowen. 2 vols. New York: Knopf, 1985.

Tomasi, John. "Individual Rights and Community Virtues." *Ethics* 101 (April 1991): 521–36.

Tönnies, Ferdinand. *Community and Society*. Translated by Charles P. Loomis. East Lansing: Michigan State University Press, 1957.

———. *Fundamental Concepts of Sociology*. Translated by Charles P. Loomis. New York: American Book Company, 1940.

_____. *On Social Ideas and Ideologies*. Edited and translated by E. G. Jacoby. New York: Harper and Row, 1974.

Toulmin, Stephen. *Human Understanding*. Vol. 1. Oxford: Clarendon Press, 1972.

Tribe, Laurence. *American Constitutional Law*. Mineola, N.Y.: Foundation Press, 1978.

Ulrich, Laurel Thatcher. *Good Wives: Image and Reality in the Lives of Women in Northern New England, 1650–1750*. New York: Knopf, 1982.

Veysey, Laurence. *The Communal Experience: Anarchist and Mystical Counter-Cultures in America*. New York: Harper and Row, 1972.

Vinovskis, Maria A., ed. *Studies in American Historical Geography*. New York: Oxford University Press, 1979.

Walker, Mack. *German Home Towns: Community, State and General Estate*. Ithaca: Cornell University Press, 1971.

Wallach, John R. "Liberals, Communitarians, and the Tasks of Political Theory." *Political Theory* 15 (November 1987): 581–611.

Walzer, Michael. "The Communitarian Critique of Liberalism." *Political Theory* 18 (February 1990): 6–23.

_____. *Spheres of Justice*. New York: Basic Books, 1983.

Ward, David. "Immigration: Settlement Patterns." In *Harvard Encyclopedia of American Ethnic Groups*, edited by Stephan Thernstrom. Cambridge, Mass.: Harvard University Press, 1980.

Waterman, Thomas Tileston. *The Mansions of Virginia, 1776–1777*. Chapel Hill: University of North Carolina Press, 1946.

Weber, Max. *Economy and Society*. Edited by Guenther Roth and Claus Wittich. Berkeley: University of California Press, 1978.

_____. *From Max Weber*. Edited and Translated by Don Martindale and Gertrude Neuwirth. New York: Free Press, 1957.

_____. *The Protestant Ethic and the Spirit of Capitalism*. Translated by Talcott Parsons. New York: Scribner, 1958.

Wellman, Barry, Peter J. Carrington, and Alan Hall. "Networks as Personal Communities." In *Social Structures: A Network Approach*, edited by Barry Wellman and S. D. Berkowitz, 130–84. New York: Cambridge University Press, 1988.

White, Morton. *Philosophy of the American Revolution*. New York: Oxford University Press, 1978.

_____. *Philosophy*, The Federalist *and the Constitution*. New York: Oxford University Press, 1987.

Wiebe, Robert H. *The Opening of American Society*. New York: Vintage Books, 1985.

Williamson, Chilton. *American Suffrage: From Property to Democracy, 1760–1860*. Princeton: Princeton University Press, 1960.

Wolfe, Alan. *Whose Keeper? Social Science and Moral Obligation*. Berkeley: University of California Press, 1988.

Wood, Gordon S. *The Creation of the American Republic, 1776–1787*. Chapel Hill: University of North Carolina Press, 1969.

_____. "Interests and Disinterestedness in the Making of the Constitution." In *Beyond Confederation: Origins of the Constitution and American National Identity*, edited by Richard Beeman, Stephen Botein, and Edward C. Carter, II. Chapel Hill: University of North Carolina Press, 1987.

Wood, Gordon S. *The Radicalism of the American Revolution.* New York: Knopf, 1992.

Wright, Louis B. *The Cultural Life of the American Colonies.* New York: Harper Torchbooks, 1962.

Wrigley, E. A., and R. S. Schofield. *The Population History of England, 1541–1871: A Reconstruction.* London: Edward Arnold, 1981.

Wuthnow, Robert. *Meaning and Moral Order: Explorations in Cultural Analysis.* Berkeley: University of California Press, 1987.

Wyatt-Brown, Bertram. *Southern Honor: Ethics and Behavior in the Old South.* New York: Oxford University Press, 1982.

Young, Alfred F., ed. *The American Revolution: Explorations in the History of the American Revolution.* De Kalb: Northern Illinois University Press, 1976.

Young, Iris Marion. *Justice and the Politics of Difference.* Princeton: Princeton University Press, 1990.

Zilversmit, Arthur. *The First Emancipation: The Abolition of Slavery in the North.* Chicago: University of Chicago Press, 1967.

Zuckerman, Michael. *Peaceable Kingdom: New England Towns in the Eighteenth Century.* New York: Random House, 1970.

# INDEX

Adams, Abigail, 76
Adams, John, 54, 59, 63, 171–72
Adams, Samuel, 54–55
Adkins, Arthur W. H., 217n, 218n, 219n
agricultural base: in classical Athens, 130; in early America, 27; in Middle Ages, 91
Allen, David Grayson, 33, 37
America, early, 27–60, 63–80
American Revolution, 52–60; background in Massachusetts, 53–55, 58–60; background in Virginia, 55–60
Appleby, Joyce, 154, 200n
Aquinas, St. Thomas, 170
Arendt, Hannah, 166
Aristotle, 5, 13, 15, 83, 121–29, 131–32; and virtues of agriculture, 57
Athens, classical, 5, 129–48
attachment, 11, 190–93
Auerbach, Jerold, 117

Bachofen, J. J., 86
Bailyn, Bernard, 153, 200n
Baron, Marcia, 226n
Beard, Charles A., 153
Becker, Carl L., 153
Becker, Lawrence C., 225n
Beeman, Richard, 201n
Beitz, Charles, 210n
Belknap, Jeremy, 69
Bellah, Robert N., 4, 6, 11–14, 25, 63, 65, 175, 184, 195, 198n, 220n
Bellamy, Edward, 7–8
Beller, Steven, 166
Bender, Thomas, 28, 212n
Benhabib, Seyla, 181
Bertelson, David, 204n
"best," "most worthy" vocabulary in classical Athens, 131
"better sort," "middling sort" vocabulary in early America, 28, 33
Billington, Ray Allen, 42
Black, Antony, 212n
Bloch, Marc, 22, 154, 192–93, 212n, 213n, 220n

Boston, Massachusetts, 38–39
Boyer, Paul, 40, 203n
Braybrooke, David, 199n
Breen, T. H., 202n, 204n
Brown, Robert E., 74, 153, 204n
Brown, Katherine B., 204n
Brown, Thad A., 207n
Buchanan, Allan E., 186, 225n
Burke, Peter, 220n
Burnaby, Andrew, 205n
Byrd, William, 51

civic republicanism, 154
Carroll, Peter N., 207n
clan: as basic element of early society, 87; myth of, 94–95
classical Athens, 5, 129–48
clergy, in Middle Ages, 90–91, 105
common good, 5, 10, 15; Aristotle on, 123–24; in classical Athens, 168–69; in early America, 69, 71, 171–72; in Middle Ages, 99, 169–71; liberal conception of, 187–88. See also public good
common history, in early America, 65–66
commonwealth, in the Middle Ages, 84–85; 102–4
communitarians, 4, 122, 150–57, 167–68, 175–76; and mistaken beliefs about the past, 150–56
community, 3–9; abstract flavor of conceptions of, 7; and tolerance, 157–58; breakdown of, 28–29, 149; conditions for, 156–63; danger of pursuing communitarian ideal of, 163–67; ingredients of communitarian ideal of, 10–18, 20–21; relevance of for life today, 8, 167–74
communities, personal, 190–91
Comte, August, 5, 81
Connolly, W. E., 200n
Cook, Edward M., Jr., 67–68
Cooper, William, 63
Cornell, Drucilla, 181
Cott, Nancy F., 202n
culture: as monolitic, 151–156; significance of, 154

243